GW01048706

Closing the Gap

Allerd Stikker

Closing the Gap

**Exploring the
History of
Gender Relations**

Amsterdam University Press · Salomé

Cover design & lay out Kok Korpershoek, Amsterdam
Cover illustration *The kiss*, Brancusi, 1908. Limestone, Philadelphia Museum of Art, Philadelphia.
page 2 *God's hand*, Auguste Rodin, c.1898. Marble, height 92,9 cm, Musée Rodin, Paris.

ISBN 90 5356 574 4
NUR 740/757

© Amsterdam University Press, Amsterdam, 2002

All rights reserved. Without limiting the rights under copyright reserved above,
no part of this book may be reproduced, stored in or introduced into a retrieval system,
or transmitted, in any form or by any means (electronic, mechanical, photocopying, recording
or otherwise) without the written permission of both the copyright owner and the author of the book.

Contents

I

Introduction

For the past fifteen years I have been involved in industrial and commercial projects linking technology, economy and ecology. I have been impressed by the great amount of time and energy it has taken the political and industrial world to begin to accept that ecology and economy are closely linked and cannot do without each other. An economic activity cannot survive without resources, be they financial, human or natural.

Acceptance of the fact that ecologically responsible management is also economically responsible in the long run (and often in the short term as well) is a change in mind-set that does not come easily to male-dominated political and industrial leadership. There appears to be a strong link between the traditions of culture having dominion over nature, male over female and economy over ecology.

Changing the simplistic perceptions of masculinity and femininity in our political and social structures and in our personal roles could turn out to be the most vital factor of all in our bid to achieve a sustainable future for human society.

A company that presents a relevant case on this subject is Deloitte & Touche, America's third largest accounting, tax and consulting firm in the early nineties. They published their findings in the December 2000 issue of Harvard Business Review. When the CEO of the group concluded that an in depth investigation was necessary to find out why so many women were recruited and trained and so few eventually stayed, he launched an Initiative for the Retention and Advancement of Women.

After several years of searching, through internal workshops, it was discovered that a great number of erroneous assumptions that existed in the male culture about career women, was the overriding reason for wasting women's talents and their high turnover.

When these assumptions were corrected, the number of women partners rose over the years from 4% to 14% and the trend continues today.

Accepting flexible working hours and removing the myth that more than 60 billable hours per week were a requirement for promotion, were among these corrections. Also the unwritten rules that women were evaluated on their performance and men on their potential, that women were passed over for certain assignments, assumed to be to tough for them, and that travel puts too much pressure on women, were recognized and removed.

By these measures and many others, taken over years of culture change, performance and productivity of both male and female partners increased, while substantial savings were realized on recruitment and training costs.

8 The purpose of this volume is to explore whether the relationship between male and female and that between feminine and masculine in human society and within individual human beings, as we experience them today, are exclusively natural 'facts of life' or whether they result from attitudes, choices and habits developed during human history. If the latter were to be the case we could in principle choose to change the relationships if they did not seem appropriate for a sustainable future. Change would be no easy task, but if our quality of life is at stake, it would be worth the challenge.

Why might the present relationship between male and female in today's world not be appropriate for a sustainable future for mankind?

I am of the opinion that the male dominating mode that prevails in most cultures on our planet is to a great extent responsible for the suppression of female qualities, for the destructive abuse of natural resources and for the forces of demonic aggression evident in conflicts between peoples.

In the history of mankind the perception has developed that female is to be identified with nature and male with culture, that culture is superior to nature and that as a consequence nature and women are of a lower order than culture and men.

Abuse of nature has a long history, but a new element is that the scale of magnitude of the world population and its rate of growth reach proportions far beyond any level experienced in the past.

With today's world population standing at about 6 billion and still growing by about 80 million per year, wars over depleting uncontaminated resources are likely to increase in intensity and geographical spread. The demographic consequences of the resulting massive migrations are awful to contemplate.

Although great efforts are being made to restrain warfare, to limit damage to the environment and to tap natural resources only within the limits of their renewal, it seems to me that in the end they will all be of no avail if we do not investigate and solve the underlying, fundamental issue of male dominance in our social structures and individual roles.

The suppression of women also has a long history, and two feminist waves, one in the late nineteenth century and one in the mid-twentieth have initiated changes, but the emphasis has been on either radical difference or perfect equality between male and female, while still taking man as the measure. Unfortunately, there are still conflicting and confusing views on what constitutes woman and man and on the overall concepts of masculinity and femininity.

The process of gender balancing, however, is now capable of assuming a new dimension and a new momentum in the context of sustainable development; the whole idea implies a fundamental change in our attitude towards nature and culture.

Is the male/female relationship subject to cycles? Is the present male domination an unavoidable and irreversible model, or did we ourselves set the rules and can we therefore change them? Those will be the questions to be addressed. The answers will not be black and white, given the great variety of models in different cultures, but searching for answers may give us a clue as to whether and how we can change these models in order to secure a sustainable future. The present models will probably be revised by political, economic and technological innovations, but although these factors are vital and essential, they alone will not suffice. First and foremost, attitudes will have to change.

In the following pages I shall attempt to shed some light on how male/female phenomena emerged in the history of nature, how perceptions of feminine and masculine emerged in the history of human civilisations, and whether it can be argued that there is a link between the resulting male dominance and the ecological and gender issues in our present world.

I think it is important to point out that this book does not mean to deal primarily with the position of women in society. It is equally concerned with the position of men. It is all about rediscovering the human being in women and in men, and redefining their roles based on the assumption that all human beings have, in varying degrees, masculine and feminine characteristics, be they more masculine in men and more feminine in women.

63
CHI CHI
Completion

Chinese hexagram.

In the Chinese Book of Change (I Ching), the trigram for feminine-related water consists of two outer yin lines and one inner yang line, whereas in the trigram for masculine-related fire it is the other way around. This symbolism implies on the one hand that feminine is predominantly yin but also contains yang, whilst masculine is predominantly yang but also contains yin.

The combination of the two trigrams form a hexagram which is the symbol for perfection, for completeness when the water trigram is at the top and the fire trigram at the bottom. In this combination they represent a perfect balance, with a subtle hierarchical primacy of the feminine.

In other words, in this perception of feminine and masculine there is a distinct difference but no radical distinction between woman and man, whilst in combination they represent integrity. This is a very essential concept; a concept we have to rediscover as it seems to have gone lost in the course of human history.

As the subject of this book and the time span it covers are both vast, I have chosen to limit the texts to summarizing various findings in primary and secondary sources in the literature and my own interpretations as to their interconnectedness. Ariadne's thread if you will, rather than any attempt to repeat what has already been written on the subject and related issues in a great number of excellent and relatively recent publications.

I have tried to present a bird's eye view of trends in relationships between male and female and masculine and feminine over the ages, first in the evolution of nature and then in the evolution of human civilisation and the human individual. I offer my personal interpretation of these trends and some speculative thoughts on future options.

I hope that this book may contribute to a more general awareness of the history, the present and the future of gender relations and its impact on sustainable development.

II

Sexes: An Innovation in Evolution

Long before the arrival of the human being on earth, there was no such thing as sex. No male, no female.

There was light and dark, spirit and matter, positive and negative poles and many other complementary dualisms in creation, but no male and female. They emerged 'only' some 1.5 billion years ago, when the earth was already 3 billion years old.

When our solar system and the earth were created about 4.5 billion years ago out of one of the many supernova explosions that occurred and still occur in the universe, there was only inorganic matter. The word inorganic means matter other than plant or animal: combinations that were built up in the early course of evolution and that formed crystals, minerals and rocks. The counterpart of inorganic is organic; it is related to matter found in and derived from living organisms.

> The chemical elements or atoms, 92 of them, were formed from subatomic particles in the initial stages of the origin of our universe, supposedly about 15 billion years ago. They start with the simplest atom hydrogen, atomic number 1, and end with the largest naturally occurring atom uranium, atomic number 92.

On earth all of the elements were and are present as such. They also existed initially in exclusively inorganic molecules. At the start of the earth's existence, the core, the surface and the surrounding atmosphere all consisted of these atoms and inorganic molecules, crystals, minerals and rocks. No life, no plants, no animals, no sexes.

The growth process of atoms, molecules and crystals consisted of combining sub-atomic and subsequent particles in ever greater combinations over the course of time by linking and binding them under the influence of forces of attraction. In atoms these forces, gravitational, are very strong; in molecules, electromagnetic forces are weaker, and in crystals the electrical cohesion forces are weaker still.

Growth continued over a long time span and led to a stupendous diversification of atoms, molecules and minerals with colours and crystalline structures of increasing complexity. Each atom, molecule or mineral created in this process represented a new type, with new properties. This continued until structural or physical limits to growth were reached.

For atoms the natural limit was arrived at atom number 92 (uranium); inorganic molecules were also restricted in their size, as their structures became too complex and unstable.

For crystals the situation was different because growth was achieved by merely adding more of the same. Here limits did not depend on the stability of the new structure but on practical, physical circumstances.

At some point in time, possibly less then one billion years after the earth came into existence, a new category, organic molecules, were formed or arrived from space via meteorites. These molecules could reach a higher level of complexity than inorganic ones and still remain stable. They are of a different chemical constellation, containing a high level of hydrocarbon derivatives, and are bonded by weaker forces. They introduced a new wave of differentiation but also a higher level of fragility.

The evolution of organic molecules and compounds continued over time, leading to amino acids, proteins and nucleic acids, the carriers of genetic codes, and then to DNA and chromosomes. It was from these organic molecules that suddenly and inexplicably the first symptoms of the phenomenon of life emerged. Life may be defined as the state of a material complex that has the capacity to perform such functions as metabolism and reproduction, and that shows some form of ecological responsiveness or adaptability.

At the same time it appeared that a limit to complexity and stability had been reached in molecules such as DNA and that more complex structures or systems would disintegrate. Therefore, if no new and fundamentally different structures, systems and mechanism had been created, evolution would have come to a halt, just as would have been the case when the atom system had reached its limit and the molecule system had not been 'invented'.

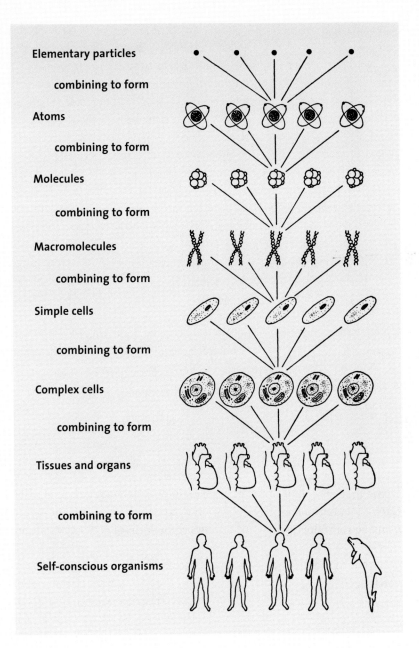

Elementary particles

combining to form

Atoms

combining to form

Molecules

combining to form

Macromolecules

combining to form

Simple cells

combining to form

Complex cells

combining to form

Tissues and organs

combining to form

Self-conscious organisms

Evolution as a progressive collecting together of units into larger systems.

The new invention at this point in time, somewhat less than one billion years after the earth came into existence, was the cell system, where complex molecules could coexist and interact with each other in a new organisational structure. An essential molecular component of the cell is the chromosome. Chromosomes are made up of DNA molecules and contain the genetic codes of each type of cell. They do not exist singly in a cell but in identical pairs.

The cell structure consists of a microscopically small mass enveloped in a thin, delicate and somewhat rigid permeable wall. These first cells had only one pair of chromosomes; they did not have a nucleus and are called prokaryotic cells.

14   These cells were and are living entities that can multiply through division, technically know as mitosis. One of the first manifestations of the prokaryotic cell system was the virus. The virus represents a transitional phase that can still crystallize like molecules, but can also duplicate like cells. This was followed, during what was in all likelihood a relatively short and chaotic period of instabilities and failures, by the development of a limited number of prokaryotic cells that still represent a vast proportion of the living cells on earth today.

They are simple unicellular organisms: anaerobic bacteria, yeasts and fungi. The oldest prokaryotic cell fossils found date from a little more than 3.5 billion years ago.

> The division of a cell into two identical 'daughter' cells was the only instrument for 'multiplication' in the early community of living 'organic' creatures. In our perception today we apparently look upon them as mother/daughter communities, which is an interesting sidelight on the female origins of creation that will be discussed in Chapter VII.

Whereas the development and growth of elemental atoms and inorganic and organic molecules had consisted of creating larger and endlessly new substances, and also more of them, the growth mechanism of cells initially consisted in the main of producing more of the same, by repeated division. Modified types of cells that resulted from 'errors' in the process of division were put to the test of natural selection with a small probability of surviving.

This would seem to represent a setback in the process of evolution. Whereas in the previous period there had been a strong and creative quantitative and qualitative growth, with ever new complexities, the new mechanism of cell division produced mainly quantitative growth.

An interesting situation apparently occurred during the growth process when the supply of nutrients, made up of all kinds of organic compounds, became gradually depleted. Between 3 and 3.5 billion years ago nature then invented photosynthesis, which was able to combine carbon dioxide and water under the influence of sunlight to form carbohydrates and oxygen. The process was catalyzed by a new organic compound, chlorophyll. Carbohydrates became a practically inexhaustible source of food for cells because of the abundant presence of water and carbon dioxide. The by-product, oxygen, was a new and poisonous gas in the earth's atmosphere, which at that time contained hardly any oxygen. However, by taking cover under water and soil and by gradual adaptation, organisms survived. Photosynthesis eventually led to a dynamic equilibrium level of 22% oxygen in the atmosphere around the earth, without which we would not survive today. On the other hand, the burning of fossil hydrocarbon fuels originating from photosynthesis is today worrying environmentalists because of a growing surplus of the by-product carbon dioxide. The easy conclusion that nature will again somehow invent a way of resolving this problem, just as it did with oxygen, does not seem valid, because of the enormous difference in time span available for a correction to evolve: a few decades versus a few billion years!

Although in retrospect it appears that the cell was to prove an essential step towards furthering the process of evolution, it took as long as 1.5 billion years for this innovation to mature and pave the way for a new leap forward.

This new leap occurred with the arrival of the more sophisticated 'eukaryotic' cell with a nucleus separated off by a membrane and containing more than one pair of chromosomes. The oldest eukaryotic cell fossils found date from 2 billion years ago.

With this newcomer a further threshold was passed in the evolutionary journey. It laid the foundation for the phenomenon of sex. Eukaryotic cells were characterized by a new process of division whereby two 'haploid' cells resulted, each carrying only one set of chromosome pairs possessed by the original cell. When one of the haploid cells meets a similar cell from a different ancestral stock, they fuse and form a new individual whose genetic make-up is unlike any that existed before. This fusion or conjugation ushers in a donor/receptor mechanism, the first and seemingly unromantic manifestation of a male and female relationship.

While the sex phenomenon is observable in rare cases at a rudimentary level in some advanced prokaryotic cells, the eukaryotic cell system provided all the conditions for intensive development of the sexual mechanism. It also opened the way to the formation of multicellular organisms.

Of the total number of chromosome pairs in eukaryotic cells, the so-called sex chromosomes comprise one pair. The sex chromosomes in this pair are designated by scientists as x and y. In popular terms most male individuals have one x chromosome and one y chromosome, whereas most female individuals have two x chromosomes.

Exceptions include birds, butterflies and moths and at least some fish, amphibians and reptiles, where the female sex chromosomes have the xy configuration and the male ones xx. Other exceptions are bees, wasps and ants, which do not have sex chromosomes, but whose sex is determined by a so-called haplodiploid mechanism. In this system unfertilized eggs produce males, an interesting example of parthenogenesis, and fertilized eggs produce females.

In human beings the sex chromosomes comprise one pair of a total of 23 pairs. The nearest animal to human beings is the chimpanzee, which interestingly enough has 24 chromosome pairs and is nearly identical to humans in its DNA configuration.

The leap in evolution towards the eukaryotic cell involved a transition from a simple, linear, slow development mechanism to a complex, non-linear and rapid one. It apparently took about one and a half billion years to take place.

After the new eukaryotic cell system had sufficiently matured around 600 million years ago, it speeded up the evolutionary process at an unprecedented rate. The simple explanation for the acceleration is the fact that when in the conventional cell division and reproduction process of the prokaryotic cells ten mutations occur in a given time, the probability of one being favorable is very small. However, in the case of cell fusion, the cross combinations of ten mutations can produce more than a thousand variants; thus the probability of one surviving is greatly enhanced.

The eukaryotic cell system therefore caused an enormous explosion of different unicellular and later multicellular organisms over the last 600 million years, starting at

16

the beginning of the Cambrian period in the geological time scale. It led, through many ups and downs, many failures and extinctions, to ever-increasing diversification, complexities and creativity. The world became exotic, colourful, adventurous and full of threats and opportunities. New species appeared, first plants, then fish, reptiles, birds, butterflies, flowers. The last three arrived only some 125 million years ago and for the first time a great variation of colours brightened up our planet, it thus far having been mostly greyish rocks, green plants and blue water.

The first divergence of the mammalian and avian lineages, between 240 and 320 million years ago, marked the beginning of x-y differentiating out of an ordinairy pair of autosomes that eventually evolved towards the human sex chromosomes we have today.

In the October 1999 edition of *Science* two American geneticists revealed that in the above period the small (male) y chromosome with only a few dozen genes evolved from the much larger (female) x chromosome that contains thousands of genes.

This implies that from a scientific point of view the feminine identity was there first and the masculine identity was a derivative. Symbolically, this is quite the opposite of the story of Genesis 2, which claims that man was there first and woman was created from him, according to the 'rib' story. An intriguing observation, given the fact that the subordination of women in Christian tradition is closely linked to this story.

I have not been able to find any evidence in the scientific literature on how the fundamental xy and xx differentiation in male and female evolved and how this differentiation developed into specific sex organs in plants and animals, including humans. Maybe my search was too superficial, but friends of mine more specialised in this field also could not give me the answer. This question is, however, of lesser significance for the purpose of this book.

As evolution then proceeded explosively, organisms became increasingly complex in their make-up and at the same time manifested gradually increasing levels of consciousness, a phenomenon Teilhard de Chardin called the complexity/consciousness law.

The most complex organism on earth today, the human species, emerged from the non-linear process of mutations, adaptations and extinctions about 3 million years ago. It acquired the capability of self-reflective consciousness and gradually became aware of existence and evolution, of eternal space and historic time.

As a sideline it is worth mentioning that Teilhard in his major work *Le Phenomaine Humain* (translated in English in 1955 as *The Phenomenon of Man*, only to be corrected to *The Human Phenomenon*, a revised edition in 1999) also questions how and when the male/female orientation came about in evolution, when our present knowledge was not available to him.

Concurrent with the development of sexual reproduction another new element was introduced, the phenomenon of natural death after a short individual existence. This contrasts with the highly improbable termination of the existence of, for instance, an atom, which can result only from natural radioactive loss over an extended period of time, from astrophysical explosions in the universe or from artificial fission or fusion.

Single molecules and prokaryotic cells only 'die' from radiation, extreme heat, or mechanical and chemical destruction, brought on by natural disasters or human interference. Normally speaking, these molecules and cells continue to exist through duplication and multiplication and do not 'naturally' disintegrate when getting old.

> To die through rapid ageing was to be the fate of the new, fragile individual multicellular organisms, plants and animals. The time horizon changed for them from duration and continuity to cycles and finality.

Thus, we see three new phenomena emerging in the later stages of evolution: sexual reproduction, consciousness and natural death.

These three elements were destined to play a major role in the animal world and especially in human behaviour.

To be sure, the exploding diversity of organisms in the last 600 million years and their growing need for food have led to complex ecological interdependence and 'food chains' with a sophisticated and exceedingly cruel predation system in the animal world, where one species depends on eating others for survival. Although in the beginning animals consumed only vegetable food, they later complemented this diet by eating recently dead animals, which gradually led, out of necessity, to the killing of live animals. Anybody who has followed documentaries on 'Discovery Channel' on predating practice in nature knows how horrifying that can be, regardless of the philosophical and theological observations of those like Thomas Aquinas that this is all part of the grand design.

However, male violence within the human species is of a very different and even more horrifying order, with abuse, rape and genocide, and until recently it was regarded as an exclusively human feature.

As mentioned in the introduction, it is arguable whether human behaviour as we experience it today is a question of nature or nurture, in other words whether human behaviour is the result of natural and genetic forces or the result of culture and environment or possibly of both. This has become an intriguing issue over time. It also relates to male and female roles, the theme of this book.

Before speculating on possible answers, we will first have a short look at some aspects of our recent human evolution.

The bonobos, living in Africa, have peaceful and egalitarian community lives with very little violence and no inter-community aggression. Friendly relationships are enjoyed among both males and females, with strong mother-son ties.

III

Our Family Tree

Research into animal behaviour concentrated in the last decades has revealed that, out of four thousand mammals and more than ten million other animal species studied, only two live in patrilineal, male-bonded communities with a system of intense, male-initiated territorial aggression. Such behaviour includes lethal raiding into neighbouring communities in search of vulnerable enemies to attack and kill.

These two species are chimpanzees and humans.

Recent research has also discovered that the genetic codes of chimpanzees and humans are so much alike that we must be much more closely related to apes than was previously assumed, as schematically shown in the family trees of the primates in the figure on page 22.

This implies that all the species mentioned are from the same lineage and that the human branched off much later than was originally thought to be the case, in fact about 5 million years ago, before the chimpanzee and the bonobo. The bonobo is a seperate species in the lineage, only discovered in 1928 to be so.

The fact that chimpanzees and humans are of common stock and show striking similarities indicates that similar evolutionary forces continue to be at work, maintaining and refining intergroup hostilities and personal violence by demonic males.

Of the other members of the family, the orang-utang, mostly found in Indonesia, and the gorilla in Africa, have also demonic males who practise rape and infanticide, but lethal intercommunity raiding and killing is absent, and family lives are generally more peaceful.

The bonobos, living in Africa, are the exception to the group.

They do not show any of the demonic features of the other members and have peaceful and egalitarian community lives with very little violence and no inter-com-

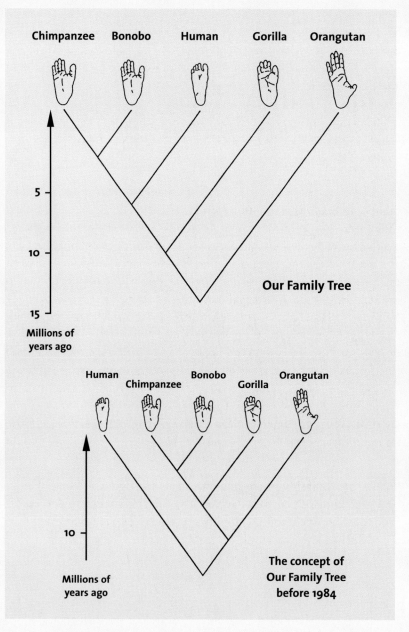

Our family tree

munity aggression. Friendly relationships are enjoyed among both males and females, with strong mother-son ties. They have sex not only for procreation but also for pleasure and friendship, they practice lesbian relations and, interestingly enough, live in a matrilineal social system with strong female bonding-based coalitions as a safeguard against male domination.

In answer to the question of why these various species from the same lineage show such differences in social behaviour, studies of the ape communities have prompted the following observations.

In the first place a common ancestor with a supposedly genetic propensity to violence within the species must have had an influence on their behaviour.

Secondly, diet and variations in the availability of food play a role, because this can lead to a split into male and female groups with different tasks. In general, the more distant the food and the more conflicts over resources, the more male-dominated social structures emerge. On the other hand, when conditions are less rigorous, communities remain more coherent, and egalitarian social structures arise, provided stronger female bonding is matched by adequately affirmative male roles and if there is mutual acknowledgment of economic and political functions.

While the gorillas, orang-utans and bonobos live in ecologically balanced habitats such as rainforests, the chimpanzees and humans moved, probably as a consequence of climate change, to woodlands. This implied a change in choice of food from fruits and foliage to roots, meat and occasional fruits.

In the third place, intelligence plays a role in social behaviour as it influences the clever organisation of survival, power and politics.

> A common trait in the primate family is the expanded brain, that of the humans being the largest. The human brain started to expand explosively some 1.8 million years ago and reached its present size about half a million years ago.
>
> As the chimpanzee also has a brain capacity more advanced than that of the other members, there could be a link between intelligence and violent male dominant behaviour.

From the above analysis it appears that behaviour of the primates, including humans, depends in great part on genetics, ecology and intelligence. In other words, on nature, nurture and culture.

It would be reasonable to assume that the more intelligent species should be able to reflect on these influences and draw conclusions.

If we want to stop the genetically conditioned tendency to male domination and aggression that threatens our human society, we will have to apply our intelligence to understanding why we have nurtured this pattern of behaviour in the course of human history and what we can do to correct it.

Although we cannot compare ourselves to the bonobos, we see in them a hopeful sign that in principle it is apparently possible for a member of the same lineage to cope in a peaceful way with the genetic potential of male violence.

IV

Major Trends between 25000 BCE and 500 CE

Studies of prehistoric human societies, that is before 3000 BCE, and of later evolving civilisations in antiquity in Western Europe and Asia Minor clearly show a growing trend towards male domination in mythology and social life. Recent extensive literature analysing this trend, mostly written by feminist women and female anthropologists, contains theories of ancient matrifocal, goddess-centred societies free of violence and wars. Although these theories may be coloured by biased viewpoints, there are nevertheless impressive arguments to support them.

The trend towards male domination is clear, but how and when it all started is less so, because convincing archaeological evidence for the earlier preagricultural period is lacking. Study of 150 contemporary indigenous non-Western cultures in North Alaska, the Pacific region and Africa, living in isolated conditions presumably similar to those of prehistoric times, shows a mixed picture. About one-third of the cultures are characterized by gender equality, meaning a peaceful and stable balance of female and male power; one-third by a conflicting and unstable balance of power, historically leading to male dominance, and one-third by markedly male domination in every way: social structures, rituals and myths.

Genetic, ecological, nutritional and intelligence aspects all play an important role in determining social behaviour, in line with the analysis of the primate family in the previous chapter.

It appears, again, that the genetic propensity to male violence in the human race is controllable if there is reasonable access to food, no serious competition for resources and mutual acceptance of complementary and well organised power roles.

In this study we will assume, therefore, that gender equality is achievable, not so much on the basis of some idealistic notion of a lost paradise that has to be regained, but recognising that in practice not only genetic but also other circumstances do play a role and that we can make choices. Choices in the sense of the ecologically responsible handling of natural resources, well organised food supply and distribution, equal respect for male and female capabilities and roles, and consequently, a dynamic and constructive balance of power.

Before elaborating on what we can do to achieve gender equality in present-day Western society, it may be useful to make an attempt to understand how we arrived at where we are today and what we can learn from that.

This chapter will briefly introduce the period of the prehistoric late upper palaeolithic, mesolithic and neolithic eras between 25000 BCE and 3000 BCE, antiquity from 3000 BCE to 500 BCE, and the period from 500 BCE to 500 CE. These three periods are chosen because in each of them decisive mutations took place in the development of female/male relationships in the geographical area of what is today England, France and eastern Europe in the palaeolithic and mesolithic eras; and Italy, Greece, Turkey, Israel (Palestine), Lebanon, Saudi Arabia, Egypt, Libya, Sinai, Syria, Iran, Iraq, between the Tigris and Euphrates rivers, the areas around the Indus and the Ganges in ancient India and the large island cultures of Crete, Cyprus, Malta, Sicily and Sardinia in the remaining eras up until 500 CE.

What happened in all these areas had a major effect on the female/male relationships in present Jewish, Christian, Islamic and Hindu civilisations.

Developments in other regions such as the Far East, Africa and South America are only incidentally referred to, but are obviously of equal importance for a global picture.

The end of each of the three above-mentioned periods is marked by a fundamental transition that contributed to the eventual erosion of the female position. A history of decline: from the spiritual, social and creative centre of society to the inferior citi-

26

zen without religious or political status, with limited social functions and a life restricted to household and family.

◄ 4000 BCE	3000 BCE	1500 BCE	500 BCE ►
one Goddess	Goddess goddesses	goddesses gods gods goddesses	one God

The first, upper palaeolithic era, roughly from 25000 BCE to about 10000 BCE, was characterized by a predominantly female and goddess orientation with a less pronounced male profile in the hunter-gatherer societies of northern and eastern Europe in the cold and barren habitat of the last glacial period.

Then came 2000 to 3000 years from which hardly any archeological findings are available and during which profound climatic changes took place due to the receding glaciers in Europe. But from approximately 7000 to 3000 BCE a warmer climate in southern Europe, Anatolia, Mesopotamia and Egypt led to the creation of new, also female and goddess-oriented, horticulture-based societies. These were concentrated around the river basins that were to become the foundations for later powerful civilisations in those areas.

Then, between 3000 and 2000 BCE, a number of major developments took place that were to profoundly change the female position in the above-mentioned regions.

In the first place, as previously small communities became larger, the domestication of animals and the development of larger-scale agriculture took over from gathering, hunting and small-scale gardening. This created new roles for men in agriculture.

Secondly, the new roles were further strengthened by the discovery of technologies for converting minerals into copper and bronze (iron came later, around 1000 BCE) and these metals were used to make agricultural tools that increased the scope and scale of food production. Excess food production in certain areas led to trade, which added a new dimension to human communities. Commerce, arts and crafts became more sophisticated, which led to the growth of towns, kingdoms, dynasties and class distinctions as societies became larger and more diversified. This outward oriented expansion led to a decreased influence of the more inner oriented role of women.

In the third place mythologies and 'celestial pantheons' began to play a role in spiritual world views, and the nameless Mother Goddess was seconded by many more goddesses, and occasionally with male partners.

Fourthly, northern patriarchal invaders entered the goddess-oriented civilisations, and introduced their weather and sky gods which led to mixed goddess/god mythologies. This marked the beginning of cultures where eventually gods and men were to become the rulers in both the divine and the secular world and where male creation stories started.

As a result, the spiritual and social prominence of womanhood in the invaded areas diminished dramatically between 3000 BCE and 500 BCE.

The transition to a third phase at around 500 BCE was marked by what Jaspers called the 'axial period'. By this he meant that within a relatively short time the mythological and quasi-historical accounts of increasingly male-dominated creation stories crystallized into religious and philosophical concepts. These were to become the bases for all religions and philosophies that still exist today. The word 'axial' was used because the transition occurred independently and concurrently in Greece (Thales, Socrates, Aristotle), Palestine (the Prophets), Iran (Zoroaster), India (Buddha) and China (Lao Tse and Kung Fu Tse), along an imaginary axis stretching around the world.

The religious and philosophical concepts were, except for Taoism, predominantly male-oriented, following the trends in mythology and society, and were instrumental in causing further deterioriation of the goddess culture. After a transition period of mixed goddesses and gods, a single God became the symbol of the new paradigm of male superiority in the West and Near East.

As Christianity emerged in the first decades CE, the process of devaluing the female continued rapidly through ill-conceived ideas propagated by most of the Church Fathers, who preached the 'natural' inferiority of women and the 'cultural' superiority of men.

The end of this third period was marked by the closing down of the last goddess temples by the Christian emperor Justanianus of Rome and Byzantium around 500 CE.

The next chapters will explore in more detail these three periods and what they contributed to the male/female relationship in society.

V

From One Goddess to One God

According to recent literature and judging from archeological findings, artefacts, tools, cave drawings and some 30,000 figurines from the late upper palaeolithic period in northern Europe, the female/male relationship in many hunting/gathering groups was one of a complementary, mutually dependent nature, without hierarchy or domination of either of the two sexes.

In most of that period the climate was governed by the Fourth Glacial (Wurm) stage and varied from cold steppe, or even Arctic tundra, to northern temperate, similar to parts of Siberia and Canada today. These climatic conditions made hunting and gathering vitally important in the search for food for survival, an essential part of a nomadic lifestyle in which both sexes were in all probability jointly involved.

The predominantly female figurines dating from that period appear to be symbols of fertility representing the vital role of the female in the process of (pro)creation. On the other hand, they also reflect the magic and divine dimension of the nameless Great (Mother) Goddess, the source and destiny of creation. The Goddess embraced heaven and earth, the cycles in nature, the cosmic dimension and the origin of life and death.

> The Goddess, in this perception, *is* Creation (as opposed to the God in later times, who *made* Creation).

The cave drawings from this period, discovered mainly in France, lay emphasis on hunting and animals, with scarce representation of other human activities.

Clay figures of the Mother Goddess, originating from Crete and India.

No signs are evident from the paintings that would indicate hierarchy or warfare.

The element of sexual intercourse is nowhere to be found, neither in animal nor in human illustrations. It is very likely, backed up by contemporary evidence from some of the thirty-odd hunting/gathering cultures in today's world, that the relationship between impregnation and childbirth was not understood at that time. The magic power of women to create children probably placed them in high esteem as they guaranteed the essential continuity of the community.

It does seem likely that ignorance of the mechanism of procreation is the original source for the concept of parthenogenesis, procreation without interference of a man, present in practically all European and Asian mythologies and in the biblical myth of the Virgin Mary.

No figurines or cave drawings of the late upper paleolithic period have been found dating from after around 10,000 BCE.

Further evidence of human activities, beliefs and cultures reappear again from the neolithic period, starting around 7000 BCE. It is found throughout much of southern Europe and south-west Asia, especially south-eastern Europe and the Mediterranean islands near Anatolia (Turkey), Crete and the Cyclades in the east, and Malta and Majorca in the west, but not in central or north-west Europe.

The external factor accompanying this revival is the fact that the glacial conditions in Europe receded, and the post-glacial period started somewhere around that time. The spread of forests and improved climatic conditions favoured horticultural settlements in the south, replacing the nomadic hunter/gatherer culture. Such a development, due to the milder climate, had occurred some thousand years earlier in the Middle East and India.

The figurines from former Anatolia, dating from 6250 to 5500 BCE, and those from Crete, dating from 5500 to 3000 BCE, are still predominantly female, but there are also distinctly male figurines and some without male or female features.

The figurines from the Cyclades, dating from a period of roughly between 3000 and 2000 BCE, represent a more refined and sophisticated image of women, without pronounced sexual features. Male figurines are also found but in much smaller numbers.

It is speculative to draw definite conclusions from these examples, but there seems to be some consensus among the specialists that the nature of the figurines relates to a continued belief in female deities and possibly a Great (Mother) Goddess.

In neolithic times the nomadic lifestyle was replaced by living in settlements, villages and even cities, such as the very early city Catal Huyuk in Anatolia in the 6th millenium BCE. More emphasis on food growing than on hunting implied a continuing pronounced role for women. They were now not only vital for procreation but also played a major role in the growing of food which was still small-scale and horticultural.

The women in the community also maintained order in the household, in the broader sense of the 'oikos', which stands for the ecosystem of the dwellings, the yards, the people, the animals, the crops and their interdependence.

Men went on hunting expeditions outside the yards and retrieved incidentally big game, which however made a diminishing contribution to the food supply.

A matrilineal society developed as a result of the new role of women in the growing communities. Girls were taken into the closed female groups and boys were sent out with the men. Fathership was still not fully recognized and was a sort of collective condition.

> Although women were clearly at the centre of things, they did not seem to have assumed a dominating position. Women were apparently able to play a 'matrifocal' role in 'horizontal' partnerships, as opposed to later 'patriarchal' communities where men chose 'vertical' dominance. There is no indication that one could speak of a matriarchy in those days; this notion simply did not arise. It is probably a present-day invention to translate the reality of patriarchy backwards into a theoretical concept of matriarchy.

Here is something to remember when we come to the later chapters of this book on the challenges for the future. All the indications are that there does not exist, nor has there ever existed, anything like a matriarchy.

As communities expanded, tribes were formed, gardens became larger, and a start was made on the domestication of animals.

The mechanism of procreation came to be vaguely understood, and women and men started to form pairs and families.

Hitherto men had been of secondary significance, but the changing conditions offered opportunities for them to find new roles, to become more important. They were probably quite frustrated with the matrilineal and matrifocal lifestyle of an inner circle, which put them into second place, as outsiders. Opportunities arrived when the 'outer' activities became more and more extended due to the increased scale and scope of food production, the need for more land, and the fact that women stayed 'at home' to look after the family.

The increase in food production was possible because the techniques of plant growing were observed and better understood by the women who were caring for the gardens daily. There is evidence that it was the practical intelligence and ingenuity of women that led to the 'invention' of agriculture in these early societies of the neolithic period.

The irony of history is that although agriculture was invented by women, that invention eventually led to their downfall, as we will see later.

The making of stone tools advanced and became more sophisticated, and this led to the first steps being taken in the mechanisation of food growing.

It is hardly surprising that over the following ages these trends accelerated, and between 3000 and 2000 BCE, when copper and bronze became available, the tools for food growing and harvesting became technically superior and more efficient. Eventually, ploughs came into use, and the domestication of animals led to the employment of oxen for pulling them.

◄ Cycladic figurine, c. 2500 BCE.

The new role for men included conquering more territory for food production. For this purpose they developed weapons to defend themselves, and to fight, kill and destroy the enemy, applying the same metals and technologies used for hunting and cultivating tools.

In order to handle crop cultivation and harvesting on these larger territories, more labour was needed, and it is at this time that we see the first indications of trading in slaves. These were predominantly the women and children of the conquered territories where the men had been killed in the fighting.

The cultivation of land and the sowing of seeds led to the understanding of an association between the seeds of plants for crops and the semen of male animals and humans for procreation.

This probably had a profound influence on the mentality of men who recognized that seeds contained all the elements essential to form a plant and that the soil was there to nurture it and make it grow. The fact that women were becoming associated with this function of the earth and men with being the primary source of procreation extended a powerful influence on the perception of male and female roles.

Associating female with nature now turned into a disadvantage for them, and men started to upgrade themselves as the source of creation and the carrier of culture. Woman became identified with the earth and with the moon with its monthly cycles; and man, conversely, with heaven and the sun.

This was probably one of the most important moments in the history of the female/male issue that led to a persistent misconception through the ages; that women represent the cyclical, unpredictable and dangerous character of nature, destined to bear, nurse and serve, while men represent the straightforward, reliable and intelligent character of culture, destined to fertilize, govern and command.

The simple and misleading formula that female is identified with nature and male with culture was taken to unfortunate extremes throughout the ages.

It is interesting to note that the matrilineal system came into existence originally because it was beyond doubt who was the mother of a child, and this led to a natural lineage and bond. Later patrilineal societies tried to eliminate this exclusive bond by denouncing sexual intercourse except for procreation and by unilaterally forbidding women to see other men after marriage, for the obvious reason that otherwise the patrilineal system would break down. The man wants be sure that he is the father, and the woman is a vehicle for bringing forth 'his' new generation. Female monogamy was, in other words, not a moral issue but a political one.

The Bronze Ages, occurring at different times in the Mediterranean, Mesopotamia, Egypt, Asia Minor and India, and also in other parts of the world, reveal more information about daily life than the prehistoric period. This is because archeological and anthropological assessments of excavated cities make it possible to understand better how people lived, how they organized their households and what their personal backgrouds were, as evidenced by records on tombs. With the advent of the art of writing we also get accounts on 'tablets' of temples and, at a later stage, records of the administration of towns and cities and stories of wars, political struggles and intrigues.

A great many studies have been published since the 19th century on the changing roles of men and women in the Bronze Ages. There seems to be a reasonable consensus that, as a result of the change from hunting and gathering to horticulture and agriculture and the shift from agriculture to urbanisation and rule by dynasties, the following phenomena are likely to be observed within changing human society:

increase in size of communities
use of metal
wars over expanding territories
killing of male adversaries and capture of women
land becoming male property
trade in surplus agricultural production
trade in slaves, initially women
urban centres
patriarchal invasion from the North
social and political hierarchies of male power
male-led dynasties and kingdoms
male-dominated temples
large irrigation projects

luxury and fine arts in elite circles
arranged marriages, young brides
women confined to household and handicraft
women excluded from education
prostitution
gender legislation based on men's superiority
class stratification

These phenomena represent some of the main trends evident between 3000 and 1000 BCE in societies not only in Mesopotamia, Anatolia, Greece, Egypt, Asia Minor and India, but also in China, South America and Africa, although not always coinciding in time and, of course, variously accented.

The question is whether these apparently universal trends are the unavoidable outcome of human civilisations emerging from primitive communities or whether we are dealing with temporary overshoots of male domination that get corrected at some time in history.

It would seem that emerging civilisations did pose a threat to gender relations in society but that they also presented opportunities, as I shall attempt to demonstrate. Unfortunately, however, these opportunities did not lead to sustainable corrections, because every time a new dimension or notion in gender relations held out the promise of restoring the balance between male and female, a counterforce annihilated the proces and male dominance prevailed.

In later chapters dealing with the first and second millennia BCE, it will be seen that history repeats itself time and again. It seems therefore that we are dealing with a law of nature. The challenge is whether we can break this law in the third millennium, if indeed that is what we want.

As gender roles changed in the secular world, this coincided with the arrival of gods in the world of mythology.

Originally, the female element was predominant and remained so throughout most of the neolithic period. But profound changes gradually took place between 3000 and 1500 BCE that hereafter opened the way to a shift towards increased male dominance.

Mythologies as we read them today are based on the various stories, artefacts, paintings and sculptures that have been found over the course of time, and the timetable of the mythological stories does not always coincide with the place and time of writing or the time of the artistic creations. In other words, it is by no means always clear when something is supposed to have happened in the celestial world of fantasy. In addition, invading tribes and conquered civilisations mixed up their respective stories, and thus the picture becomes even more incoherent.

Nevertheless, the oversimplified scheme on the following pages shows in brief how sequential transitions from an original one Goddess to an ultimate one God could be visualised over time in the mythologies of the aforementioned geographical regions.

As indicated earlier, the concept of the nameless Great Mother or Great Goddess was conceived as the original and universal source of creation, the cosmic force reigning over heaven and earth and associated with the sun and the moon. It is possible that women in real life were somehow identified with these divine gifts and powers.

In prehistoric times the Great Mother remained central in all the regions, but she sometimes bore different epithets, such as the Queen of Heaven, Lady of the High Place, Celestial Ruler, Lady of the Universe or simply Her Holiness.

Over the course of time, between 3000 and 1500 BCE, additional goddesses started to play a role in the various mythologies, charged with certain symbolic tasks and functions. As these mythologies are not always linked specifically to very precise historical times and areas, the names of goddesses sometimes appear in different sequences and in various 'stories' in different regions. Therefore, any chart or scheme describing how mythologies evolved is doomed to be incomplete and controversial. Nevertheless, the scheme on pages 38 and 39 presents an impressionist picture of the trend from the One Goddess to the One God. This trend was influenced by the arrival of creation stories, about which more will be said in Chapter Seven.

Many of the goddesses procreated through parthenogenesis, bearing children without male interference, which could reflect earlier prehistoric stories, orally transmitted, from the times of ignorance of how procreation works.

The goddesses eventually had male partners on occasion, mostly younger men but always in somewhat confusing relationships, at least for today's reader, being sons, husbands and gods. In the beginning these gods always had less prominent positions and were sometimes even smaller in size. After a time, however, the gods became more dominant, and the goddesses lost their status, becoming wives, lovers or spinsters.

From feminine/matrilineal orientation to masculine/patriarchal domination in Soutern Europe and Asia Minor.

Age	Paleolithic		Neolithic	
	◄ 8000 BCE		4000 BC	
Civilisation	nomades hunters gatherers partnership matrilineal cave art fugurines		settlements hunting horticulture families matrilineal domestication artifacts	
Mythology	one Goddess	Godesses	lower Godesses	
India	w	Devi	Kali Durga	Aditi Agivi Devisri
Sumeria	i	Nammu	Inanna Ninhursag	Ki Nintur Ninmah Ningal Ningirsa
Mesopotamia/ Babylon/Syria	t h o u	Tiamat	Istar	Kubiba Damkina Ninlil
Anatolia (Turkey)	t	Anath	Astarte Cybele	Potnia Estan Lotan Arina
Canaan (Israel) Egypt	n a	Sophia Nun	Ashera Isis	Astarte Nut Hathor Maat
Greece	m e	Gaya	Aphrodite Artemis	Hera Demeter Hestia

Bronze	Iron	Antiquity
2000 BC	**1000 BC**	**500 BC ▶**
villages	dynasties	nations
cities	kingdoms	empires
agriculture	patriarchal	religion
metal	slavery	philosophy
handicrafts	wars	male domination
patrilineal	creation stories	
writing/script		
lower Gods	**Gods**	**one God**
Indra	Shiva	w
Visnu	Brahma	
Agui		i
Ur	Anu	
Tammuz		t
Attis		
Damuzi		h
Enki	Marduk	o
Ashtar		
Apsu		u
EA		
Istanu	Hepat	t
		n
Baal	Yahwe	a
Atun	Osiris	
Ra		m
Hades	Zeus	e
Poseidon		

39

In the course of the shift in power, the female-related symbol of the serpent became identified with danger and death as opposed to the original image of wisdom and renewal.

The gods in Canaan, Baal and Yahweh fight serpent Lotan; god Marduk in Babylon fights serpent Tiamat; the gods Zeus and Apollo in Greece fight Typhon and Python.

Here are additional signals of the profound change in the evaluation of the female function, forerunners of the later story of Eve and the evil serpent Sophia.

40

Over time the increased importance of gods led to monotheistic and male-oriented creation stories and to the one and only God replacing the one and only Goddess of the prehistoric past.

Although a final and total turnaround did not happen overnight, Friedrich Engels characterized the mythological and secular changes that occurred around 3000 BCE as the period of 'the world historic defeat of the female sex'.

The change from horticulture to agriculture, the application of bronze and copper, the first writings and the revolution in the perception of goddesses and gods in this period coincided with another series of events which had a powerful effect in both the secular/social and divine/celestial spheres. Between roughly 3000 and 1500 BCE the arrival of aggressive invaders from the North played a major role in a final and fundamental transition to a male-dominated civilisation. The invaders came in several waves and over an extended period in various parts of South-East Europe, Egypt and Asia Minor. They imported their mountain and weather gods, like Zeus in Greece, Indra in India and Marduk in Mesopotamia.

These incursions from the North and the emergence of 'creation stories' reflecting the winds of change in the invaded civilisations all influenced the shift from female orientation to male domination, from Goddess to God.

The next two chapters will illustrate these two influences in more detail.

VI

Machos from the North

Between the fifth and the third millennium BCE, nomadic tribes, usually referred to as Indo-Europeans, Indo-Aryans or simply Aryans, came down in several waves to southern Europe and the Middle East from the Baltic area, Russia and the Caucasus.

The peaceful civilization of Old Europe which had flowered undisturbed for 2,000 years, from 6500 to 4500 BCE, was suddenly disrupted by the invasion of these nomads. The first arrivals, who were later known as Indo-Europeans (or Aryans), were in fact neither Indian nor European. Archaeologist Marya Gimbutas names them as the Kurgan peoples and suggests that their homelands were the steppe land between the Dnieper and Volga rivers. These pastoral tribes worshipped sky gods wieling the thunderbolt and the axe, and rode the horse, which they had domesticated as early as 5000 BCE, enabling them to cover vast distances at a previously unimaginable speed.

We can only speculate as to how these nomadic bands grew in number and ferocity and over what span of time.

Over millennia they were apparently out there in the harsh, inhospitable, colder, sparser territories at the far corners of the earth, while the first great agricultural civilizations were spreading out along the lakes and rivers of the fertile heartlands. To these agricultural peoples, enjoying the early peak of evolution so gladly achieved, peace and prosperity must have seemed the blessed eternal state for humankind, the nomads no more than a peripheral oddity.

But suddenly the battle-axe and the dagger appeared in the civilized regions. The invaders encountered goddess-oriented, often still matrilineal, cultures with thriving urban centres and written languages. Although it is not clear whether the nomads were mainly barbaric and lacking in culture, it seems that they readily adapted the advanced cultures to their own. Consequently, millennial traditions were truncated: towns and villages disintegrated, magnificent painted pottery vanished as did shrines, frescoes, sculptures, symbols and script. The taste for beauty and the sophistication of style and execution withered. The use of vivid colours disappeared in nearly all Old European territories apart from Greece, the Cyclades and Crete, where the old traditions continued for three more millennia, to 1500 BCE.

The resemblance of their goddess sculptures to much earlier goddesses, and to each other, shows that Old European culture did not entirely die out but continued in some form on the western coast of Anatolia and the Cycladic islands of the Aegean, passing to the Minoan and Mycenaean civilizations and then to Greece.

The Kurgan tribes that entered the lands of Old Europe in waves of infiltration changed the course of European prehistory by imposing a culture that was stratified, mobile and war-oriented on a culture that was agricultural, sedentary, egalitarian and peaceful.

> The repeated incursions and ensuing culture shocks and population shifts were concentrated in four major thrusts: the first in 4300-4200 BCE; the second in 3400-3200 BCE; the third in 3000-2800 BCE (dates are calibrated by dendrochronology) and the fourth into what is present-day Greece, in 1500-1000 BCE.

As Aryans in India, Hittites and Mittani in the Fertile Crescent, Luwians in Anatolia, Kurgans in eastern Europe, the incomers gradually imposed their ideologies and ways of life on the lands and peoples they conquered.

> In present-day Greece the invaders came in three waves over a period of about 500 years between 1500 and 1000 BCE, first the Ionians and Mycaneans, then the Archaeans and later the Dorians. They overtook the goddess-oriented civilizations of the Cyclades, the mainland and Minoan Crete.

Zeus in Greece, Indra in India and Marduk in Mesopotamia are examples of the Indo-European mountain gods that were introduced by the invaders from the North.

Thus, the Vedas texts, originating from the hymns and rituals of the northern nomads, were written sometime between 1500 and 1200 BCE in the Indo-European

Indra, Lord of the Mountains, riding the white elephant Airavata while fighting Krishna. ❯

Sanskrit, using scripts they possibly borrowed from the Akkadians and the prevailing Harappa culture in India. These texts are male-oriented and do not allow for a goddess culture. They led to a degrading of the female goddesses and of female prestige.

Indra, the Indo-European Lord of the Mountains, is quoted in the Rg Veda: 'The mind of woman brooks no discipline. Her intellect has little weight.'

There were other nomadic invaders as well. The most famous of these are a Semitic people we call the Hebrews, who came from the deserts of the south and invaded Canaan (later named Palestine for the Philistines, one of the peoples who lived in the area). The moral precepts we associate with both Judaism and Christianity and the stress laid on peace in many modern churches and synagogues now obscures the historical fact that originally these early Semites were a warring people ruled by a caste of warrior-priests (the Levite tribe of Moses, Aaron and Joshua). Like the Indo-Europeans, they too brought with them a fierce and angry god of war and mountains (Jehovah or Yahweh). And gradually, as we read in the Bible, they too imposed much of their ideology and way of life on the peoples of the lands they conquered.

Wherever and whenever they arrived, the invaders made no great effort to ignore the Goddess, but they gradually brought about Her deposition.

As 'creation stories' were conceived from 2000 BCE onwards in the various regions and cultures observed so far, the changes in female and male roles led eventually to a further transition to male monotheism in religion and male domination in society.

VII

Creation Stories

Creation stories are found in Mesopotamian and Egyptian texts (3000-1000 BCE), Hellenic mythology and Indian Vedas (1500-1000 BCE), and the Hebrew Torah and Old Testament (1200-100 BCE).

> A more impersonal, philosophical and less anthropomorphic approach to questions of origins and the laws of Creation is taken by later Greek and Taoist philosophers (600-350 BCE).
>
> Later again, the Church Fathers combined stories and philosophy and laid down the dogmatic foundations of the Christian and Islamic religions (100-800 CE).
>
> These stories, philosophies and dogmas were all profoundly influential in shifting the perception of the female/male dualism from female orientation towards male dominance, except in the case of the Taoist philosophers' world view.

In the previous period, let us say up to about 3000 BCE, the mysteries of life and death seem to have been experienced as collective, natural, cyclical and mystical phenomena of Creation and were not linked to origins and futures. But from 3000 BCE onwards, coinciding with the development of written language, there appears to have been a change towards examining individuality and posing such questions as who creates life, who directs our destiny, what is the origin of evil, do we have individual access to a God? Also, the sense of historicity or developmental time was introduced in addition to perceiving time in ever returning cycles.

Civilisations in those millennia were undergoing changes from agricultural to urban life, from communities to dynasties, from producing to trading, from static societies to dynamic societies. Class differences were emerging, and people began experiencing time in historic and revolutionary events. It seems likely that all these changes contributed to the need for questioning the purpose and meaning of Creation instead of just accepting it.

In any event, creation stories emerged all over the world.

This chapter will deal with those from the Mediterranean area, although it will also touch on the stories from India because of the common influence of the northern invaders.

In the next chapter the antique Chinese world view will also be investigated because of its surprisingly different nature compared with the stories from the West and in view of the potential importance of the Chinese nation in the quest for global sustainable development in the 21st century.

Creation stories were meant to address new, existential questions, but they also reflected concepts and realities in human society, including female/male relations. The stories later developed into texts and rituals that were to become the basis of all the main religions and philosophies that still influence our present civilisations and cultures.

In general, it seems that in these creation stories, the world view moved away from the traditional female orientation towards one of male domination. Babylonian and Hellenic stories still start with a female-oriented origin of the universe in the primordial stage; the Hebrew story starts with androgynous origins, but in the Christian religion a male God creates the cosmos ex nihilo, and the first human He creates is a man.

Intermediate androgynous creatures appear in several stories, but grosso modo in all of them, except in the old Taoist philosophy, Creation finally emerges as a predominantly male affair.

Thus, the road travelled in Europe and India, from the one Goddess to the one God, seems have taken an irreversible turn.

Although it is impossible to pin down any moment in time when the Creation story originated, it can be reasonably assumed that the first signs appeared in the early stories of the Sumerian civilisation (fourth and third millenium BCE). In these stories a primal Great Goddess is the source of all being, the origin of the universe and the begetter of gods and goddesses. We also find this concept in early stories from other parts of the world as well as in those of present-day aboriginal tribes.

In later Creation stories the original Goddess is often described as the Mother Goddess and linked to the primal waters.

The feminine principle ruling over the life-giving force of water is for instance manifest in the Sumerian goddess Nammu, goddess of the primordal ocean, whose ideogram or hieroglyph is the sea. The Egyptian goddess Nun is described as 'the flowing unity of celestial primordial waters'. The Cretan goddess Ariadne and the Greek goddess Aphrodite have both arisen from the sea. In Babylonian myth the goddess Tiamat is identified as the primeval sea.

Also in the Taoist world view, water and the mystic female are closely linked as both the origins and symbols of life, because of their similarity in character and function within nature and society.

In these concepts the primal force in nature is water, linked to the mystery of creation and the renewal of life, to which the female holds the key.

47

The Babylonian Creation Story

The Babylonian Creation story: *Enuma Elish*, meaning 'from on high', originated at the beginning of the second millenium BCE and was partly related to the earlier Sumerian tales. This story was to become the root of all three patriarchal eschatological religions of today, Judaism, Christianity and Islam.

As we have seen in the previous chapters, around this time northern invaders with predominantly male gods had entered or were about to enter various agricultural civilisations around the river basins, and they began to influence the position of women in real life and the goddess in mythology.

This is also the time that the first Babylonian dynasty, from the 19th to the 16th century BCE, started to celebrate the ascendancy of the city of Babylon and its deity, the god Marduk, over other cities.

In Babylonian myth the goddess Tiamat is identified as the primeval sea. In the guise of a dragon she went to battle against the god Marduk, who eventually defeated her.

The essence of the Enuma Elish story is the violent conflict between the older mythologies of the Mother Goddess and the new myths of the Aryan and Semitic Father Gods.

This struggle for supremacy can also be found in other stories in Mesopotamia, Persia, Anatolia, India, Canaan, Greece and to a lesser extent Egypt, but the Babylonian creation story is the first where this led to the defeat of the goddess Tiamat and the victory of the god Marduk.

Real life was here linked to mythology in that the rise of dynasties and cities out of agricultural communities led to the need for the organisation of political and social power and for control over land and water against 'chaotic' natural forces such as droughts and floods. These powers were sought by the urban elites, priests and priestesses, kings and queens, who started to identify the Goddess with chaos and the new gods with order. Therefore, the Goddess had to become subordinated to Marduk, the weather god of the northern invaders.

> In the Babylonian creation story the Sumerian goddess Nammu, 'the cosmic waters', gave birth to the cosmic mountain An-Ki, heaven and earth, son and daughter, two in one as a unity, an androgenous concept. This parthenogenetic birth is followed by the 'normal' birth of a son, Enlil, by An and Ki. Enlil then separated his parents into two individuals, male and female. Only after that were gods, plants, animals and humans created.

The separation from one into two can be interpreted as the initiation of dualistic distinctions in our world. Dualism arising from primordial unity and leading over the course of time to 'ten thousand things' as the Taoist creation story has it.

From then on, the Sumerian and Babylonian stories relate a complex series of births and events, with conflicts between generations and also between 'second generation' goddesses, such as the Sumerian goddess Inanna and the Babylonian goddess Tiamat and their consorts, sons or lovers.

In the Babylonian story this eventually leads to the final battle between Tiamat and her great-great-great-grandson Marduk. He extinguishes the life from her body, from which he then fashions the cosmos, separates the sky from the earth and creates and enslaves humans. He, the God, is the creator and the master of the universe, and He thereby reflects and protects the power of the emerging dynasties in the real

The powerful Egyptian sun god Ra depicted on a mural in the Sennedjem tomb, Thebes, 13th century BCE.

world. This marks the decline of the female image of the Bronze Age and the beginning of male superiority in the Iron Age.

At the time when this Creation story evolved, around the 17th century BCE, the end of the Sumero Babylonian civilisation was in sight. This does not seem to have been a coincidence. The course of events leading to the dethroning of the Goddess through intermediate stages of degraded goddesses who have consorts, sons and lover gods, culminating in the victory of a God who creates and governs the world is a pattern recurring in most of the following stories.

Egyptian mythology, dating from the same period as the Sumerian, deviates from this pattern in that the 'second generation' goddess Isis maintains a central position in the world of the gods and goddesses and in the dynasties of Egypt from around 3000 BCE onwards.

Although eventually taking second place to Osiris, Isis remains the throne Goddess, manifesting her descent from the Great Goddess Nun.

Interestingly enough, in Egyptian mythology a goddess, Nut, was the sky goddess and a god, Geb, was the earth god. In nearly all the other mythologies in the world, the sky is always identified with male and the earth with female deities; the sun with a god and the moon with a goddess. The only other exception is found in ancient Japanese mythology, where Amaterasu is the sun goddess and Tukiomy no Mikato the god of the moon.

As we have seen in the previous chapter, changes occurred in the male/female relationships in Egyptian mythology, such as Nut being replaced by her son Atum who becomes the sky god, and Ra becoming the sun god, but the female presence remained stronger than in other mythologies.

Bearing in mind the strong identification of the feminine with water, perhaps the river Nile, being the principal source of life in the ancient Egyptian civilisation, played a role in this resilience of the feminine. At any rate, Isis remained a major and influential goddess in Egypt and later in Greece and Rome, into the early centuries CE.

The Creation stories after the Babylonian, such as the Indian, the Hellenic, the Hebrew, the Greek and the Christian, increasingly ignore a primal Great Goddess origin and move through stages of androgyny towards the concept of a God Creator.

The Egyptian goddess Nut was depicted on amulets that had to protect the mummy. When a pharaoh died he was to be incarnated in her body.

◄ The Egyptian god Osiris was refered to as the great god of the dead, a mighty king that every Egyptian hoped to join in the afterlife. He once possessed human form and lived upon earth. On this mural Osiris is portrayed with his royal attributes: the flail, the Egyptian crown and sceptre.

The Indian Creation Story

The oldest known civilisation in India is the Indus or Harappa civilisation, of which archeological findings date back to 2500 BCE, showing evidence of a goddess culture. The present Hindu goddess Devi, as Kali or as Durga, originates from this pre-Aryan, pre-Vedic period of the third and second millennia BCE in the Indus Valley.

Northern Aryan invaders penetrated into the already declining Indus or Harappa civilisation in the second millenium BCE. Between 1200 and 800 BCE they introduced their war god Indra and the ancient Sanskrit Rg Veda texts. Between 800 BCE and 200 BCE the Upanishads were incorporated into the religion and culture of a new, male-dominated civilisation. The Rg Veda and the Upanishads contain creation stories similar to the others mentioned in this chapter, where the perception of a goddess-'given' Creation is shifting to that of a god-'made' one, through stages of goddesses and gods, sometimes with androgynous features.

The Indian story, leaning on the sources in the Vedic texts, presents Brahman as the wholeness of Creation; both the relative, manifest aspect of the universe and the absolute, non-manifest aspect, All in One, similar to the concept of the Tao in ancient China. The Vedic texts indicate a dualism containing both male and female elements in alternating roles. For instance they say 'sound is the Shakti, the creative energy, of the Absolute, and through the power of sound, Vach, the whole Universe is created'. From later texts we know that Shakti is always identified with the feminine and associated with the goddess Devi Shakti. Also Vach, sometimes identified with the word, appears as a female deity called the Queen of the Gods.

But the texts also say 'first there is Brahman, Lord of all, with whom is Vach, the word; and the word, verily, is Brahman'.

Then Brahma becomes the first-born among the gods and is the creator of everything. He is 'born from the silent womb of the all-seeing, the all-knowing Brahman, whose meditation is infinite wisdom' and 'he moulds the swelling life-force into matter, name and form'. There is a similarity here with the Hebrew story where Elohim is the more conceptual and abstract God and Yahwe is the material God Creator.

◄ Kali, the Black Goddess. She is the creative and destructive breathing of the universe itself and personifies female strength.

In other texts mention is made of two complementary principles in the cosmos: the masculine Purusha, the cosmic spirit, and the feminine Prakriti, nature. *He* is the subjective aspect of existence, the essence of mind; *she* is the primal substance, the undifferentiated matter-energy from which the entire objective Creation arises. In this dualism there is no strife between the female and male origins, but dynamic coexistence with a primacy for male.

The masculine Purusha is described as the source from which breath, mind and senses, air, light and water and lastly earth are born, the last being the foundation for all; and also the solar energy and rain, from which plants and food emerge. An early recognition of photosynthesis!

54

'Nourished by plants and food, the male pours seed into the female. Thus the whole multitude of beings come ultimately from Him (Purusha). From Him arise all hymns and chants, all rituals and initiations, all ceremonies and offerings, the many deities, the angelic beings, the human, the beasts and birds, the rice and corn, the air we breathe, meditation, stability, purity, order, truth, the seven senses, the mountains and the sea, the herbs and the juices. Purusha is truly the whole universe, the immortal soul of all Creation'.

The story goes that Purusha was lonely and wanted a companion, 'so he grew as large as a man and a woman entwined, and then divided himself in two, creating a husband and wife', for 'this body is but half of oneself, the other half is woman'. This androgynous concept is also reflected in some figurines of the god Shiva, his left half showing female and his right half male characteristics.

The constituents of the feminine Prakriti: rajas, tamas and sattva, are the three basic tendencies inherent in all Creation. They are associated with the Vedic deities Brahma, Shiva and Vishnu, who are mostly presented as male gods, although sometimes also androgynous.

An early nineteenth-century painting of Vishnu, the embodiment of the universe and one of the main deities in Hinduism. ➤

The vindictive Indian goddess Kali, also known as the Mother of Eternal Time, decapitating a man.

Although in all these tales a feminine presence remains, the primacy of the masculine is apparent. We have already seen that Brahman is called the Lord, but in other texts he/she is described as Prajapati, who is woman, man and maiden, but also old man. In Hinduism the main deities are the gods Brahma, Shiva and Vishnu, who have influential female companions that can mostly be traced back to new names and forms of the pre-Vedic Great Goddess Devi.

Brahma has a much worshipped wife Sravasti, the River Goddess. Shiva overpowered the independent goddess Kali, and she now worships him from her place beside him in the temple.

Of Shiva and goddess Parvati it is said 'there is Shiva in all things male, Parvati in all things female. They are the cause of Creation. The universe is their descendant'.

In other places Sati, the Golden Goddess, is described as a powerful wife of Shiva, resembling the relationship between Isis and Osiris in Egyptian mythology. Vishnu, who in Hindu tradition is the protector and preserver of the world and the restorer of moral order (dharma), is often depicted in the presence of his consort Devi Sri (also called Laksmi), the goddess of prosperity.

◀ A current Bombay portrait of the 'divine family':
Shiva, 'in all things male', his counterpart Parvati,
'in all things female', and their child Ganesha.

The Indian Goddess Durga in a fight with Mahisha, a buffalo demon who threatened the gods.

So the goddess has retained a significant place in Hinduism, regardless of the male-oriented Creation story and the subsequent strong patriarchal bent of the culture due to the dominance of the Shiva and Vishnu cults. Indeed, Durga ceremonies and Kali worship are still familiar routines in Indian life.

Goddess Durga is one of the most formidable and popular deities of the Hindu pantheon. Her primary mythologycal function is to combat demons who threaten the stability of the cosmos. She appears late in the stories, around the 4th century CE but, as discussed earlier, Durga seems to derive historically from the indigenous non-Aryan, pre-Vedic cultures of India.

> Kali is often depicted as the Black Goddess, the essence of perishable things. She is the creative and destructive breathing of the universe itself and 'rivers of blood flow from her'. She is also known as the Mother of Eternal Time.

Thus, the Indian Creation stories imply a shift from a goddess culture to a god culture, but they retain a strong goddess presence.

The Hellenic Creation Story

In *Greek mythology* we find a Creation story in 'Theogony' by Hesiodos of the 8th century BCE. This first comprehensive account of the goddesses and gods of Greece also describes the history of the cosmos and of the earth and its inhabitants and is therefore also a 'cosmogony'.

From this text, and from Homer's poems the Iliad and Odyssey dating from about a century before, it seems plausible that the Greek creation story originated in the latter part of the second millenium BCE.

This coincides with the time that the Mediterranean Aegean civilisation, with its centre in Crete and originating from the third millenium BCE, was destroyed by (Indo European) Dorian invaders from the North in the twelfth century BCE.

Prior to this destruction, the Aegean civilisation had spread to continental Greece in the sixteenth century BCE, starting in the Mycenaean Argolis and initiating a cultural mix between the Cretan and Mycenaean traditions. These gave evidence of Indo-European male-dominated traits from earlier invasions into the mainland.

In the original goddess tradition of the Aegeans, which lasted the longest of all goddess traditions, the chief deity was feminine; nameless, the Great Goddess, the Universal Mother. All the universe was her domain, representing the whole Creation. I have described this phenomenon of the one Goddess without name in a broader context in Chapter v.

In the course of time, also in Crete, a pantheon of goddesses and gods was eventually formed, and later accounts mention an Aegean god Asterius or Asterion, king of Crete, as the subordinated consort of the Great Goddess, who was by then apparently worshipped as Rhea.

With anthropomorphic concepts of divinity and under the influence of foreign cultures, Zeus (the nomadic weather god) was made Rhea's son and subsequently a

LEFT Ares, the god of war. Replica of the lost 'Ares Borghese' made by Alkamenes.

CENTER The Greek goddess Aphrodite, Roman copy of an original made in the third or second century BCE.

RIGHT The Hermes of Olympia. Replica of an original by Praxiteles.

daughter, Britomartis, was born who captured the heart of Minos, the ruler of Crete. We then enter into typical Greek stories of intrigues, mixing divine and secular worship, with the increased presence of the male element and the introduction of historic, developmental time.

When the Dorians finally destroyed the Aegean-Mycaenean civilisation, pantheons of goddesses and gods were already in place, and male dominance had entered the celestial and secular world. The time was ripe for a creation story to consolidate the position of male power.

In Hesiodos's account of the prevailing Greek creation story, in the beginning there was Chaos, vast and dark. Then appeared Gaea, the deep-breasted earth, and finally Eros, 'the love that softens the heart'. Chaos, a word with a Greek root meaning 'gape', simply means open space, a pure cosmic principle devoid of god-like characteristics.

Gaea is a well-defined manifestation of Creation, the earth.

Hesiodos's Eros has only a metaphysical significance: he represents the force of attraction which causes beings to come together and has nothing to do with the Eros of later legends.

From Chaos were born Erebus and Night who, uniting, gave birth to Ether and to Hemera, the day.

For her part Gaea first parthenogenetically bore Uranus, the sky, 'whom she made her equal in grandeur, so that he entirely covered her'. Then she created the high mountains and Pontus, 'the sterile sea with its harmonious waves'.

Now that the universe had been formed, it remained to be peopled. Gaea united with her son Uranus and produced the first celestial human race, the Titans. There were twelve of them. Six were male: Oceanus, Coeus, Hyperion, Crius, Iapetus and Cronus. Six were female: Theia, Rhea, Mnemosyne, Phoebe, Tethys and Themis. The youngest son Cronus castrated his father at the instigation of his mother and became the head of a new dynasty. By his sister Rhea he was the father of three sons, Hades, Poseidon and Zeus; and three daughters, Hestia, Demeter and Hera.

In the above account it is interesting to note that in the sequence of creation from the one goddess Gaea, the human race comes first, albeit in a celestial setting, and the deities come after.

In subsequent accounts in Greek mythology, Zeus, the youngest son of Cronus, was born in Crete, in the thick forests of Mount Aegeum. This was the result of a conspiracy between Rhea and her parents Uranus and Gaea, who were determined to protect him from being swallowed by Cronus. It had been predicted that

Zeus would overthrow his father, who understandably wanted to prevent this.

When Zeus reached adulthood he indeed overthrew his father Cronus and with his brothers drew lots for the partition of the empire of the world. Zeus received as his share the sublime regions of the Ether, Poseidon the tumultuous sea and Hades the sombre depths of the earth. The three sisters were not involved in this distribution of power.

Mount Olympus was to be held in common by all the deities and would become their dwelling place.

Once the Olympian pantheon of three gods and three goddesses has been established they formed a society with its own laws and hierarchy, leading to a reorganisation and a reshuffling of positions.

From then on, the top consisted of six gods and six goddesses:

Zeus, Poseidon, Hephaestus, Hermes, Ares and Apollo

and

Hera, Athena, Artemis, Hestia, Aphrodite and Demeter.

It will be noted that there are 7 additions to the original core of the six brothers and sisters and that Hades did not maintain his position but remained in his subterranian empire.

The newcomers are partly 'pre-hellenic' goddesses such as Aphrodite and Artemis, who now lose the authority they had in the former Aegean goddess culture. They continue to play subordinate but influential roles in the new setting.

At a later stage Hestia is deposed and replaced by Dionysius; consequently the symmetry is lost and the gods are in a majority position.

In the new society Zeus reigned as sovereign and authoritarian ruler, having secured for himself divine supremacy and all the

◄ Figure of the Greek god Apollo from the west pediment of the temple of Zeus at Olympia, *c.* 460 BCE.

The Demeter of Knidos, c. 340-330 BCE.

Head of the Greek goddess Athena from the west pediment of the temple of Aphaia on Aegina, c. 490 BCE.

gifts required to be the new creator. He had obtained 'supreme wisdom', for instance, by swallowing his first wife Metis, who was the daughter of two Titans Oceanus and Tethys. She personified wisdom and, according to Hesiodos, 'knew more things than all the gods and men put together'.

Zeus's authoritarian style differed sharply from that of his father Cronus, who had reigned on terms of mutual understanding with gods and men, although apparently not with goddesses and women.

Still, when the victorious dynasty of the Olympians was established, Gaea's prestige was not lessened because it was she whom the gods and goddesses invoked when making oaths. Gaea remained the omnipotent Goddess, who created the universe and bore the first human race and the first race of gods. Later, as other divinities rose in the estimation of men, the role of Gaea gradually became less important, when for instance the Oracle of Dephi was passed from her into Apollo's hands.

In his self-appointed role as the new creator of the universe, Zeus appointed Prometheus and his brother Epimetheus, who belonged to the celestial Titan race living in the Golden Age, as creators of mankind on earth.

From the texts it appears that in this earthly human race only men were important, as agriculturists in the Silver Age, as warriors in the Bronze Age and, according to different accounts, as victims of misery, crime, injustice, infidelity and lack of respect and virtue in the Iron Age. We see here a clear link between mythology and the history of human civilisation as described in Chapters IV and V. It should be noted that at the time when most of the mythology was written, which was around 1000 BCE, the Iron Age had just started.

Typical of the misogynous atmosphere that was infiltrating human thoughts and fantasies is the story of Pandora. According to the wishes of Zeus in order to punish the theft of fire by Prometheus, Pandora was created by Hephaestus to be the first earthly woman, with a dazzling beauty equalling that of the immortal goddesses. In the story, all the divinities contributed their especial gifts to this new creature, except Hermes who put perfidity into Pandora's heart and lies into her mouth.

When Pandora was welcomed by the enchanted co-creator of mankind, Epimetheus, against the advice of his brother Prometheus, she opened a jar (not a box!) she was carrying with her, and all the terrible afflictions with which the vase was filled escaped and spread around the world. Thus, with the arrival of the first woman, misery made its appearance on earth.

In summing up, the Greek Creation story implied a shift from one supreme Goddess without name, representing Creation, to one supreme God with a name, Zeus, the Creator.

The Hebrew and Christian Creation Stories

The *Hebrew story*, with roots in the Babylonian story resulting from the first exile in Babylon, can be traced back to the period between the 12th and 5th centuries BCE. It starts with Elohim creating the cosmos in six days. Elohim is a Hebrew term with a feminine base but ending in a masculine plural and signifying a dualistic 'Goddess and God'. There is no strife in the story between the Creator and the primal Mother. She is reduced to a concept of 'primal stuff', coexisting with the Creator, who is in serene control of the process.

Elohim first creates light, separating it from darkness. Then, like Marduk did, he creates the sky, to separate the waters above from those below. Next he creates dry land out of the water and then the seed-bearing plants. On the fourth day he creates the stars, the sun and the moon to govern day and night, and on the fifth day he creates the fish and the birds, followed by cattle, reptiles, wild animals and humans. On the seventh day Elohim takes a rest.

A relief representation in black chalkstone of Marduk the warrior, c. 1100 BCE. The Gods gave him the emblems of kingship to make him conquer the goddess Tiamat.

The first human was created in the image of Elohim 'both male and female', correctly translated from the Hebrew text 'sakar-u-nekeba', which are adjectives and not nouns as later translations would suggest.

From the text it can be understood that the first human is still a celestial androgynous being, named Adam-Kadmon. Later Elohim transforms this celestial human creature into an earthly human, who is then split up into man and woman, Adam and Eve. It is only at that point that the name Yahwe starts appearing in conjunction with Elohim, Yahweh as co-creator of earthly mankind. In later texts only the male god Yahweh prevails, although in earlier texts Hokhmah (Sophia), signifying wisdom and spirit in Hebrew, represents the female and 'spiritual' part of his being, complementary to his 'material' creations. In still later texts, however, this female element of Yahweh disappears from the scene completely.

In the Christian perception of Creation, as opposed to older Hebrew texts, God is alone and does not coexist with the 'primal stuff'. He creates ex nihilo. The remnants of the feminine origin have now been totally eliminated. The female wisdom, Hokhmah (or Sophia), is absorbed in anonymity. Androgyny is abolished, and the male God reigns exclusively in splendid divine isolation.

Genesis 1, appearing at a late stage in the Hebrew Torah texts in the 6th century BCE, and part of the present text of the Old Testament:

> 'And God said, let us make man in our image, after our likeness: and let them have dominion over the fish of the sea, and over the fowl of the air, and over the cattle, and over all the earth, and over every creeping thing that creepeth upon the earth.
>   So God created man in his own image, in the image of God created he him; male and female created he them'.

offers possibilities for an androgynous interpretation, reflecting the image of Elohim and the early Yahweh. But Genesis 1 has never been emphasized in Christian religion, nor has it been portrayed in art.

In Genesis 2, however, now assumed to be an earlier text than Genesis 1, Adam is created first. Then, to relieve his loneliness, Eve is created from one rib of the man's body. Although here also one could argue that both male and female are incorporated in the 'human' Adam and this human is then separated into male and female, the Creation myth in Genesis 2 has not been interpreted that way in the history of the Christian religion.

Thus, the story that the first human being was a man has become the accepted version in Western Christianity, contributing to a male-dominated culture.

The Christian view was influenced by the Creation story in Plato's dialogue – the Timaeus – dating from the 5th century BCE. This story is more abstract and philosophical than the other stories described in this chapter and will not be treated in detail, but considering its profound influence on later Christian thinking, it should be briefly mentioned here.

Timaeus makes a radical distinction between the visible, temporal, imperfect and mutable world and the invisible, eternal, perfect and transcendent reality. The last category represents Forms, known only to God, the Unmovable Mover.

The visible world had a beginning when an intelligent and omnipotent God moulded the world from the Forms and created the world's soul, placed in the circles of the heavenly bodies. Subsequently, the gods and the immortal and rational elements of the human soul were formed. The human body and the lower components were then generated through the intermediacy of the 'created gods' (i.e. the stars).

As the Creation needed space, 'chora', the metaphysical nature of this space required the recognition, over and above God or mind, of an element called necessity, 'ananke'.

This transcendent cosmology in the creation story of Plato, supported in great part by Aristotle, was of great importance in the history of science and Christian dogmas, although metaphysically of secondary interest. The implicit and exclusively male nature of Plato's and Aristotle's God has had a substantial impact on the mindset of the Church Fathers who were the architects of the Christian religion and to whom we will return in chapter XII.

◄ Adam and Eve under the figtree. A leaf from the Codex Vigilanus in Madrid. The snake is coiled around the trunk of the tree, its head facing Eve to whom it is talking. Adam pricks up his ear to eavesdrop. Both Adam and Eve cover their nakedness with large figleaves, signaling that they have already lost their innocence.

觀音大士

VIII

From China:
A Different Story

Although the creation stories in this book are limited to the Mesopotamian/Mediterranean area, I could not resist the temptation to have a look at some of the stories about Creation that can be found in other parts of the world, such as China. Their story differs substantially from the one described in the previous chapter.

> The Chinese history of civilisation shows many similarities to those of Europe and India, such as a neolithical population around 12000 BCE, the shift from nomadic, pastoral, tribal cultures to agricultural lifestyles from 5000 BCE onwards, and the development of villages in subsequent millennia, followed by the growth of cities, kingdoms and dynasties.
>
> Findings dating from about 2500 BCE reveal a knowledge of textiles, carpentry and ceramics. Around 1600 BCE, in the Bronze period, we see the emergence of refined arts and crafts and the arrival of feudal systems.
>
> During the above period there were, according to Joseph Needham, signs of a shift from matriarchal to patriarchal control, although in my own research I have not come across any records of matriarchal cultures in ancient China.

◀ Kuan Yin, the most revered and popular Chinese deity, came to China as a male in the first century CE, a bodhisattva from Southern Asia. From the 7th to the 12th century a process of change occurred, at the end of which Kuan Yin had become female.

Interestingly enough, there are no records of Creation stories in China like those that appeared in the Mediterranean and Indian civilisations described in the previous chapter. The reason could be that in the Mesopotamian, Egyptian, Roman, Greek and Indian philosophies, the intellectual power of man has been projected into his concept of one Deity, a God as the All-wise, the intelligent Creator of an intelligible universe, whereas in the Chinese perception of reality, neither man nor the universe needed a conscious controller.

With the early Chinese it was the physical side of animal and human beings, the power of procreation, that gave the first clue to the mystery of nature. The here and now, they said, is the source of new life. Spontaneity is for them the original law of Creation.

For the Chinese it was only natural to extend this known principle in the material world to an unknown immaterial world and hence to believe in the dual powers of nature, Yin and Yang.

This dualistic principle, later enlarged upon by the Taoist philosophers, to whom we will return later, is not a dualism of mind and matter, nor of good and evil, but of male and female. The Chinese literati never recognized a clear distinction between spirit and matter; they believed in spirit and matter as one indivisible whole and were therefore sceptical as to the existence of spirit or spirits as distinct from matter. For this very reason there exists no particular word in the Chinese language meaning 'religion', thus leaving no scope for a separation of religion from life, of heaven from earth.

This illustrates the fundamental difference in their perception of the origin of things between the Chinese and the Mediterranean schools of thought. In the latter the spirit or soul was considered to be a captive of the body and liberated from this captivity at death, while the Chinese saw the organic unity of heaven, earth and human being as inseparable, and not to be untangled into separate realms of dominance, either intellectually or emotionally.

Stories, in the conventional sense of a mixture of history, fantasy, deities, consolation, devotion, intrigues, power and prestige, are very much part of Chinese mythology, but they can only be understood in terms of organic unity, alien to the concept of one God ruling from outside.

The proliferation of many female and male deities fits within the Chinese cosmological concept, where stories of real life and mythologies freely interconnect, inspiring and reassuring people that they have personal access to and are part of the mysticism of a cosmic, organic whole.

On the evidence of ancient records, two different concepts of ultimate reality were entertained in early Chinese civilisation: on the one hand, the popular and deistic, influenced by the shamans of the northern invaders from the second millennium BCE, and on the other, the philosophical and impersonal, originating from the philosophers in the time of the Warring States in the second half of the first millennium BCE. The two concepts later merged into the mosaic of present-day Taoist 'religion'.

The popular and deistic stories, probably originating from before 1500 BCE, posit Chinese mythology in an undefined age of the Five Sovereigns, to which belonged Yao and Shun, the earliest of all figures mentioned.

> The Sovereigns, sometimes described as being half snake, half human, such as Huang Ti and the female Nu Kua, were instrumental not only in establishing the order of the sun, the moon and the stars, but also in leading the people from the darkness of the caves out into the light and teaching them fishing, hunting, agriculture and language, as well as organizing the calendar and the forms of marriage, filial pity and perfect order.

The myth of the Sovereigns, also called Emperors, led to the emergence of Yao, the supreme Yellow Emperor, yellow being the imperial colour, symbolic of the highly fertile loess which covers large areas of Northern China. The Yellow Emperor is the deification of the earth, of the harvests and of the moving heavens that govern the seasons.

Although a strong female identification with Creation can be found throughout the ancient and recent histories of Chinese thought, we find in the above story of the Yellow Emperor the first clear indication of a perception of male primacy, on earth and in heaven. Subsequent emperors, kings, princes and magistrates were considered 'Sons of Heaven' who derived their positions in the later dynasties from 'a mandate from Heaven' and were related to male deist ancestors.

Mythology stories were translated gradually into history, as out of the reign of the Yellow Emperor emerges the first and probably legendary royal dynasty, the Hsia, of which no archeological evidence exists. According to myth the Hsia dynasty fell when successive generations weakened and was replaced by the Shang dynasty. The Shang has actually been identified as commencing around 1700 BCE in the three northern provinces of Shansi, Hopei and Shantung.

LEFT Huang Ti, 'The Jade Emperor', is known as one of the founders of Chinese civilization. Tradition has it that he invented the compass and the potter's wheel. He became immortal at the age of hundred.

RIGHT Nu Kua, an ancient Goddess of Creation, married Fu Xi after she rescued humanity from the Flood.

During the Shang dynasty pictographs began to be replaced by brush-written characters. These later developed into written language at the beginning of the 11th century BCE, during the Chou dynasty, who conquered the Shang around 1027 BCE.

Records indicate that the strong patriarchal family system of the later Chinese had not yet fully developed in the prevailing primitive feudal society, where the religion was still one of agrarian fertility.

It is supposed, but not confirmed by evidence, that in the middle of the 11th century, the founders of the Chou dynasty, King Wen and his son the Duke of Chou, formulated the sixty-four hexagrams of the 'I Ching', the Book of Changes. This document, albeit primitive, represents the first Chinese, reference to cosmology and destiny. According to some historians, it was the revised edition of a work by a legendary Emperor of antiquity from the third millennium BCE, Fu Shi, who supposedly originated the Yin-Yang concept of universal dualism.

The 64 hexagrams in the I Ching, combining different groupings of 8 trigrams consisting of undivided Yang lines ——— and
divided Yin lines — —, symbolize the orderly universe as a realm
of perpetual activity, in constant change, where things are forever
interfused and interconnected through the simple interaction of
Yin and Yang.

As stated earlier, whereas Creation stories do not appear in
ancient Chinese culture, the I Ching probably contributed to the
development of Chinese philosophies concerning the nature of
man and his existence within a natural and cosmic context.

The Book of Changes grew out of the ancient practice of divination. It is not philosophical and very cryptic, but alludes to a well ordered and dynamic universe. Change,
for which the Chinese word is 'i', meaning also 'easy', summons the two forces Yin
and Yang, representing the passive feminine
and the active masculine in nature, and their
interaction gives rise to all multiplicity in
the natural world. The creation of life from
the female and the male is an extension of
the universal principle of Creation, without
the need for a separate Creator. Creation is
a continuous manifestation of an undefined
and impersonal ultimate reality. No beginning, no end.

This cosmology may seem naive and crude,
but the philosophical spirit is clear: Creation exists in a natural operation of forces
in the here and now and is neither initiated
nor controlled at some specific point in time
by a spiritual force from outside. It follows that Chinese
mythology was not preoccupied with an anthropomorphic Creation story; it left the Creation in peace, with its
resilient female character.

The well known Chinese yin and yang-
symbol represents all the opposite
principles one finds in the universe. Each
of these opposites produces the other.
Heaven creates the ideas of things under
yang, the earth produces their material
forms under yin.

It appears that this ancient organic Chinese cosmology with its complementary Yin/Yang had no discernible influence on gender relations in the Chinese society of the period covered so far, as nowhere in the literature have I been able to find any references to the realities of daily life of women and men within this context. From scattered information in historical texts and stories, however, one may conclude that women in society were, as in other parts of the world, inconsistently stereotyped as inferior, weak, timid and sexually exploitable, and at the same time dangerous, powerful and sexually insatiable. Also, like everywhere else, during their menstrual periods women were considered unclean and not allowed to participate in religious rituals. How they fared within the strongly patriarchal family cells in those days is unknown.

An interesting point is that, again as in other cultures, the comparison is made between the seed of a plant growing in the soil and the male semen growing up in the female womb. But the functions of the semen and the womb are regarded very differently from the way Aristotle saw them in Greece.

The Chinese interpretation is that, whereas a seed itself turns into a grown plant, semen merely starts the growth process. What turned into the body of a child was supposedly the menstrual blood of the mother. In contrast to the Aristotelian view, therefore, the woman played a substantial qualitative role in procreation.

Coming back to the Chou dynasty, they systematized the incipient feudal society bearing the thoroughgoing agricultural character of the unfolding Chinese civilisation. A new aristocratic class ruled the Empire, as it had now become, through landownership by local nobility in a way very similar to the feudal system that existed in Europe two thousand years later. This implies a continuation of male dominance and female subordination in an increasingly patriarchal and patrilineal society. So it seems likely that the same conditions existed as in the third and second millennia BCE in Mesopotamia, and later in Greece, where ruling class women had certain privileges but no rights and where the peasants, soldiers, artisans, merchants and slaves disappeared in anonymity and poverty, without any historical record.

The Empire collapsed in the 8th century BCE, and the period of the 'Warring States' followed. It ended when the first unified Chinese Empire was created in 221 BCE by Prince Cheng of the State of Chhin. As the first Emperor of a united China, he adopted the title Chhin Shih Huang Ti. Huang Ti was the name of a supreme agrarian male deity.

The strongly centralised and authoritarian Chhin Imperium lasted only fifteen years, but it set the new imperial stage onto which China had irreversibly trodden.

It declared an end to feudalism, organized a nation state and safeguarded itself from northern invasions and cultural export by building the Great Wall of China.

In the period from 1000 to 200 BCE, ancient China went through far-reaching societal and political changes, but that was not all. The invention of iron-working technologies (from 500 BCE) introduced new warfare methods and agricultural practices, while massive irrigation projects were built.

These changes reinforced the male-dominated organisation of society, with increased hierarchical and territorial conflicts. Hence the period of the 'Warring States' from the 5th to the 3rd century BCE.

Between 500 and 250 BCE China entered its greatest period of intellectual development with the 'hundred schools' of philosophers. In the same century that Plato founded the Academy (named after Attic hero Academus) in the Greek capital Athens in 387 BCE, Prince Hsuan founded the famous 'Academy' (our western nametag) of the Gate of Chhi in the Chhi state capital in 318 BCE.

The 'hundred schools' included the school of Confucianism, based on the Analects dating from the 6th century BCE, and the school of Taoism, based on the Tao Te Ching and probably dating from the 4th century BCE.

Both philosophies adhere to the principle of the universal law, the Way of Heaven, the Tao. In Confucianism the emphasis is on culture; in Taoism on nature.

For Confucius Heaven is not an arbitrary, governing, divine, supreme Deity, but the embodiment of a system of legality.

Confucius's thoughts on the codes of morality, democracy and equal rights to education remind one of the concepts of his Greek contemporary Socrates, except for the fact that Confucius embeds his ideas in an axiomatically and exclusively male setting. His works were to become very influential on the way Chinese society was destined to be organized. Unfortunately, they further reinforced the male-dominated mode in Chinese history and civilisation.

In the Confucian system the basic cell of society is the family, at the head of which stands the eldest adult male as a sort of patriarch. The state is an extension of the family. In the days of Confucius, the state meant the class of ruling feudal lords, who are Sons of Heaven. So the hierarchy of the system is the father in

> the family whom the wife, sons and daughters unconditionally obey without rights; the ruler to whom the head of the family unconditionally submits; and the ruler who derives his religious and social authority from Heaven.

Thus, in Confucianism the cult of Heaven, the family system and the state are welded into a unity through an exclusively male lineage. This became the foundation of Chinese society up to the present day, although China has also experienced feminist movements from time to time over the past thousand years, and feminism has started to gain some ground since the end of the last century.

As Taoism, both philosophical and religious Taoism, has more roots in nature as opposed to Confucianism's roots in culture, their perceptions of reality and of human nature are in many ways quite different and sometimes even contradictory. Although Confucianism seems to have been more influential than Taoism in the organisation of society, Taoism had and still has considerable influence on individual life and religious experience in society.

> The fundamental characteristic of Taoist thinking is that the ultimate reality, the 'Tao', literally translated as the 'Way', cannot be defined and thus loses its meaning when we start to define it. This is the essence of Chapter 1 of the Tao Te Ching.
>
> Tao is stream, change, process, transcendent, imminent, always present, an undefined phase before and beyond the non-existing void, from which existence emerged. Tao represents pre-ontological, primordial experience, present in the cosmos, in the natural world, in the human body.

In Taoist thinking, initial existence is symbolized by the One, the T'ai Chi, which then leads to the Two: Yin and Yang. From them the Three were born, and they lead to the Ten Thousand Things in our world. In this process the Tao represents the creative power, which is perceived in essence as feminine.

◄ An eighteenth century Chinese painting of Confucius, Buddha and Lao Tse. For Confucius heaven is the embodiment of a system of legality.

Essential in the creative process is the all-pervading presence of an energy, ch'i, also called material force or cosmic spirit, comparable to Bergson's elan vital or the Greek pneuma in its original meaning.

> According to Taoist cosmology, in the beginning there was original Chaos, 'Hundun', the eternal maternal uterus that conserved the whole Creation in a diffuse, potential condition containing all ch'i energies, intermingled within darkness.
>
> Through the influence of the element of cyclical change in the Tao, the uterus breaks open, and the ch'i energies are liberated. They untangle themselves into light energies to form the Sky and heavy energies to form the Earth. Together they unite into the Middle. It is at this point that the Ten Thousand Things originate, leading to the Five Planets, the Twenty-eight Houses, the Thirty-six Stars in the Sky and the Seventy-two Stars on Earth, who together form the One Hundred and Eight Celestial Phenomena. These generate new phenomena in new classes, and so Creation continues. In this process the human being is the most complex organism, consisting of countless essential elements, although amounting to nothing more than an intricate part of the whole.

The Taoist story is one of movement and change within continuous cycles of interaction between the feminine and masculine forces. Important manifestations of this interaction are water and fire, wood and metal, unified in the fifth and central element, the Earth. Water and fire, in Chinese thought very much connected with feminine and masculine symbolism, are represented by two symmetrical trigrams:

The water trigram consists of one inner Yang and two outer Yin lines; the fire trigram of one inner Yin and two outer Yang lines. If we were to take these symbolic representations of the feminine and the masculine literally and translate them into our perceptions of female and male, female has two outward Yin appearances with an inward Yang core, and male has two outward Yang appearances and an inward Yin core. I think that symbolism expresses what we, women and men, are beginning to understand about ourselves: there is masculinity in a woman and femininity in a man, a notion we have been educated to ignore.

> In the I Ching the hexagram combining the two is called incomplete when the water trigram is put below the fire trigram, because water goes down and fire goes up and therefore the two do not meet. However when the water trigram is put on top of the fire trigram, water and fire meet and mix, and the resulting hexagram, number 63, is identified as complete and perfect!

In the stories in the Taoist book of Chuang Tzu, the cyclical movements are also explicitly linked to evolutionary transformations, but neither the beginning nor the end of Creation plays any role. In the Taoist and ancient Chinese perception of ultimate reality, cosmic organic unity and the undefined origin of the Tao simply do not invoke the questions of where we come from and where we are going; Chuang Tzu considers the events of life and death as moments in the ongoing and universal process of transformation.

We cannot investigate the secret of the Tao; all that man can do is to describe and study the natural world, including the human experience of life and the eternal and universal dance of the Yin and Yang, of the feminine and the masculine, creating today's world.

Taoist philosophy implies dynamic harmony between the feminine and the masculine, both in society and in the human being, within an organic nature of the universe.

> In the Taoist 'religion' that developed later over the ages, this principle of the equity of male and female, masculine and feminine, man and woman and the essence of interaction has been

maintained in the resilient Taoist/Buddhist spirituality, with a multitude of male and female deities and rejection of celibacy in the male and female priesthood.

The most revered and popular deity in present China is still the goddess Kuan Yin, comparable to Mary in the West. She evolved in the course of time from an original male bodhisattva called Avalokitesvara from Southern Asia to a semi-androgynous goddess in China within the process of male-oriented Buddhism infiltrating female-oriented Taoism.

The society-oriented Confucianist doctrine, on the other hand, followed the same path as the West by emphasizing the dominance of the male in the family, society and government.

Although Taoism and Confucianism have the same origin and in many ways similar interpretations of the Yin/Yang dualism, they clearly translated these differently in respect of their views on human society.

For the present, the male domination view has clearly won the day in the organisation of the State in China, but the resilience of the Taoist religion manifests itself strongly at the level of the people's daily lives.

Therefore, in contrast to the West, where male domination in society and religion ran in parallel, Chinese society developed into a kind of hybrid coexistence of gender neutral spirituality in a male-dominated world.

Since the Communists seized power in 1947, they have done everything to destroy temples and spiritual practice, but according to China experts, such as Zurcher and Schipper and recent literature from Taiwan (where all the temples are still very much intact and in use), the resilience of this spirituality is very robust.

Maybe the recent public appearance of the Falun Dafa movement in China, promoting the Falun Gong principle, which is based on Buddhist/Taoist spirituality, is a sign of this resilience, much to the dismay of the Communist authorities who have taken radical measures to eradicate the movement. They obviously fear the effect these kinds of developments could have on the power of the male-dominated communist system.

IX

Ups and Downs in Greece

Previous chapters have dealt with changing perceptions of male and female roles in prehistoric and neolithic times and in the Bronze Ages, as manifested in artifacts, paintings, mythologies, Creation stories, epics and visions.

These manifestations most probably reflect the moods, the trends and the daily preoccupations of human societies of the period.

The works of Homer, the *Odyssey* and the *Iliad*, written in the 8th century BCE are based on orally transmitted stories and epics of Bronze Age Greece. They are also a source of information about life in that period, later matched by archeological findings.

In the Bronze Ages women of the elite in Sumerian, Babylonian, Assyrian, Egyptian, Cretan and Mycenaean societies did not have formal powers or status. They were confined to the households and premises of their masters, obliged to obey and perform their subordinated functions. They did have the opportunity, however, to influence policies and decisions of state through marital arrangements and what we call today their 'network', their informal power.

Women also had considerable spiritual influence, because goddesses still maintained a resilient presence in the cultural and spiritual world of that time, and women played a major role as priestesses in the temples.

The oldest, Sumerian, civilisation collapsed in 1800 BCE, due to over-irrigation and consequent salination of agricultural land, destroying its food base.

Nevertheless its culture and societal institutions and customs continued to be influential in the Babylonian and Mycenaean civilisations that flourished subsequently and later still, after the Dark Ages (1200-800 BCE), in Greece.

We know from the records, the stories and the surviving art that in these civilisations women of the elite had increasingly greater freedom, access to education, inheritance and economic means. They also enjoyed social respect because of their

positions as mothers, wives, sisters or daughters of the ruling emperor, king or magistrate, and the associated ownership of land and wealth.

Whether women were happy with their lot in those times, is difficult to say, but at least some must have enjoyed their ambiguous position and potential to compromise. Conversely, men must have felt uncomfortable at times, when their public image of power in the dynasty or temple was out of tune with the reality of their private life in the palace or home, a familiar thought in our present, still mostly patriarchal society if we read corporation for dynasty, church for temple and office for palace.

The struggle of the elite to remain in control through arranged marriages offered clear opportunities for women to match male power. But it cannot have been easy to break through the vested interests of the institutional male hierarchy, especially as the overwhelming obligations of the domestic motherhood role were so limiting, and such informal powers as women possessed were dependent on formal male authority.

In archaic (800-500 BCE) and classical (500-335 BCE) Greek urban life, separation of the sexes was a logical consequence of the new organisation within the non-agrarian household, distanced from nature. It provided separate quarters: those where women were supposed to feed and breed, the 'gynaikonitis', and those where men were supposed to wheel and deal, the 'andron'. This arrangement admittedly afforded solidarity and safety to women, having 'their own place', but at the same time it reinforced the radical distinction between the sexes.

Despite the increased, but marginal female influence in upper-class circles, a fundamental breakthrough in society did not occur, although there were incidental and temporary exceptions where a strong woman made her mark in a weak dynasty.

In archaic and classical Greece, which was to have such a great impact on Western civilisation, developments were taking place that contained both opportunities and threats to the female/male balance. In 8th century BCE Greece the city states (polis) were created, autonomous units mostly run by noble landowners, but with a certain amount of people's involvement in electing the exclusively male governing officials. Each polis had its own patron god or – very often – goddess, whose temple stood on the acropolis, where the polis's religious ceremonies took place and where priestesses were important.

The polis system introduced the principle of decentralisation of power to Greece and some modest elements of democracy. The advent of democracy, however, was destined to have a negative impact on privileged women's informal power roles, as we shall see later.

◄ Goddess and child, Attica c. 700 BCE. The amply decorated throne emphasizes the divine nature of the female figure, whereas the schematic modeled child accentuates her motherhood.

Another new development, in the 7th century BCE, was the rise of natural philosophy and physical science in Ionia at the periphery of the Eastern world, in southern Italy and in Sicily. Mythical explanations of natural phenomena were no longer accepted by some thinkers of that time, and they started to analyse natural processes via logical reasoning. They did not repudiate the mythical deities but added the new dimension of rationality, which was to become the basis of Western scientific thought. Renowned representatives of this new school of thought were Thales from Milete and Pythagoras from Samos.

> As I am writing this on the 26th of February 1998 on the isle of Bonaire, where today we experienced a total solar eclipse at 14.11 pm in the presence of a large international group of scientists, it is appropriate to remember that Thales predicted with astonishing accuracy the solar eclipse of May 28th in the year 585 BCE.

The breakthrough to scientific thought in Greece developed further from the 6th century BCE onwards with the start of the classical period. This was marked by a continuing tendency to turn away from mythologies in favour of philosophies and religions.

As will be shown, this trend was also helping to turn the tables on womanhood, leading to a new era of gender relations with new ambiguities.

In order to place these developments in context, something more needs to be said about classical Greece.

Daily life for men and women in the Ionian polis of Athens in classical Greece was in many ways similar to that of earlier ages, but the rights of the privileged 'citizen' women with respect to marriage, dowries, divorce, inheritance and education were more protective and better formalized in laws. Even so, the position of women remained politically, socially and legally inferior to that of men.

Also, slavery was formalized and endowed with certain rights, including the opportunity to regain one's freedom.

Prostitution and homosexuality were accepted practices, and it seems that various factors played a role here. In the first place, the arranged marriages were not necessarily happy ones.

Secondly, married upper-class women were keen to limit the number of their children as motherhood was attended by great risks and a high rate of childbirth

mortality. So limiting sexual intercourse was to their advantage. On the other hand, men were free to go to prostitutes or sleep with slaves or male friends. They could also spend evenings with higher-class free women, the 'hataerai', female companions who were well educated, intelligent, and usually artistic and beautiful, comparable to the later courtesans in China and geishas in Japan.

The School of Athens (1508-10) by Raphaël. Vatican, Stanza della Segnatura, Fresco, 770 cm at the base.

And so life in aristocratic Athens was a mixture of formal and informal gender relations, full of compromises and contradictions, but fundamentally a man's world. Unfortunately, very little information is available as to the true state of gender relations in the other social classes and slave communities, as no historical records exist.

Eventually, the traditions of worshipping mythological deities and entertaining in male-dominated aristocracies started to show signs of fading in classical Greece.

There was renewal in the air. A renewal involving a transformation in thinking about the individual as a human being, not merely as a member of a citizen body. Attention began to focus on each person's ethics and responsibilities, the achievement of happiness and personal religious experience. All of this coincided with the search for rational explanations of natural processes.

The new thinking introduced elements of doubt into the prevailing traditions of mythology and aristocracy. In the course of the following ages, it led to their decline and replacement by science, philosophy, religion and democracy.

This process also introduced new dimensions into the relations between men and women. As we have seen, the improved roles in the daily lives of women were related not only to the resilience of the goddess mythology, bestowing them with spiritual leadership and priesthood, but also to the prestige of the aristocracy, bestowing them with access to male power. The new trends, therefore, by diminishing faith in mythologies and aristocracy threatened the basis of improved gender relations in Greek society.

After the Persian wars and military confrontations between Sparta and Athens, Pericles established new legislation in 451-450 BCE that laid the foundations of democracy in Greece. It resulted in the curbing of aristocracy and eliminated the class stratification that separated men according to noble descent and wealth in the traditional polis. This also entailed the repression of women, at least those had flourished in the aristocratic society. Because their husbands lost influence and prestige, they did too. And then their husbands had to find new ways of proving their superiority; turning on them was an obvious resort.

In that same period the philosophical school of Socrates (469-399 BCE) and his dialogues with his pupil Plato (429-347 BCE) introduced the system of rhetorical education.

Socrates, in his search for natural ethical laws, had progressive ideas about social justice and the equality of men and women as human beings of similar nature. He therefore stressed the importance of both sexes having equal rights with regard to education.

Plato supports this position in the 'Republic' when he prescribes the same curriculum for guardians of both sexes to prepare them for their duties. The only difference between them, he claims, is that the male begets and the female bears children. He proposes state-supported childcare and the abolition of property as provisions for an androgynous lifestyle in a society of gender equality.

In the later 'Laws' he retreats from these idealistic positions and takes a more practical stand. He is still progressive as regards to women's rights but suggests that, on the whole, women are not equal to men, which weakens his point.

> Plato advises that women should not marry and bear children before the age of 16 and that men should not marry before 30. Women should have a chance of gaining a basic education before marrying, and men should engage in military service and be prepared for war in their years of mature youth.

These views and discussions of Socrates and Plato on male and female and on masculine and feminine offered new opportunities for restoring the balance between the sexes. They could have had a considerable and positive influence on the gender issues of those days, and indeed of those on following ages up to and including our twentieth century.

That opportunity was finally lost, however, when Aristotle (384-322 BCE) developed his misguided, supposedly scientific arguments about the inferior nature of women.

> The major conclusions of Aristotle's theory were, in short, that:
> – a woman provides the nourishing carrier of the male sperm and only contributes 'matter' (mater), while the male sperm already contains the complete individual person, soul and spirit.
> – women are mutilated males (monstrosities), for 'they do not have the principle of soul in them'.
> – the deliberative functions of the woman's impotent soul make her mentally and intellectually weak and in need of supervision

These, for today's reader incredible, viewpoints were derived from Aristotle's philosophical system and studies of biological anatomy. They were accepted as scientifically indisputable and therefore had a great influence and impact on the future history of women and their positioning in society.

Another part of Aristotle's philosophical system was his theory of the 'prime mover', taking the position that in the sequence of cause and effect shaping all the phenomena in the cosmos, there must be one universal cause. This concept was later used by Thomas Aquinas in the 13th century CE as a rational way of proving the existence of one God, the 'prima causa'.

This approach supported the development towards monotheism. Monotheism originated from the 12th century BCE Hebrew creation story and was formalized in the Torah in the 6th century BCE, in the same period that Aristotle postulated his theory of the prime mover.

Aristotle's views on male superiority and on one universal cause and the Hebrew concept of one male God present a remarkable coincidence, reflecting the spirit of that time. They eventually ruled out the potential for more gender equality promised in the progressive ideas of Socrates and Plato.

When Alexander the Great from Macedonia took the initiative, in the heat of discord between the Greek states, to extend territorial control over all of Asia Minor and Egypt from 334 BCE onwards, he created a vast unified Hellenistic Empire. But his rule also marked the end of free autonomous city states and a decline of the democratic system. It was the start of the Hellenistic period (334-30 BCE), with kingdoms and an oligarchy. This change offered upper-class women new opportunities to improve their position, who had lost much of their power with the advent of democracy.

After Alexander's death in 324 BCE at the age of 32, a number of kingdoms and cities of great diversity played a part in shaping Hellenistic society. Intensive intercultural exchange took place, with infiltration of the achievements of Greek civilisation in respect of the arts, literature, religion and gender relations.

The three main kingdoms (the Ptolemies of Egypt, the Seleucids of Asia Minor and the Antigoni of Macedonia), and the city states of Greece each favoured different styles of political and social life. What they all had in common, however, was a strongly oligarchic structure and a freer involvement of queens and other upper-class women in political and economic affairs.

Thus, the legal and social status of women improved, although fundamentally the primacy of male power remained. But it was especially the increase in economic wealth achieved by some women that gave them access to political and religious power as well as public acclaim. Documents and deeds of transactions from that period show a considerable involvement of women, even as magistrates. In Hellenistic Sparta women owned two-fifths of the land.

Under pressure from revolts against the oligarchy and a mounting disparity between rich and poor, which had already begun to be a problem in classical Greece, democracy was eventually restored in Athens in 307 BCE. But it was not the same as before, and the rest of the Greek city states remained in the hands of oligarchies. Short-lived bloody revolts were mounted by the poorer population, but basically the ruling upper-class system was maintained, albeit with an increased involvement of middle-class citizens.

As ancient myths about the Homeric deities had been criticized in the previous classical period, the trend towards more personal religious experience in the Hellenistic period led to a lessening of faith in the ancient Olympian pantheon members. The influence of abstract philosophical thought started to be felt, with an adapted system of more personalized deities. At the same time, Zeus was elevated in philosophical works to a more universal level, gifted with supreme divine power.

In this Hellenistic period, the contacts with the Near East and Africa led the Greeks to identify their own gods with foreign gods, even the God of Israel, and in particular the Egyptian goddess Isis.

Isis was partly 'hellenized', an adaption that can be recognized in visual arts and hymns, and she was considered to be of a higher level of divinity than the Greek deities. She was worshipped as a supreme Goddess through whom the religious and emotional needs of women and men could be expressed and satisfied.

Isis was, as we have seen in previous chapters, a national deity of ancient Egypt, where female goddesses always commanded high esteem. In the course of the classical and Hellenistic periods she had become a deity of many lands including Greece, and the cult of Isis adapted itself to local beliefs wherever it was carried.

Isis was endowed with magical gifts such as healing and achieving resurrection after death. To her was attributed the powers of not only female but also male deities, such as dominion over lightning, thunder and the winds. She was worshipped in many different ways, reflecting unlimited flexibility, at times being part of a polytheistic or henotheistic cult and at other times being a single supreme Goddess.

Plutarch cites the creativity of Isis from Plato's 'Timaeus', where her power is concerned with matter which becomes and receives everything: 'light and dark, day and night, fire and water, life and death, beginning and end'. She could be all things to all people, which explains her great popularity.

Her worship was not confined to women, but appealed equally to men. Isis became a symbol of equality between men and women. This resulted, in both the Hellenistic and the later Roman world, in an Isis cult having a larger influence on religious ideas than any other of the new movements. This cult, attracting the worship of both men and women, could have offered another opportunity to restore the balance between male and female and how each was valued in society. But it did not, because of the mounting influence of the Mithras cult.

The cult of the exclusively male god Mithras originated in Persia, where Zoroaster was introducing a monotheistic philosphy, and proved to be an increasingly strong countervailing force to the Isis cult. The concept of one male God, infiltrating from both Hebrew and Persian sources, eventually led to the downfall of Isis in the Roman Empire. The Christian Emperor Justanian finally closed the temple of Isis in Philae, the last heathen stronghold, shortly before 550 CE.

One wonders what would have happened to relations between men and women in society if the Isis cult had survived and grown into a new religious culture. Would it have safeguarded an equal appreciation of male and female values in the secular world?

In this chapter I have tried to investigate the various factors that influenced female/male relations in the Greek world and to show how, with ups and downs in the strive for more equality between men and women, the male-dominating model always emerged as the winner in the end.

The stories provide us with clues as to why this happened and what we can learn from it if we wish to change the pattern in our present societies.

Bronze figure of Isis nursing Horus. The gold mask covering the goddess' face is of substantial thickness; the wooden base is original. (Isis was a national deity of ancient Egypt, where female goddesses always commanded high esteem. In the course of the classical and Hellenistic periods she had become a deity of many lands including Greece, and the cult of Isis adapted itself to local beliefs wherever it was carried.) ➤

X

The Secret Words of Jesus

Before touching on the subject of the secret words of Jesus, I will first offer a brief sketch of the history of the Roman world into which Jesus appeared around the start of the first millennium during the reign of the Roman Emperor Augustus.

While the winds of change were blowing in Greece, a new power was gradually emerging in the West. When in 509 BCE the city of Rome, by then the largest city in Italy, expelled the Etruscan king and abolished monarchs as an institution, the Early Roman Republic was formed. Executive powers were transferred to two annually elected magistrates, later called consuls. Religious authority was passed to the 'rex sacrorum' and the 'pontifex maximus', an all-male network of power.

In the subsequent period, up to the third century BCE, the history of the republic was dominated in the main by two lengthy processes. One was the settling of powers between the patricians and the plebeians; the other was the struggle for power in peninsular Italy, where the expansion of Roman influence continued against a background of wars with hill tribes and Etruscans, Celtic raids and power struggles within the Latin League.

By 275 BCE Rome had achieved complete control of the whole of peninsular Italy, including the Greek cities in the south, in a variety of alliances with the different tribes and city states. From then on the republic grew steadily, westwards into Europe, southwards into Africa and eastwards into the Hellenistic Empire, turning the acquired territories into colonial provinces or leaving the national or tribal status intact under local vassal rulers loyal to Rome.

During this period of expansion, many internal uprisings and civil wars also had to be fought, so all in all it was an intensely militaristic and consequently masculine scenario.

◄ Jesus Christ portrayed as a classical philosopher.

Christ washes the feet of the apostles, *c.* 1000. *Otto III's evangelistary,* Bayerische Staatsbibliothek, München.

The Hellenistic Empire, what remained of it, finally came to an end when in 30 BCE the last ruler of Egypt's Ptolemeic dynasty, Cleopatra, was defeated by Octavian. Egypt was integrated into the Roman Empire, and Octavian was honoured with the name of Augustus (meaning majestic, he who has been promoted to greater power). This marked the beginning of the Early Imperial Age.

During the period of Roman growth and Greek decline, homage was paid to a colourful bouquet of mythologies, gods and goddesses, mystery religions, cults, nature gods, abstract deities and new pantheons. This was the result of adapting and integrating all the various civilisations that came to constitute first the Hellenistic and then the Roman Empire. In previous chapters some of the gods and goddesses have been mentioned that were currently popular such as Isis, Mithras and Cybele. For the Romans it meant a change in emphasis from their originally impersonal, abstract deities to personalized Egyptian, Greek and eastern gods and goddesses with romanised names, and also to new philosophical world views and monotheistic religions.

In general, the influence of Greek culture, art and literature remained strong throughout the whole age. The Romans had great respect for the Greek lifestyle which they regarded as older and in many ways superior to their own. Cultural life in Rome was thus inspired by the Greek example. It should not be forgotten that Roman history goes back no further than around 750 BCE, whereas Greek history started in the Bronze Age.

Although first century BCE Rome is often compared to classical Athens, records indicate that democracy in Rome never reached the level it had attained in Athens. As regards cultural life and the arts, however, both cities displayed exceptional quality.

Roman civilisation was based on military, political, legal and organisational genius. The Greek historian Polybus considered the combination of monarchy through the consuls, democracy through the popular assemblies, and aristocracy through the senate as the formula for the success of the Roman Empire.

In the matter of gender relations, most sources agree that women in Rome were given more freedom and shown more respect than in Athens. In the upper circles at least, women were offered more educational opportunities and private tuition. They could reach administrative positions, just but as in Athens, political power remained predominantly in the hands of men.

It is obvious that this general and brief description of the development of Roman society does not take into account the numerous differences in mythological traditions, secular lifestyles and political organisations of all the components of the vast Roman Empire with its great variety of directly administered provinces and indirectly affiliated kingdoms.

Jesus was borne in Judea, the mid-southern part of Palestine, which also encompassed Galilee in the north and Samaria further south. Between 830 and 63 BCE, after having been occupied by Assyria, Babylonia, Alexander the Great's Hellas, the Ptolemies and the Seleucids, the Jewish people asked for help from Rome. They were resisting the tyranny of the Hellenistic occupation, which was trying to force them into the service of Zeus. In 63 BCE the Romans conquered Judea, which eventually became a Roman province-kingdom under Herod the Great in 40 BCE. After his death and following the unsuccessful reigns of his incapable sons, Rome appointed a procurator and later a prefect, Pontius Pilate.

As noted earlier, Roman rulers were living in a multi-religious and multi-mythology culture that did not accept the Jewish monotheism into which Jesus was born. They later accused him of claiming to be 'King of the Jews'. On the other hand, the strongly paternalistic and patriarchal Jewish community refuted Jesus's liberal teachings on free spirituality, the equality of male and female, and the vanity of laws and hierarchy, to which I will return shortly. As we shall see later, the Christian religion that developed from this Jewish base also failed to accept the message of the historical Jesus.

In other words historical Jesus was not acceptable to the Romans, nor to the Jews, and not understood by the orthodox Christians. The last mentioned group invented the name Christ (from the Greek 'christos', the 'anointed') after his death and created a different man.

What happened during Jesus's lifetime has become clearer over the last five decades now that so-called apocryphal manuscripts have been found, translated and analysed. These manuscripts were for the most part unknown until recently because they were declared heretical by early Christian orthodox leaders and had been excluded by the Church fathers from canonisation (canon means literally 'guideline') into the New Testament (NT).

Especially significant are the 52 documents discovered in 1945 at Nag Hammadi, a location far upstream of the Nile in Egypt. They shed a new light on the message of Jesus, ranging from direct individual access to the divine and free individual spirituality to equality of male and female in all respects and no religious hierarchy in the community (ecclesia in Greek).

Although the various Nag Hammadi texts do not all support the equivalence of male and female, the words of Jesus consistently express this view.

The later Catholic (meaning universal) Christian religion, in the process of its development from the second century CE onwards, was based on the concept of access to the divine exclusively through Christ and thus through the Church and the hierarchical authority of a male bishop (from episcopos, the overseeer). Its prescription of compulsory 'confession' and the exclusion of women from the priesthood clearly did not at all match well with the texts of the documents found in Nag Hammadi.

Recent specialised literature on the Nag Hammadi papers, which were for a great part written in the Egyptian Coptic language in Greek script, comes to a consensus that they were set down in and around 375 CE and that the original Greek texts date from between 50 and 70 CE. This is the same period as that of the oldest gospel, Mark, but possibly somewhat earlier. It is certainly earlier than the gospels of Matthew, Luke and John, the originals of which date from between 70 and 100 CE, the first two possibly being derived from a common single source, the so-called Q gospels.

As the apocryphal documents were rejected at an early stage as heretical and unacceptable sources for Christian liturgy, it could very well be that they are more authentic than those that were chosen as 'inspired by God' for canonisation into the NT. The apocryphal texts were set aside and probably mostly destroyed. Those that survived, therefore, were not manipulated, whereas there is abundant proof that the four official gospels were revised, adapted, extended, interpreted and adjusted to serve the goals of the Church Fathers in creating the Catholic Church during the 500 years following the birth of Jesus. However, as we shall see, selected sayings from the apocryphal texts can still be found in the NT.

The inconsistencies in the hundreds of different manuscripts that are presently known of the four gospels and other NT texts make them a volume of debatable historical value. This is clearly demonstrated in the Scholars' Version of the Complete Gospels, published in 1994.

Although the currently available translations of the apocryphal documents date from the late 4th century CE and were undoubtedly also adapted to the moods and dreams of the time, it is highly possible that the secret words of Jesus are less distorted than the chosen words of the NT.

What were the secret words of Jesus?

I will give a few quotations from the manuscripts of Nag Hammadi which illustrate something of what Jesus tried to convey and which are especially relevant to the subject of this book.

The Four Evangelists, Jacob Jordaens,
c. 1625. Oil on canvas, 133 x 118 cm,
Musée du Louvre, Paris.

In logion 22 of the *Gospel of Thomas*, Jesus answers a question put by his followers as to how they will enter the Kingdom of God:

> 'When you make the two into one, and when you make the inner like the outer and the outer like the inner, and the upper like the lower, and when you make male and female into a single one, so that the male will not be male, nor the female be female, ...then you will enter (the kingdom).'

A similar notion can be found in another historical Christian document by Clement of Alexandria, one of the early Church Fathers who in 190 CE makes reference to God in feminine as well as masculine terms and with respect to human nature postulates that 'men and women share equally in perfection, and are to receive the same instruction and the same discipline. For the name 'humanity' is common to both men and women; and for us in Christ there is neither male nor female'.

Clement was alone in his attempt to match orthodoxy with Gnostic dualism and was later overruled by his contemporary Church Father Tertullian.

The concept of duality out of oneness, of completeness both in pre-existence and in existence, is essential to the message of Jesus if we acknowledge logion 3 of the *Thomas Gospel*:

> Jesus said, 'If your leaders say to you 'Look, the kingdom is in heaven', then the birds of heaven will precede you. If they say to you 'It is in the sea', then the fish will precede you. Rather, the kingdom is within you and it is outside you. When you know yourselves, then you will be known, and you will understand that you are children of a living father. But if you do not know yourselves, then you will dwell in poverty, and you are poverty.'

The essence of this saying is that the Kingdom of God is also within every human being. It is not only 'out there', outside this world, but is both within and without, originating from pre-existence. It can be known through knowledge of the self.

In Luke 17:20-21 a vague allusion is made to this idea when he records Jesus as saying, in answer to the Pharisees asking when God's imperial rule would come, 'You won't be able to observe the coming of God's imperial rule,........ on the contrary, God's imperial rule is right there in your presence'.

Just for comparison the Taoist philosopher Mencius said 'All things are already complete in oneself'. To which he added 'Ability possessed without having acquired it by learning is innate ability, and knowledge possessed without deliberation is innate knowledge'.

These sayings are often associated with so-called Gnostics, who claim that we can, through insight, achieved by individual experience of pre-existence, have awareness and knowledge of the original complete fullness, the pleroma, that preceded the cosmic reality.

But whereas the traditional Gnostics, like the Essenes, often translated this experience into rejection of the real world, because it was polluted by matter, and consequently decided to live an ascetic life, Jesus was very much of this world and did not choose the road of radical dualism.

In the *Gospel of Mary*, Mary Magdalen is depicted as one of the apostles, favoured with visions and insight that go beyond those of Peter.

In the *Dialogue with the Saviour* she is described as the apostle who excels all the other twelve. She often explains Jesus's sayings to them, as she seems to understand him and his message better than anyone else.

In *Pistis Sophia*, Peter complains that Mary has priority in the conversations with Jesus and that he and the other apostles should take first place. Mary is quoted as saying to Jesus: 'Peter makes me hesitate; I am afraid of him because he hates the female race', to which Jesus answers 'Whoever the Spirit inspires is divinely ordained to speak, whether man or woman'.

Peter is typically annoyed at Mary's presence, when according to the *Gospel of Thomas* he says to the disciples 'Let Mary leave us, for women are not worthy of Life.' Jesus replied, 'I myself shall lead her, in order to make her male, so that she too may become a living spirit, resembling you males. For every woman who will make herself male will enter the Kingdom of Heaven'.

This seemingly discriminating text can be understood as confirming the strong patriarchal culture of the prevailing Jewish community, against which Jesus takes a position by assisting women to enter the man's world as equivalent persons.

The image of Mary Magdalen in the Nag Hammadi texts is quite different from the presently prevailing idea that she was a converted whore, declared holy for her rehabilitated role as an example to 'fallen' women. Although Vatican II withdrew this interpretation in 1969, few Christians today view Mary as the 'apostle of the apostles', relating her holiness to the fact that Jesus appeared to her after the resurrection.

Positive Gnostic texts usually make reference to Genesis 1:26 and 1:27 which suggest gender equality in the creation of humans. Orthodox texts, on the other hand, lay stress on Genesis 2:21-23 which describes how Eve was made from a part of Adam, and created for his fulfilment. This is also the text favoured by the Jewish religion.

In two Nag Hammadi texts we can read stories about Adam and Eve that offer a different interpretation from what we have been taught in the Christian culture. In *On the Origin of the World* and in *The Essence of the Archons*, the taking of the fruit from the tree of knowledge by Eve is seen as a blessing and not a sin. A blessing because it brings intrinsic knowledge and consciousness to humanity, thus transmitting a spark from the ultimate divine, the pre-existential, universal and androgynous source of Creation. It was a sin in the eyes of the male demiurges, the creators of matter, earth and life, who were jealous and afraid that they would not be able to control human beings anymore when they had acquired divine knowledge and consciousness.

Here we are confronted with a belief that was widespread in those days and which is frequently mentioned in the apocryphal papers, namely that there are two levels of Creation: the pre-existential androgynous level that we also find, under the name of Elohim, in the Hebrew texts that were described in Chapter VI; and the level of the earth and its inhabitants, which represents the work of the male archons and demiurges, in Hebrew text under the supervision of Jahweh.

If we read in Genesis 1:26-27; 'Then God said 'let us make man in our image, after our likeness'..... in the image of God he created him; male and female he created them', the reference surely is to the ultimate androgynous Creator. The Creator in

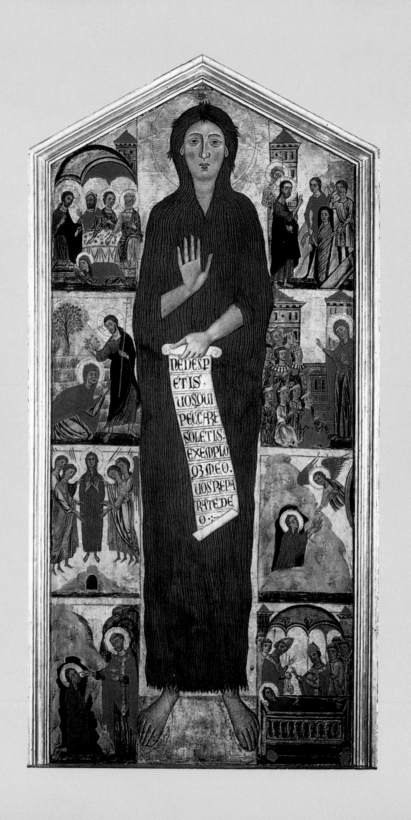

Genesis 2, where man (Adam) is created first and Eve from him obviously refers to the level of the male demiurge.

The practically exclusive and subjective reference in Christian culture to Genesis 2 has had a fundamental effect on the perception of gender in Christian society. In the Nag Hammadi stories, the serpent and in some cases Eve represent the wisdom of Sophia, who is the female complement to the male component in the ultimate Creator. Eve's taking of the fruit is symbolic of a major step in the process of evolution when through self-reflexive consciousness and knowledge, human beings became co-creative in the evolutionary process, thereby distinguishing themselves from all other creatures on the planet. The downside is that self-reflexive consciousness also brings with it the element of doubt, of choosing between good and evil. This can lead to sin, but can be prevented by knowledge of the self.

In the *Gospel of Mary* Jesus says, when asked by Peter what sin means in the world, 'Sin does not exist' and explains that humans 'make' sins. In other texts in the *Dialogue with the Saviour*, he says that sin is nothing other than ignorance (see Lucas), not knowing.

Thus, the apocryphal manuscripts shed a totally different light on the story of Adam and Eve which, if conveyed in this way to the Christian community, could have caused gender relations to be viewed very differently from the way they are now perceived in Christian culture.

The words of Jesus in the apocryphal manuscripts did not fit the agenda of the Church Fathers. His pronouncements on individual and direct mystical experience, on the futility of laws as opposed to intrinsic knowledge of oneself, on Mary's role in spreading the word of his visions, and on male and female equivalence were all at variance with what the Church Fathers had in mind.

After Socrates and Isis, Jesus presented yet another opportunity to correct the trend towards male domination. As we shall see in the next chapter, however, this chance was also missed. In the 400 years following Jesus's death, the Christian religion was built on a male-dominated, hierarchical and legalistic base, in direct opposition to His words which were kept secret for nearly 2000 years.

◀ In this representation Mary Magdalen stands frontally before the beholder with a scroll in her hand. It reads: 'Do not despair if you have sinned. Follow my example and make your peace with God!' On the eight small scenes around Mary Magdalen the most important stages of her life are pictured.

105

XI

Misogynic Church Fathers

In the previous chapter the historical Jesus arose from the apocryphal texts as a man with a message directed at obtaining divine knowledge through self-knowledge and at rediscovering human integrity from within by following the laws of nature and not of man. His views on human integrity implied the equivalence and complementarity of male and female, man and woman as equals in Creation and in the world. It was a gnostic vision in a sense, but did not reject the material world as some gnostic movements of his time did.

After his death, the disciples were to become apostles, and the message of Jesus was gradually transformed into the message of Christ. Over the course of time the two messages became very different. The life and sayings of Jesus were described and transmitted in stories, narratives and sacred texts. Over a period of about 400 years these laid the base for the official text of the New Testament.

Church Father Athanasius, Archbishop of Alexandria, published his Easter Letter in 367 CE in which he listed for the first time in Christian history scriptures that were claimed to be divinely inspired and therefore deserving of sole recognition as authentic for Christian belief.

The scriptures were and still are today the four Gospels, the Letters of the Apostles, the Letters of Paul and the Revelation of John. These were all endorsed as final texts of the New Testament at the council meetings of Hippo Regius in 393 CE and of Carthage in 397 and 419 CE, after which the case was closed and has remained so ever since.

It seems that during those 400 years the tendency to subordinate the female sex became stronger and stronger as time went by. The same trend continued right into the Middle Ages when the Church Fathers Albertus Magnus and Thomas Aquinas, adopting Aristotelian theory, 'discovered' that woman was a 'minus perfectum'.

The road to the endorsement of Christian Bible texts had gone through a number of stages. A great many different and geographically dispersed initiatives had been undertaken to create a religious follow-up to Jesus's ideas after his death, especially in the first centuries, within a still pluriform and mythologically oriented Roman Empire. As Christians refused to publicly worship the Roman state gods, they were accused of bringing down the wrath of these gods on the Empire and of forming a state within a state with their religious communities under clerical hierarchies.

Up to the beginning of the 4th century CE, when Constantine the Great came to sympathise with Christianity, the early Christians were confronted, prosecuted, expelled and murdered in Egyptian and Roman territories, where not only the Isis cults but also the Persian Mithras and Asian Cybele traditions were still flourishing up to the 4th century CE. Christians were also fought and prosecuted by the patriarchal Jewish communities.

But at the end of the road, the Christian faith won over the cults of Isis, Mithras and Cybele and strode ahead of the Jewish religion.

Instrumental and highly influential in the direction of the Christian movement were the Church Fathers, those early theologians who also shaped Christian perceptions of masculine and feminine characteristics, and of male and female roles in the church, society and marriage.

These views resulted in a general culture of male domination.

Such a culture contrasted with the prevailing trend towards an improvement, albeit still modest, in male/female relationships in Egypt and Rome, where from 200 BCE onwards the social, political and legal status of women had already advanced in relative terms. At the beginning of the first century, for instance, patriarchal forms of Roman marriage were replaced by ceremonies with new legal rules involving voluntary and mutual vows between man and woman.

This gradual progression towards more equity between men and women could have received a positive boost from the words of Jesus, but it was reversed by the Church Fathers by their direction of the Christian movement after Jesus's death.

Again a critical moment passed and a chance for change was missed, just as 300 years earlier the opportunity presented by Socrates had been reversed by Aristotle. The turnaround started with Peter, as we have seen in the previous chapter, and was continued by Paul, although in an ambivalent way. It was then further shaped by the Church Fathers, specifically by:

- Clement of Alexandria and Irenaeus of Lyon in the second century CE;
- Origen and Dionysius of Alexandria, Tertullian of Carthage and Hippolytus of Rome in the third century, and
- Ambrosius of Milan, Hieronymus of Rome, Athanasius of Alexandria and Augustine of Hippo in the fourth century.

What did all these men do and think in those times?

Peter thought and behaved according to his Jewish patriarchal background, and he therefore saw no role for women in fulfilling the message of Jesus. From the apocryphal texts it appears that Jesus tried to explain to him why he was wrong, but one gets the impression that Peter neither understood nor accepted this. When Jesus commissioned Peter to lead the campaign after his death, this resulted in an exclusively male-directed process that was to be continued by all the popes that came after Peter, acting as the sole representatives of God through Jesus Christ.

In the middle of the first century CE, Paul, a former prosecutor of Christians under the name of Saul, assumed the role of super apostle. Although he had never known Jesus, he claimed to have been inspired by a vision of Him.

Paul's opinions on gender issues are recorded in various texts of the New Testament. Although scholars in the field of Bible studies are increasingly doubtful about the authenticy of many of the sayings and letters ascribed to him, his endorsed message on the role of women, is sometimes ambivalent but on the whole clearly misogynistic.

> Paul is quoted as confirming in Galatians 3:28 that 'in Christ.... there is neither male nor female', but he is ambivalent when it comes to the practical implications of human equality. Although he allowed women more religious functions in the church than the Jewish congregations did, he did not propound equality in social or political activities.
>
> In 1 Corinthians 11:7-9 he says: 'a man....is the image and glory of God; but the woman is the glory of the man. For man was not made from woman, but woman from man. Neither was man created for woman, but woman for man'.

◄ Church Father Ambrosius, Sforza-book of hours, Italy 1521.

But in 1 Corinthians 11:11-12 he adds: '...in the Lord woman cannot be without man, nor man without woman; as woman comes forth from man, so man comes forth from woman and all come forth from God.'

With respect to marriage, Paul is not against the union between man and woman, but he considers celibacy and continence the better option. However 'it is better to marry than to burn (with desire)', according to 1 Corinthians 7:9.

In 1 Corinthians 14:34-35 the text reads 'the women should keep silence in the churches. For they are not permitted to speak, but they should be subordinate... it is shameful for a woman to speak in the church.' In line with this, by the year 200 CE when the foundations of the Catholic Church were laid, the majority of Christian communities endorsed as canonical the pseudo-Pauline letter of Timothy in Hippolytus, ref 6.9 : 'Let a woman learn in silence with all submissiveness. I permit no woman to teach or to have authority over men; she is to keep silent'. Statements of this kind can also be found in *1 and 11 Timothy, Colossians and Ephesians*.

If we compare these texts with those in the previous chapter citing the words of Jesus in the Gospel of Thomas, for instance regarding the right of women to speak, the position of Paul presents a sharp contrast, regardless of the fact that he acknowledges women as his equals 'in Christ'.

As mentioned in the previous chapter, it seems likely that the four Gospels in the New Testament were originally written in the second half of the first and the early part of the second century by evangelists (literally 'messengers of good news'). They were not apostles, and they wrote their stories many decades after Paul. The original texts are not known, as the earliest transcripts we have access to today date from the late 4th century and must have gone through many adaptations and 'corrections'. But if we take them as they stand, they too reflect the male-dominated scene, although in some texts we can still recognize the original Jesus; for example, his view that the Kingdom of God is not 'out there' but around us here and now, and his respect for women, especially in the stories about Mary Magdalen.

Augustinus surrounded by saints, 1415. ➤

ær augustine. precas niaf

sulapx. ec peccas ꝯ dicon.

Saint Petre and Saint Paul, Masolino da Panicale, c. 1428.

In the following period, the second half of the second century CE, there are still two categories of Christians, the gnostics and the orthodox. Both place more emphasis on the risen Christ, the spiritual being whom Jesus represented, than on his biography, but the gnostics are nearer to the sayings of Jesus in the apocryphal scripts than the orthodox. The gnostics acknowledge that every human being has direct access to the mystic experience, whereas the orthodox claim that only the apostles and their chosen successors have such access. There are other profound differences, such as the matter of one or two Gods (the abstract and the demiurge) or the symbolic versus the factual interpretation of the resurrection, but they will not be discussed here.

With regard to sexual attitudes, two very different patterns emerge. Gnostic Christians describe God in both masculine and feminine terms with a complementary description of human nature. They refer to Genesis 1 for their belief in equal or androgenous Creation, often translating their principle of equality into the religious, social and political structures of their communities. Orthodox Christians, however, describe God only in masculine terms and relate to Genesis 2, subscribing to the idea of the primacy of man over woman and translating this into religious and daily practice.

In those early Christian days there were many different gnostic and orthodox movements. It was a time of exploring the truth, and some orthodox Christians like Clement could live perfectly well with gnostics like Valentinus. In fact, Clement demonstrated in his works that the elements of gnosticism could be worked into fully orthodox teaching. In Paidagogos 1.6 he characterizes God in feminine and masculine terms, and also in Paidagogos 1.4 where he writes: 'men and women share equally in perfection, and are to receive the same instruction and the same discipline. For the name 'humanity' is common to both men and women; and for us in Christ there is neither male nor female'.

He urges women to participate with men in the community, citing women who have won great political, literary, artistic and philosophical achievements.

Clement strongly opposed ascetic gnosticism and had a positive opinion on marriage, although he insisted that sexual intercourse should take place only for the purpose of procreation, comparing it in Paidagogos 2.10,102 with the farmer who sows his crop only when the field is fertile. This comparison is no coincidence as the identification of earth with female and seeds with male stems, as we have seen in earlier chapters, from the period of the degradation of the female sex more than 3000 years ago, repeated by Aristotle and now picked up again by the Church fathers.

In *The Second Letter of Clement* which was partly retrieved in the *Codex Vaticanus* we find a text clearly related to the gnostic Gospel of Thomas:

'The Lord was asked by someone when his kingdom would come and He said: 'When the two are one, and the outer as the inner and the male and the female will not be male and female any more'.

But Clement's view that orthodox teaching could extend to affirmation of the feminine element and condone the active participation of women was not accepted by the majority of Western Christian communities in Asia Minor, Greece, Rome, Gaul or even provincial Africa. His contemporaries Ireneaus in France and Tertullian in Carthage followed a strict orthodox line and condemned any form of gnosticism as heresy and blasphemy. Irenaeus expands on this in five volumes of his *Refutation and Overthrow of falsely so-called Gnosis*. He notes that it is women especially who are attracted to heretical groups. Tertullian makes a similar criticism when he complains in *De Virginibus Velandis 9* that 'these heretical women have no modesty, engage in argument, enact exorcisms, undertake cures and, it may be, even baptize'.

For Tertullian, women are daughters of Eve and are therefore directly connected with sin, as he explains in his De cultu feminarum 1 1,2.

Clement fled Alexandria in 202 because of severe persecution of Christians. He died around 215, and although declared a saint shortly afterwards, his name was removed from the saints' calendar in 1600 by Pope Clement VIII.

His successor in Alexandria, Origen, also contemplated matching gnostic and orthodox Christian thinking. He emphasized individual human responsibility and creativity, and postulated the idea that without knowledge (in the gnostic sense) there could be no belief. Origen was an inspiring teacher and had many women followers.

In the beginning he was an accepted Christian scholar and was ordained to the priesthood, but later he was excommunicated by his own bishop, Demetrios, because of his deep mysticism linked to gnosticism. During the fifth ecumenical council, in Constantinople In 553, Origen's teachings were officially condemned as misleading.

Many fundamental orthodox teachings followed, such as those of Hippolytus in *Refutatio Omnium Haeresium* at the beginning of the third century, only partly discovered in 1842 in Athos. They all contributed to the fact that by the middle of the third century orthodox thinking had become the predominant factor in the Christian movement. Virtually all feminine imagery for God had vanished, and nearly all the secret texts which gnostic groups had revered were omitted from the canonical scriptures.

In the fourth century orthodox thinking was further reinforced and consolidated. In 325 CE Constantine the Great convened the first ecumenical council in Nicea in order to put an end to the great divisions within Christianity, for instance the question of whether Jesus was more of a God or more of a man, the choice between Christ and Jesus.

In 367 CE Church Father Athanasius of Alexandria wrote his Easter Letter, referred to at the beginning of this chapter, leading to the final canonisation of the New Testament in council meetings between 393 and 419 CE.

At the Synod of Nimes in 394 it was decided that women were no longer allowed to perform diaconal functions or to sing in church.

The three powerful anti-feminine Church Fathers in the latter part of the 4th century and the beginning of the 5th were Ambrosius of Milan (339-397), Hieronymus of Rome (342-420) and Augustine of Hippo (354-430).

In the previous 300 years the anti-feminine character of the Christian movement had remained to a certain extent ambivalent, more concerned with aspects of male primacy in Creation and in the world, but over time the element of sexuality became more and more of an issue. While the early Church Fathers like Paul, Clement and Origen had relatively tolerant views on marriage and gave their approval to sexual intercourse in its procreational function, these attitudes were later dismissed in favour of total rejection of marriage, especially by Hieronymus. To be eligible for redemption, sexual intercourse was to be denied. According to Augustine in his monumental work *De Civitate Dei* (On the City of God), the sin of Eve had resulted in a profound shift from Creation by God to procreation by sex. Every act of sexual intercourse between men and women was a repeat of the original sin of one woman (Eve), who was in turn responsible for all the suffering and calamities of the world. Augustine derives the authority for making statements of this kind from the *Letter of Paul to the Romans* 5:12, in which the apostle writes that just as sin has entered humanity through one human being, so death has entered all human beings because they have all sinned. However, when Augustine translated this originally Greek text into Latin, he changed the words 'death' into 'sin' and 'because' into 'therefore', which fitted his own views better!

According to the Church Fathers, women were to blame for the sexual drives of mankind, initiating sinful feelings of lust and appealing to the lower instincts that should be contained and suppressed. *In Soliloquia* 1.10, Augustine writes that 'nothing degrades the male spirit from its high level so much as caressing a woman'.

The obsession with sex led to another obsession: virginity as supreme purity, necessary for achieving redemption. The Church Fathers became victims of a kind of virgin cult, applicable to both men and women. Hieronymus went so far as to say that the only benefit gained from human procreation was that it produced virgins.

Symbolically at first, but more and more historically, the sins of Adam and Eve were considered to be in receipt of absolution by the ascetic Jesus and the virgin Mary. Augustine claims that Jesus was so pure that he did not have libido. As for Mary, she was considered a virgin before, during and after the birth of Jesus (represented by the three stars that are present on later icons of the Mother of Christ) and had therefore preserved her purity. According to the late 4th and early 5th century Christian institutions, the purity of Jesus and of Mary set an example to every Christian seeking to be eligible for salvation. Through baptizing with water the inheritance of sin could be washed away.

This symbolism of sin and purity, and the underlying ideas fostered by the Church Fathers, bishops, cardinals and popes, were destined to dominate gender relations in Christian culture.

One wonders how it could have been possible for these fantasies, based on such thin argumentation and naive misinterpretation of the laws of nature, to become the dogmatic and institutionalised belief that has led to more than 1500 years of unequal feminine/masculine relations in Christian society.

How different a world might we be inhabiting if the teachings of Socrates, the words of Jesus and the attempts by the Church Fathers of the Egyptian region to reconcile gnostic and orthodox thinking had been understood and put into practice. A better balance between female and male in society would surely have been possible.

It is hard not to conclude that the leading thinkers in the first 400 years of Christianity had a decisive and adverse influence on gender relations and laid the foundations for a male-dominated religious, social and political society.

XII

Middle Ages and
Middle Classes

The Middle Ages can be roughly divided into two periods, 500-1000 CE and 1000-1500 CE. The first period is generally described as the Dark Ages, while the second was marked by political and economic revival and a cultural awakening, leading eventually to the Renaissance.

We have only selective information on the realities of gender relations in the early Middle Ages such as can be gathered from religious and legal regulations, records and histories, land ownership deeds, marriage arrangements and anecdotal stories. And these all relate to the upper classes, not to the anonymous masses of the rest of the population. We cannot, therefore, form an accurate picture of how things really were, but the trends about the second period of the Middle Ages here described are probably not too far removed from reality. More information is available, especially about the rise of middle classes, although there is still little known about the daily life of farming and village families.

As will be clear from the following texts, I must first give a brief account of the general political, religious and social conditions prevailing in the various periods in order to put observations on gender relations in the right context.

At the end of the fifth century CE the Roman Empire finally collapsed when the last emperor Romulus Augustus was deposed by Odoacer in Ravenna in 476 CE. Constantinople had already gained capital status in 333 CE, becoming the 'second Rome'.

The deposing of Romulus Augustus meant the end of the unity between the Latin western and the Greek eastern parts of the Empire. The eastern part continued to survive as the Byzantine Empire right up to the 15th century CE, when the Turks conquered Constantinople in 1453.

The collapse of the Roman Empires marked the end of a long struggle against sustained pressures from northern and eastern pagan tribes who were moving westwards and southwards, looking for better climatic conditions, a movement that had started long before, at the beginning of the first century. Although at first the Romans successfully opposed the invasions, the tribes gradually took over the territories and undermined the civilisation of the Empire. The final stage of the decline culminated in the sacking of Rome by the Visigoths in 410 CE.

In 430 CE the Vandals invaded the African territory, where Church Father Augustine died as one of the victims of the conquest of Hippo. The barbarian Germanic general Odoacer was appointed King of Italy by his soldiery in 476 CE.

Europe then underwent a period of turmoil with many wars and struggles for power by the newly decentralized political and ethnic kingdoms in Italy, France, Germany and England involving the Franks, the Alemanni, the Saxons, the Gauls, the Goths, the Celts, the Vandals and, from central Asia, the Huns.

In general, these Dark Ages were characterised by a decay of cultural values and a breakdown of the extensive and ingenious networks and technologies with which the Romans had built up their cities, aqueducts and roads, their mining operations, their urban and water management skills and their legal, administrative and political systems. The population of Rome declined from 1 million in its heyday to as few as fifty thousand in the Dark Ages.

The Christian Roman Empire had been able to convert many of the former tribes to Christianity, although they at first adhered to Arianism. However, when the Gothic leader Clovis adopted the faith in 496 CE, much influenced by his wife Clotilda, who was an orthodox Burgundian Christian, it marked the beginning of a surge to Catholic Christianity that would eventually take in the whole of Europe.

The major unifying force in a politically disintegrating Europe proved to be the Catholic Church. This increasingly influential institution filled a political vacuum, established a spiritual base and joined the struggle for power in a contest that would lead to continuous tensions between secular and religious leaderships in a new era.

As a result of these developments in Europe, the powerful forces in society were a centralized Catholic Church, a decentralized feudal aristocracy and a multitude of converted tribal kingdoms, with a clear series of interrelationships between the dignitaries and leaders of all three. It was these elites that determined the roles of the sexes.

Benedictus (480-553). Pen and ink
drawing, 1138-1147.

The nature of male/female relationships had been quite firmly established by that time, embodied in that of the Hellenistic and Roman civilisations as described in earlier chapters. But the legal rights of women with respect to marriage, inheritance and education were affected to some extent by compromises between conventional centralized Roman legislation and decentralized tribal customs. This was not necessarily to the disadvantage of women because the Germanic tribes were mostly matrilineally based; they were agriculturally oriented cultures and were used to tribal community decision-making by consensus.

The Catholic Church, then, took the lead in striving for unity in Europe and in preserving the cultural and spiritual achievements of the past, with the aim of creating an all-Christian Continent. But as was made clear in the previous chapter, this so-called Christendom was going to be a male-dominated, hierarchical and profoundly anti-feminine stronghold.

Between 500 and 1000 CE an intensive missionary drive initiated by Pope Gregorius I led to the further conversion of the whole of Europe of Christianity, including the northern Scandinavian and eastern Slavonic regions.

The missionary drive included the establishment of about 800 monasteries all over Europe for the theological education of monks, initially dedicated to spiritual, Christian devotion and ascetic lifestyles. But the monasteries were also used to create unity in liturgy, in canon and monastic observance, and in the preservation of literature, philosophy and administrative skills. In a later stage, pioneered by St. Benedict of Nursia in the 6th century at the monastery of Monte Cassino, a formal organisation of monasteries and the principle of self-sufficiency were introduced, along with the practices of horticulture and craftsmanship and a more outward-oriented attitude. These monasteries became the forerunners of institutions of broader education, adding law, medicine and other disciplines to their fields of study. This eventually led to the establishment of schools for general education, taking in also laymen, and to a certain extent replacing the public education system of the former Greek and Roman days. In the 9th century this development led to the founding of the first university, in Salerno, Italy. Still later, in the second half of the Middle Ages, cathedral schools and local parish schools were added to the range of Christian educational service, and education became an integral part of Christendom.

As the Church fathers had created an overwhelmingly male-oriented foundation in organizing the Church and had adopted eccentric views on sexuality, their world-views permeated the whole of European society and negated the opportunities for women to benefit from the educational facilities. This was a clear setback compared with the past, when education for women had become increasingly available in the Greek and Roman civilisations.

Boniface, a prominent missionary agent, saw the need for women in mission and in 782 recruited a woman from England called Lioba to develop Benedictine monasteries for females. Despite her outstanding and unique achievements, however, this movement ended with her death, and Roman Catholic women reentered mission service only in the 19th century. Once again an opportunity to restore the balance of the male and female roles was lost. Nevertheless, nunneries and monasteries for women continued to be established, albeit under the strict control of the male Church hierarchy. These institutions offered unmarried women, young girls sent there by their fathers, and female orphans a relatively safe haven for personal and educational development and an alternative to married life.

In the secular world the aristocratic and feudal elements in Europe's leadership were faced with the familiar problems of preserving their positions in land ownership and securing the future of their dynasties. The resulting marital arrangements and inheritance rights of women led to the female population of the upper class gaining increasing affluence and influence. It is very likely, judging from many anecdotes such as that of Clotilda, the wife of Clovis, that these women played a considerable part in the making of political and economic decisions, but it seems doubtful to me whether this had any significant effect on female roles in the broader context of society and on decision-making in general. The women in high places were in all likelihood rarely motivated by social and philosophical considerations, being fully engaged in the battle for power, money, prestige and sex that preoccupies most human beings in those conditions. When we come to the second half of the Middle Ages, we will encounter examples of prominent women who did make a difference, even though their influence was later suppressed by countervailing forces from Rome.

In the meantime, another event caught the attention of Christianity when in 610 CE Mohammed had his vision in Mecca which led to the birth of the Islamic religion. Over the following hundred years this movement conquered Syria, Persia and, via Egypt and North Africa, Spain. The Muslims were finally halted in 732 by the Franks at Poitiers and were thenceforth denied further penetration into Europe at that time.

The Christian community was alarmed by this new force which threatened to wipe out its culture in many lands.

One outstanding Islamic philosopher, who occupied a position comparable to the status of Church father in the Catholic world, was the Cordova-born Averroes. He was commissioned by the Caliph to review and comment on Aristotle's philosophy as a reference for Islamic thinking.

The interesting thing is that Averroes's interpretation of Aristotle was quite different from that of St Augustine, especially on the subject of the immortality of the individual soul, in which he did not believe. In his view, only the individual's contribution to universal intellect, *the nouos*, was immortal. In considering gender, he also had a different and strongly held opinion on the equality of men and women, concurring with Socrates and with Plato in his *Republic*. He very much regretted the male-dominated ethos of Islam as expressed in the interpretation of the Koran in Islamic social practice.

The Islamic philosopher Averroes occupied a position comparable to the status of Church father in the Catholic world.

His opinion was that the unjustified degradation of the female in Islamic society led to economic waste and poverty.

Both the orthodox Islamic leadership and the orthodox Catholic Church authorities were displeased with the unorthodox views of Averroes and turned against him. Later on, in the 13th century, Thomas Aquinas, commissioned by the Pope to combat the philosopher's negative influence on Christian belief in academic circles in France, strongly opposed Averroes's interpretation of ancient Greek philosophy.

I think that if the Islamic and Catholic traditions had taken Averroes's observations and warnings seriously, male/female relationships would have developed quite differently from the way they did, the consequences of which we still see today. The anti-feminine interpretation of the messages of both the Bible and the Koran continue to offer an affront to feminine potential in present-day societies.

The codes of the Koran are laid down in 114 chapters or Surahs, of which Surah IV is on Women. It seems a one-sided chapter wherein it is exclusively men who seem to be addressed, dealing with their role and responsibilities towards women. Although there are allusions to essential equality between men and women and to granting and protecting women's rights such as with regard to inheritance, divorce and economic activity, in essence the chapter has been misinterpreted in Islamic traditions as providing a licence to compel absolute subordination of the female in society, similar to the misinterpretation of the Bible.

It is worth mentioning in this context that a prominent woman Islam scholar, Riffat Hassan, born in Pakistan and presently professor at Louisville, Kentucky, in the United States, has studied, published and lectured extensively on the literary texts of the Koran and their actual meaning. The texts are, she claims, clearly not misogynic, on the contrary, they represent a correction to the strongly patriarchal tradition of the Middle Ages. Whereas Muslims believe the Koran to be God's Word transmitted through the Angel Gabriel to the Prophet Muhammad, *Sunnah* (the practice of the Prophet Muhammad), *Hadith* (the oral traditions attributed to the Prophet Muhammad) and *Fiqh* (jurisprudence) have, according to Riffat Hassan, been interpreted only by Muslim men who have arrogated themselves the task of defining the ontological, theological, sociological and eschatological status of Muslim women.

So there is an apparently essential difference between the original divine message and a subsequentedly distorted male interpretation in the Islamic tradition.

The Koran differs from the Bible in many respects: for instance there is no story of Adam and Eve and no such thing as original sin. Therefore, there is in Islam no need for redemption and no universal blame heaped on women. But motherhood and family care are the only areas where, according to the Koran, women have a duty, whilst men have the responsibility to provide economic conditions. Islamic society has concluded that therefore women can have no political or economic functions and no leave to appeal against men's absolute rule in society. Also here, Riffa Hassan claims, the meaning of the text has been distorted by for instance interpreting the word 'qawwamun' as ruler, whilst linguistically it means provider.

Surah IV explicitly recommends husbands to lock their wives up in the sleeping quarters and beat them in the event of their showing the lack of respect for men's efforts to maintain them. Apparently here the root-word 'daraba' is interpreted as beating, whilst it has many different possible meanings in the Arabic language.

Anonymous, Glorification of St. Thomas Aquinas, S. Caterina, Pisa. Under Thomas lies Averroes. ❯

سورة البقرة مدنية وهي مائتان وست ثمانون آية

خواص سورہ بقرہ سات مرتبہ واسطے دفع آسیب وجن ودیو پری کے اس سورہ کو صدق دل سے پڑھنا مفید ہے اور نیز

| حروفہا | کلماتہا | ایاتہا | رکوعہا |
| (۲۵۰۰۰) | (۶۲۲۱) | (۲۸۶) | (۴۰) |

مرض صرع زمرگی کے لیے اس سورہ کو لکھ کر بازو پر باندھنا فائدہ مختتام ہے و

بِسْمِ اللَّهِ الرَّحْمَٰنِ الرَّحِيمِ

الٓمٓ ذَٰلِكَ الْكِتَابُ لَا رَيْبَ فِيهِ هُدًى لِّلْمُتَّقِينَ

الَّذِينَ يُؤْمِنُونَ بِالْغَيْبِ وَيُقِيمُونَ الصَّلَاةَ

وَمِمَّا رَزَقْنَاهُمْ يُنفِقُونَ وَالَّذِينَ يُؤْمِنُونَ بِمَا أُنزِلَ

إِلَيْكَ وَمَا أُنزِلَ مِن قَبْلِكَ

So the new force that came into the world in the first half of the Middle Ages only made things worse as regards the imbalance in male/female relations in Europe, North Africa and Asia Minor.

Another missed chance, similar to the distortion of the words of Jesus by the male interpretation in the Christian tradition.

In general, the Dark Ages were not only dark from the point of view of economic and cultural decline, apart from a brief period in the 9th century under the reign of Holy Roman Emperor Charlemagne. They constituted a dark period too for male/female relations, in which progress suffered a severe setback from the admittedly slow but growing trend towards more equality in the Greek and Roman civilisations.

Let us now investigate what happened in the second half of the Middle Ages, between roughly 1000 and 1500 CE, and how this affected the positions and roles of men and women. A number of factors can be identified as having had a great impact on social change in Europe during this period. Let me mention a few, not necessarily in any preferred order of time and importance.

– A widening breach between the eastern and western Christian churches and the final split between the two churches in 1054 CE. This occurred, among other reasons, because of radically different views on celibacy, the divinity of Jesus and the organisation of the church leadership.
– The construction of 80 monumental Romanesque-style cathedrals and 500 large churches in western and eastern Europe between 1050 and 1350 CE, celebrating the expansion of Christianity. These edifices were built in white stone and with ever larger windows in order to reflect St. Augustine's dictum that light is the most direct manifestation of God. This 300-year building campaign has been called the 'cathedral crusade', an impassioned counterpart of the equally costly great military Crusades to recover the Holy Land from the Muslims.
– The continued building and expansion of monasteries and nunneries, along with cathedral schools and other religious institutes of education, triggering the emergence of monasterial universities, starting in Italy and spreading to France, Germany, Sweden, Switzerland and Holland in the 10th and 11th centuries CE.
– A stronger hold by the Church on the disciplines connected with the institution of marriage, which was declared sacramental around the turn of the 12th century CE.

◄ Beginning of sura (chapter) 2 of
the Koran. Delhi, mid 19th century.
Illuminations by Qamar al-Din.

– In the 11th century CE an upsurge in devotional celebration of the Virgin Mary (declared *theotokos*, Mother of God, at the Council of Ephesus in 431 CE) and of Mary Magdalen. At the same time, not by coincidence, the phenomenon of courtly love arose in aristocratic circles, with the emergence of knighthood from the wealthy class of landowners.

– In the 13th century a record number of women were declared saints, one-third of the total.

– An increase in trade and commerce, the creation of craftsmen's guilds, better communications, a general upswing in the economy and the growth of larger cities and towns. With all this came a new class of citizens: a self-sufficient and thriving middle class established itself in urban areas, becoming an important factor in society alongside the clergy, the aristocracy and the population at large in farming communities and villages.

– Universities began to shift from monasteries to cities in the 11th century.

– The population of Europe increased significantly from the 11th to the 14th century. This was due to better health care and a substantial increase in food availability through the expansion of agricultural land for the large-scale growing of beans, an important new addition to the food package of the common people. A serious setback was the plague or Black Death of the mid-14th century, which wiped out between a quarter and one-third of the European population. It caused a major recession, especially for the lower classes, and aroused great concern as signifying a possible act of punishment by God and the end of time.

– The appearance of strong female personalities between the 11th and the 13th century, making women more visible in the fields of politics, religion, literature and commerce. It was followed by a reaction leading to a new wave of female repression, in concordance with the works of Thomas Aquinas in the mid-13th century. He repeated Aristotle's and St. Augustine's devastating philosophical, 'scientific' and theological views on the nature and biology of women and their lower order relative to men, as described in chapters X and XI.

– Emerging religious unrest in the 12th century CE, leading in the following century to separatist religious movements like the Beguines, initiated by women, and the Cistercians, Waldensians and Cathars, adhered to by many women. These movements were part of a search for renewal and innovation, rejecting the hierarchy and many of the canons of the Catholic Church.

– In 1231 the systematic organization of the Inquisition under Pope Gregorius IX for the apprehension and trial of heretics, marking the start of 300 years of terror and death. It culminated in the publication in 1486 of the textbook of the Inquisition, *Malleus Malefecarum*, endorsed by the Pope and at that time mostly affecting women accused of witchcraft and sex with the devil.

What trends can we detect in all these different aspects of the late Middle Ages to illustrate the theme of this book?

It seems that by the end of the Dark Ages, social, political, economic and religious developments in Europe were not favourable for balanced gender relations as the power culture of the Catholic, Islamic and aristocratic elites was strongly male-oriented, stronger than in the days of Greece and Rome.

However, at the beginning of the second part of the Middle Ages, there were changes in the air that offered new opportunities for reversing the trend and achieving a better balance.

The Virgin Mary cult and the revived popularity of Mary Magdalen, started in the 11th century CE, were signs of the desire to recognize the feminine element in religion. In the secular world the drive to liberate women of the aristocracy from their functional prison and to allow them to become individuals worthy of love was a sign of the need to recognize the feminine in society.

In professional literature there seems to be consensus that these two manifestations of revival of the women were interconnected. They were aspects of a reaction to the overemphasis of the male role in the prevailing Catholic and aristocratic cultures.

Both renewals were rather hypocritical, however, because on the one hand they pretended to restore the honour of the female in the church and the real world in an exemplary way, but on the other they eliminated the element of sexuality. The immaculate conception of Mary implied that she was a Lady unsullied by eternal sin when she bore Jesus, the incarnation of God, without having had intercourse with a man. The courtly lovers from the knighthood adored, admired and loved the married lady but the nature of the game was that, although caresses and kisses were allowed, never should the brutal act of having sex for love and pleasure, such as the lower classes enjoyed, be part of the relationship. The ladies had their lawful husbands, who had married them for rational reasons and who needed offspring for the continuity of their estates.

In other words, there was no way that normal human beings, men *and* women, longing for a normal life with love, respect and intimacy could ever identify with the metaphoric concepts of the Lady in Heaven and the lady on earth.

No wonder these constructs did not survive for long, but nevertheless they at least provided a feminine visibility, whereas before the female presence was hardly acknowledged, except in slavery and prostitution.

This visibility, however, plus the rise of the middle classes in the second part of the Middle Ages led to more women than ever coming out into the open with their opinions and writings and actively participating in the fields of religion, politics, poetry, philanthropy and craftsmanship as well as the conduct of state affairs, estate management and business.

In religion one powerful woman of the first order was the Benedictine Abbess Hildegard von Bingen, who lived from 1098 to 1179. She had founded her own convent on the Rupertsberg in Rudesheim in Germany and made no secret of her goal to reform the Church, undermined as it was by schisms, sclerosis, simony and intellectual aridity, and to restore the integrity of true religion. She was thoroughly educated in theology and philosophy, with skills in law, biology and the arts. She remained part of the feudal system and the socioreligious hierarchy, but she was also an exponent of the mystic movement, having herself experienced visions and received inspiration from the Holy Spirit. In 1147 CE she was authorized at the Synod of Trier to publish her writings on these visions, after which her fame spread throughout the whole of the Christian world.

Hildegard was tolerated as a reformer and a mystic because she accepted the male orientation of religion within the cosmic organic hierarchy. But she tried to break free from the traditional male-dominated patterns in society and was in favour of regarding sexual relationships as a natural phenomenon, uniting male and female in love and procreation. Her vision was powerful in its holistic embrace of all aspects of Creation, linking the macrocosm of the universe with the microcosm of the human being. In that sense she contributed to the organic, neoplatonic world-view of the Middle Ages: considering all dualities in the cosmos as complementary manifestations of a single divine origin, a notion we discover later in the works of Bonaventura and Aquinas in the 13th century.

There were many more mystical women in Europe – such as the Anglo-Saxon Christina of Markyate, the Italian Catherine of Siena and the German Christina Ebner and Elizabeth of Schonau – in cloisters that were chapters of official monastery orders. They managed, like Hildegard, to combine their public roles as teaching prophets of reform with the traditional female duties of Catholic orthodoxy.

In the second part of the 12th century and the first part of the 13th, women led new movements such as the Beguines, who not only pursued reform but also looked for renewal and even innovation in the interpretation of religious experience and

Hildegard von Bingen's third vision: the egg-shaped cosmos. ➤

practice. They were partly inspired by the mystic visions of the movements' leading exponents such as the Cistercian Beatrice of Nazareth and the Beguines Mechthild of Magdeburg, Marguerite Porete and Hadewijch of Antwerp. They also highlighted the need of women, especially in the growing cities, to have their own religious groupings, as access to the restricted number of established nunneries was banned to them. These nunneries were all chapters of existing male orders, such as the Dominicans, the Benedictines and the Franciscans, and one needed funds and/or an aristocratic background to join them. A third motivation was the desire to return to simplicity and poverty in the midst of the corruption and materialism prevalent in the secular and religious circles of those times. Yet another reason for these movements was that in the cities there were many unmarried women who clustered together and went looking for something to do in the name of selfless compassion.

Their growing visibility, capability and participation in all aspects of secular and religious life, especially in the cities, made women weary of the male-dominated structures and gave them more confidence to act as agents of change. In essence, they wished to re-establish a respectful attitude to the individual, with a recognition of his or her direct link to the divine. They sought a transition from a sacred and hierarchical establishment to a more liberal and individual order.

The uncloistered women who shaped and formed the renewal movements were of course more vulnerable to Church criticism than those who were working at reform from within.

Apart from these movements in the 11th and 12th centuries, we see at about the same time the emergence of the ascetic Cathars and Waldensians, who were led by male visionairies but had majorities of female adherents. These sects held views that conflicted with the established Catholic belief and went much further than those of the women's movements, which mainly objected to the Church being the only intermediary between God and the human individual.

The Cathars believed in radical dualisms such as the existence of two gods, one the creator of good and one who created evil. In their perception, both men and women could become closer to perfection by ascetic living, and the two sexes were considered more alike than different in the divine purpose and in their religious potential. As sin originated in the god of evil, Cathars considered Eve blameless in the Fall. They did not believe in the physical resurrection of Jesus, but only in the resurrection of his soul. They did not believe Mary to be the mother of Jesus and held that Mary Magdalen had been Jesus's wife.

◄ Madonna and the Child. Presumably painted in Constantinople, c. 1280.

In many respects the Cathars were followers of the radical and ascetic type of Gnosticism discussed earlier in chapter XI.

Interestingly, many women from the nobility were attracted to the new thinking. Urban middle classes were drawn to the Beguines and also to Catharism, because it sanctioned financial profit and interest, which the Church at that time opposed.

When the seperatist lay groups, movements and sects had proliferated to the point of becoming a major development in Catholic Europe, the Church decided it could not tolerate the deviations from Catholic dogma any longer, even though in many cases local Church authorities had at first been sympathetic to the mystic movements.

Inquisition against heretics was officially organized in 1231 CE under Pope Gregorius IX. This led to the total extinction of some of the new movements, as in 1244 at the siege of Montsegur Castle, the last stronghold of the Cathars, where 200 members were burned and the remainder succumbed to Catholic pressure to abandon the sect. Before that, many similar brutal massacres had taken place in other parts of Europe.

In the course of the 13th and 14th centuries the separatist movements disappeared or were reformed and incorporated into existing Catholic orders. This happened with some of the Beguines.

In the meantime, however, many prominent women who refused to submit were condemned and executed; for example Marguerite Porete, who, after being examined by a Dominican inquisitor, was sentenced and burnt at the stake in 1310 at the Place de Greve in Paris.

By the middle of the 14th century all the movements had gone. Their suppression marked the end of two ages of renewal that could have achieved changes in the male-dominated hierarchy of Catholicism and halted the trend towards corruption. But the Church struck back with ruthless violence.

Mysticism nevertheless continued to flourish for instance through the works of the Dominican mysticist Meister Eckhart (1260-1328), although revolts against the corruption of the Church remained dormant. The reforming and renewing religious women of the Middle Ages were undoubtedly the visionary forerunners of the Renaissance and the Reformation, ahead of their times and temporarily silenced.

Many others, apart from the purely religious ones described above, also played a role in making women more visible in this era.

In the field of literature, the first woman in history to make a living as a writer and whose work was accepted as authoritive was Christine de Pizan (1365-1430). She

Witches sabbath. Discourse on the crime of witchcraft. ❯

Ar leuue du diable
la mort prist entre
ou monde. Et ce le
enſuuient ceulx qui tiennent ſo

wrote prose and poems lauding women's role in society. She critizised the mockery of women implicit in the notorious *Le Roman de la Rose*, the elaborate allegory of amorous pursuit in the context of courtly love, written by Guillaume de Lorris and Jean Chopinel de Meun between 1240 and 1280. This led to an exchange of letters with male exponents of the humanist creed which started the debate, ongoing for centuries, on the position of women and the part they should play in society, known as the Querelles des Femmes. One of her major works, *Livre de la Cite des dames*, written in 1405, was an inspiring defence of women and the first effort to present a history of their sex.

Other women writers of influence in the later Middle Ages were Marie de France, who in the late 12th century CE was the earliest known French poet, revealing in her stories the growth of a new social convention in which women had a larger role and a higher function, following the cult of the Virgin Mary begun a century earlier; Helene Kottannerin who in her autobiography deals with political life and her own role as lady in waiting to the Habsburg queen in the first half of the 15th century; and Alessandra Macinghi degli Strozzi, who left a large collection of letters on the conduct of commerce, family relations and the political intrigues of Florence in the period from 1447 to 1470 CE.

Other categories of women who left footprints in late medieval history were the regent queens and the so-called 'ladies of the castle'.

Examples of the regent queens are Eleanor of Aquitaine, Regent of England during Henry II's absence and an influential patron of the arts and poetry; Matilda, Queen of William the Conqueror; and Queen Margaret of Scotland who accomplished a thorough-going reform of the Church in her Kingdom which brought it into the mainstream of the Latin Church. Then there was Blanche de Castille who, after the death of her husband Louis VIII, was the long-term Regent for her son Louis IX. A dedicated wife and mother and a strong financial supporter of the Cistercian order, she fulfilled her duties as Regent selflessly like a fully-fledged king in the first half of the 13th century, from the age of 38 until her death at 66. She handled all the decision-making in matters of war, religion and administration; all the political deals,

The Garden of Love. Miniature in the *Roman the la Rose*, Flanders, 15th century. ❯

territorial conflicts, peace negotiations and the running of her estate and finances. Her record has put her name on the list of the greater 'kings' of France. Yet another women ruler was Queen Margareta of Sweden who succeeded in uniting the three kingdoms of Sweden, Denmark and Norway during her regency in the Kalmar Union in 1397, an act that influenced the future of all   Scandinavia.

As for the 'ladies of the castle', a prime example is Eleanor de Montfor. Of noble descent and married to a French knight, she played the power and money game in grand society with relentless fervour, living in castles in France, Italy and England, spending money, giving parties and entertaining lavishly. But she was also involved in politics and wars, in legal battles with the French government and in fighting for her status and posses- sions after the death of her husband in battle. She died at the age of 60, a real-life model of a heroine of medieval drama, romance and tragedy.

Last but not least, the second half of the Middle Ages produced a strong urban mid- dle class, in which women played an important role. Not only in the larger cities of more than 10,000 inhabitants like Venice, Genoa, Pisa, Marseilles, Paris, London, Cologne, Lübeck, Frankfurt, Nuremberg, Vienna, Zürich, Basel and Prague, but also in the smaller towns of 2000 inhabitants or more, with thriving manufacturing and trading activities.

Characteristic of the life in the cities was that a great number of women partici- pated fully in business, mostly family concerns engaged in manufacture, trading, dis- tribution and finance. Men were often away, either on business or at war, and women handled the organisation and administration at home. They often also involved them- selves directly in professional craftsmanship, if that was the business they were in.

Strong family ties and equal partnerships led to improved legal arrangements in matters of ownership and inheritance between husband and wife. As women citizens went on to obtain full civil rights and freedoms in cities, they were able to have their own businesses as so-called *femmes soles* and could become members of guilds. Women were butchers, chandlers, ironmongers, net-makers, shoemakers, glovers, girdlers, haberdashers, purse-makers, cap-makers, brewers, wine merchants, skinners, book-binders, gilders, painters, silk-weavers, embroiderers, spicers, smiths and goldsmiths, to name but a few.

The fact that cities developed their own secular schools meant that women could obtain a full education, no longer dependent on the religious institutions with their limitations on admission. And women needed education in order to fulfil their multi-functional duties in family affairs.

It is not surprising, then, that during the second part of the Middle Ages, when this development was in full swing, the position of women in the cities improved considerably. It seems quite likely that in the cities of the 14th and 15th centuries more women were participating fully and on an equal basis with men in commerce, trade and manufacturing than in any city in Europe in the second half of the 20th century.

The new and increasingly prosperous middle class became a strong element in the social structure of the Middle Ages, gaining more and more influence in city administration and economical and educational affairs. Universities and financial institutions became independent of the Church and the nobility and in this environment created a whole new layer of influential citizens. With increased wealth and power many of these citizens started to play a role in the commercial and political development of their countries in the 15th century. The nation states and monarchies that emerged in the 15th and 16th centuries were mainly financed from these sources.

Examples of women prominent in middle class circles during this period are Margaret Paston of Norwich in England and Margharita Datini of Prato in Italy. A great many more are worthy of mention, but that would fall beyond the scope of this book. Their lives, recorded in letters and stories, illustrate the limits and the potential of medieval women.

In the household, on the peasant holding, commercial premises or the estate, women shared fully in managing the family base, mainly on the home front, but sometimes also in the business, and often in equal partnership with men. However, in the spheres of war, politics and law women played no part and stayed at home. An exception of course was Jeanne d'Arc who, as she believed, under the divine inspiration of the 'voices' of St. Michael, St. Catherine and St. Margaret led the French to a momentous victory over the English at Orleans in 1429. That was the turning point in the Hundred Years' War. She ended at the stake, condemned as a heretic by an English-dominated Church court in 1430.

Although the Middle Ages saw some very positive developments in gender relations and an improvement in the balance between male and female values, towards the end of the period, during the 15th century, the general trend was backwards again.

In religion the liberalizing innovations died out with the Inquisition, nunneries were decaying, the glory and the power of the regent queens and the ladies of the castle were petering out. The social improvements taking place in the cities stagnated and were even reversed as men came to feel more and more uncomfortable with the ascent of female power and started to exclude them from traditional male territories. So once again history repeated itself, and the seeds that had promised to restore some female/male equality were destroyed before they had a chance of developing into a healthy crop.

One of the reasons why women returned into the shadows was that emancipation took place only in part of the secular world. In religious communities and aristocratic society no change occurred, and this had a negative effect on women's advance. Thus, the Catholic Church, with its ferocious Inquisition and mainly anti-feminine attitude, still exerted a great retarding influence.

The misogynistic position of the Church was reconfirmed in the Middle Ages by Thomas Aquinas who in the 13th century wrote in *Summa Theologica*: 'Women are subordinate both in nature and in purpose and therefore have not sufficient strength of mind to resist concupiscence'.

Thus, despite the rising status of women in the middle classes, who in general were also dutiful churchgoers, the male-dominated powers of the Church set the ultimate tone.

It was only on Sunday, March 13th 2000, that the negative stance with regard to women was pronounced as regrettable, when Pope John Paul II asked forgiveness for the sins committed by the Roman Catholic Curch in a historical 'mea culpa' ceremony in Rome, seconded by seven cardinals. One of these sins was the humiliation and marginalisation of women. However, no consequences were attached with respect to improving the position of women in the Church hierarchy.

The liberal and individualistic movements initiated by women in the Middle Ages had begun a trend that was to return in the Renaissance, that great reawakening that developed in the course of the 15th century.

The bibliography to this chapter contains a wealth of information on cases, personalities and histories of women in the Middle Ages, of which I have presented only a random sample in order to sketch the landscape.

◄ Ingres, *Joan of Arc at the Coronation of Charles VII*, 1854. Oil on canvas, 240 x 178 cm, Musée du Louvre, Paris.

139

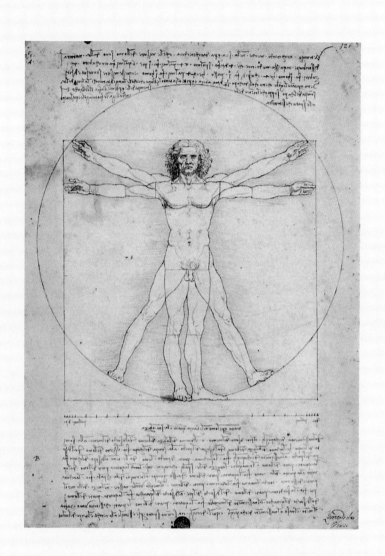

XIII

Confusion in the Renaissance

As we have seen in the previous chapter, in the second part of the Middle Ages, there were distinct signs of change, with the end of the closed and introvert Dark Ages and a renewal of religious, political and economic life. At first this opened the way for women's roles to increase, but then the tide turned once more against this emancipation due to tougher resistance from a still male-dominated religious and social order.

The process of renewal proved resilient, however, and continued into the 15th century. This was a time for further innovative developments; fertile soil for the growth of man's radically new insights into the macrocosm of the universe and the microcosm of nature and the position the human individual.

It is not my intention to delve deeply into the history of this period of European civilisation, but for an understanding of the fate of gender relations I offer a bird's-eye view of its main features.

In literature on the Renaissance, it is emphasized that we cannot speak about a radical distinction between the late medieval and the early Renaissance period. By all accounts the movement we call the Renaissance had its early roots in the 14th- and 15th-century Italy and Spain, and one can differentiate it into two branches, one aristocratic and the other popular. The first referred to a return to the reading and study of classical Greek and Roman manuscripts and the philosophies of antiquity; this included a predilection for Platonic idealism, as was developed at the Platonic Academy in Florence. The second referred to an empirical Renaissance, less traditional and hierarchical but more scientific and forward-looking, reflected in the arts, science and a new humanistic world-view.

Ever since 500 CE the Catholic Church had monopolized the realms of philosophy, science and religion in the Christian perception of reality. As a consequence, the rich

◀ Leonardo da Vinci, *Proportions of the Human Body*, c. 1490.

Greek and Roman cultures on philosophy and science were lost to medieval generations, despite Augustine's attempts to integrate Aristotelian thoughts into Christian doctrine.

It was only after the Islamic tradition came into Europe through Spain that Aristotle's ideas reappeared on the same, and the classical works of antiquity re-entered Mediterreanean minds.

The resulting late medieval world-view was a conceptional system of nature, as put forward by Thomas Aquinas about 1250 CE, combining Aristotle's ideas with Christian theology and ethics. The system was based on the organic unity of the world in all of its physical manifestations, including the human body. According to Aristotle, the physical world consisted of four elements: air, fire, water and earth, all striving to reach their true natural centres. In this endeavour, the elements of water and earth moved downwards when they could and fire and air moved upwards. These movements kept nature going, not as a machine but as a hierarchy, in which each element sought for its own fulfilment.

The heavenly bodies were considered to be of a higher order than the earth. They consisted predominantly of air and fire in a purer form, making up a fifth element, the 'quintessence', the ether. The planets followed magic paths as they circled the earth, which was the centre of the universe according to the theories of Ptolemy.

As we have seen in previous chapters, the organic hierarchical world-view of the Middle Ages implied a fixed order with God over man and man over nature. Geocentric cosmology considers the earth and nature to be the lowest, material, feminine sphere in the cosmic hierarchy and God in Heaven the highest, spiritual, masculine sphere.

In line with Aristotle the medieval world-view had rejected any rational description of the universe employing measurements and numbers.

In the early days of the Renaissance, however, when antiquity was rediscovered in its entirety, the Pythagorean approach combining mathematics and magic revived.

Concepts like pi, the fixed ratio between the radius and the circumference of a circle; or the divine section, the 'sectio divina', the aesthetic ratio of divisions observed in tree branches and plants and in the spiral configuration of the nautilus shell and in the pleasing proportions of windows and doors in architecture; or the magical harmony of sounds from different lengths of strings that Pythagoras linked with mathematical formulas. Non-rational, transcendental phenomena were shown to follow mathematical principles, ratios and numbers.

These phenomena were conceived by men like Pythagoras and Archimedes in the 6th century BCE and later by Eratosthenes who correctly measured and calculated the circumference of the earth in the third century BCE.

The return of their approach meant that while in traditional medieval thinking, miracles were observed, accepted and poetically described, in the Renaissance miracles were again investigated, explained and mathematically assessed.

It was the rediscovery of mathematics in the 'renaissance' of antiquity that proved so important in giving people a resolve to explore and exploit the real world through human inventiveness and to try to accommodate this within Christian spirituality but outside Aquinas's intellectual, scholastic and doctrinal straitjacket.

In other words, the early Renaissance looked not only at Aristotle's ideas but also at the rational and empirical concepts of antiquity. There was also a revival of Plato's notion of a fundamental duality in Creation, in the sense that all dualities originate from a singular source, that there is unity in diversity, proclaiming the organic integrity of Creation, including body and soul, male and female. The universe was a living organism according to Plato, with a feminine soul. This last element of his theories did not persist in later neo-platonic thinking.

The idea that there were mathematical laws that governed nature and the fact that humans, specifically men (I shall come back to this later), could discover these laws implied a much closer and more direct relationship with the Creator, who was supposed to be the originator of these laws. This in turn led to a feeling that the human individual had direct access to God and Creation, in contrast to medieval Catholic thinking in which access to God was only possible through the medium of the Church.

The discovery of laws was not only of scientific significance. They were also applied to the development of numerous technologies and to the design of instruments, architecture and engines of war, in all of which fields Leonardo da Vinci was an early pioneer.

The emphasis on the real world and on the human individual also found expression in the arts, where after more than a thousand years of monasterial religious texts and illustrations, liberal elements returned in poetry, painting and sculpture. Writers and artists depicted human feelings, emotions and sensuality, together with the details and wonders of the natural world, including the naked human body.

So the Renaissance reintroduced a new and positive approach to the individual lives of men and women and their potential on this earth. This same idea had been at the root of the humanist movement which originated as early as the middle of the 14th century through the artistic and literary works of Petrarch (1304-1374) and Bocaccio (1313-1375).

The 15th century city-states of Italy such as Milan, Venice, Florence, Bologna, Rome and Naples with populations of 100,000 to 200,000 were important centres of the renewal process. Their mounting influence coincided with a growing independence from the authority of the Church.

The interest in antiquity was enhanced by the fall of Constantinople to the Turks in 1453, as a result of which Byzantine Greek scholars such as Pletho and Bessarion fled to southern Europe and brought with them their knowledge of classical culture.

The variety of disciplines in which a transformation occurred illustrates the universal dimension of the Renaissance experience.

Representatives of new thought included Cosimo de Medici (1389-1464) in politics and philosophy; Leonardo da Vinci (1452-1519) in art, natural science and technology; Michelangelo Buonaroti (1475-1564) in painting; Machiavelli (1469-1527) in political ethics; Christopher Columbus (1451-1506) in navigation and Nicolaus Copernicus (1473-1543) in mathematics and science. The last mentioned was Polish, but spent some time at Italian universities as a pupil of Domenico Maria Novara, who was one of several astronomers citical of the system of Ptolemy.

What all these men had in common (no women are on record except in the arts in the late Renaissance) was that they looked at the world and saw the human individual as possessing unlimited potential and innate creativity, not imprisoned by an elaborate indoctrination or restricted to a lifetime of monastic devotion and unvarying work. They displayed a zest for studying and exploring all the details of natural phenomena and humankind, rediscovering laws in a visible world instead of myths in an invisible world.

It was also a time for exploring the geographical boundaries of the earth, with Columbus and Vasco da Gama trying to reach India in 1493 by sailing west and south over the sea instead of travelling east overland as Marco Polo had done in the 13th century CE. After India and Asia, the unexpected discovery of the American continent further opened up the world to European colonists, missionaries and traders.

The Copernican (re)discovery that the earth was not the centre of the universe but a planet revolving around the sun had a profound influence on the sun-centred culture impacted by the Renaissance. The centre of the universe shifted from the feminine earth to the masculine sun, which had more than symbolic significance.

We shall see later in this chapter why women failed to participate creatively in the age of discovery and renewal.

The only evidence we have of women's habits, clothing and culture in the Renaissance comes from paintings, mostly done by men and rarely by women, or at least that is what I first thought. One of the exceptions I could find in my literature search was Lavina Fontana. She was a late 16th-century Bolognese artist born in 1552, who was described as the first professional woman painter in Western Europe. A collection of more than 30 of her paintings was exhibited in 1998 in the National Museum of Women in the Arts in Washington.

To my surprise, however, when visiting the Museum in late 1998, I found out that there had been a long tradition of women artists in Bologna, such as painter Caterina Vigri in the first half of the 15th century, sculptor Properzia de'Rossi in the first half of the 16th century, the above-mentioned Lavina Fontana and the engraver Diana Scultori in the second half of the 16th century. Caterina was canonized around 1710 and as St. Catherine of Bologna became known as the protectress of painters. By that time there were some 25 well-known women painters in Bologna.

FILIA EX SPECVLO IMAGINEM
ORIS SVI EXTRESIT ANNO
MDLXXVII

But many more women artists were also well known and visible in other Renaissance cities. They included, in the 16th century, Sofonisba Anguissola in Cremona and Marietta Robusti, the eldest daughter of Tintoretto, in Venice, and in the early 17th century Artemisia Gentileschi in Florence. Recently, Sofonisba, who is considered the equal in portraiture to Titian, was named the first socially accepted professional woman painter rather than Lavina Fontana, according to the catalogue of the exhibition of 24 of Anguissola's works in the National Museum of Women in the Arts in 1995.

It was not only Italy that could boast woman artists in the Renaissance. Flemish painters Elisabeth Scepens and Agnes van den Bossche in the 15th century and Caterina van Hemessen and Levina Teerlinc in the 16th century were all well-known portraitists. Teerlinc was retained as court painter by Henry VIII and his three successors, the last of whom was Elisabeth I.

The paintings of all the above-mentioned women in Italy and Flanders consist largely of portraits, in line with the Renaissance emphasis on the essence of individuality and culture and the great demand for portraits from the aristocracy and the European courts. Fontana and Anguissola were held in great esteem in the courts of France and Spain.

These women also painted religious scenes, often produced to order from ecclesiastical bodies who were great patrons of women artists. And finally, they offered refined and intimate pictures of family life with music, children and details of household interiors.

Women painters were expected to remain within the limits of purity and chastity in their works of art and not to conflict with the ideology of Renaissance and contra-reformation perception of womanhood. Nevertheless, the 16th century was a time when sexuality and morality were being openly discussed, and representations of the female nude were beginning to appear, celebrating both erotic and aesthetic ideals. Fontana especially includes the sensuality and beauty of the female body in some of her paintings, although others are more prudent.

◀ Lavina Fontana, *Self-Portrait at the Spinet, Accompanied by a Handmaiden*, 1577.

Why are all of these female artists so unknown to the general public and, until not so long ago, even in professional circles?

There seem to be several reasons.

The monetary value of the works of women was lower than that of well-known male artists, who were often the fathers of the women artists who worked in their studios. The works of women were often characterized as showing a typically 'feminine touch' as opposed to the 'virile hand' of men, supposedly proving male superiority. Male critics did stick to the traditional belief that women were simply not fit to create supreme quality art, reiterating the Aristotelian opinions of men like Bocaccio and Durer who openly declared good female artists to be miraculous exceptions to the rule and were quite amazed that they performed as well as they did.

Another probable reason is that the period of a woman's artistic output was shorter because of her family duties.

All these factors combined to make it likely that many works of art produced by women either disappeared into oblivion or were assumed to have been executed by men. Often paintings were not signed by the women artists, or their identification was misread.

Many of the works of women mentioned here were only rediscovered in the late 19th century, and many had to be reattributed as late as the middle of the 20th century.

Going back to the 16th century, we see that the Renaissance advances further and reaches into northern Europe. There the humanist movement took a more reformist turn through people like Erasmus (1466-1536) in Holland, Rabelais (1490-1533) in France, Thomas More (1487-1535) in England and, last but not least and in a more aggressive manner, Martin Luther (1483-1546) in Germany.

These men all represented the mood of the time, which was a determination to reform the prevailing state of the Catholic Church culture from within. They were especially infuriated by the corrupt practice of indulgences, through which people could partake of the reservoir of grace held by the Church by donating money. But they also had different views on subjects like free will and the goodness of man versus predestination (Erasmus) and man's sinfulness (Luther) and the way reform needed to be realized.

While Italian humanism evinced no intention of a revolt against the Church's institutional set-up, northern European reformers tended to take a more confrontational stand vis-à-vis established Church practice.

◄ Sofonisba Anguissola, *Self-Portrait*, 1554. Oil on panel, 17,1 x 12 cm, Vienna, Kunsthistorisches Museum.

The northern humanist movement was more strongly oriented towards direct individual access to God through the Bible, without dogmatic interference. It advocated consulting the original biblical text as the only authority of Christian belief ('sola scriptura') and rejecting the purgatory powers of the clergy.

The humanists' approach to original sources and their rejection of scholasticism also led to a revival of ancient alchemical 'hermetic' traditions, named after their supposed originator Hermes Trismegistos, an Egyptian divine prophet. His principles are described in a manuscript called the *Corpus Hermeticum*, translated from Greek in 1460 by Marsilio Ficino, a priest and medical docter at the court of Cosimo de Medici. The document was discovered by one of Cosimo's men in Macedonia and found to contain a record of an ancient occult Egyptian religion.

This set of beliefs was supposed to embody the oldest wisdom regarding the occult powers in nature, the secrets of matter, the functioning of the soul of the world's organism, and the magical interactions between the planets, the stars and human destinies. Although it turned out a hundred years later that the document was from a later date, somewhere in the 2nd or 3rd century CE, the hermetic movement of the 15th and 16th centuries had many supporters.

So to add to the confusion of the times, there was a revival of magical sciences which rejected both the scholastic doctrines of the Church and the rational application of mathematical science. One of the outstanding early Renaissance supporters of the occult sciences was Agrippa von Nettersheim (1486-1535) who wrote a classic text, *De Occulta Philosophia*, and also a famous treatise on the superiority of women, *De Nobilitate et Praecellentia Femina Sexis*.

Agrippa, and later Paracelsus, tried to reconcile magical sciences with the spiritual foundations of Christian belief. At first, they were considered serious scholars but eventually their theories were fiercely condemned at the Council of Trent in 1563.

Nevertheless, occult sciences, given a special place as intellectual stimuli, continued to influence the Renaissance search for new world-views for a long time, even into the 17th century CE. One aspect of relevance to our subject is that alchemy implies an organic natural philosophy, seeking a revival of the primordial unity of dualities in nature, specifically reconciling the masculine and feminine elements and referring back to an androgynous origin. These dualities were considered to be complementary and equal, ideally to be united and repurified to the original state. In this sense the magical movement contained an element of gender integration that was quite the reverse of the views of Aristotle, Augustine and Aquinas.

Returning to humanism, Erasmus, who was a Catholic priest, re-translated the Bible from the original Greek texts into Latin in 1516 and found them markedly different from the officially approved Vulgate translations by Hieronymus a thousand years earlier. Erasmus felt he was offering the Bible a fresh to the common men, and he wrote in his preface: 'I wish that all *women* might read the Gospel and the Epistles of Paul'.

What he probably meant was that Latin was the official Church language to which common men had no access and certainly not women, because they were not educated in it. The small number of people, men only, with the ability to read the Latin texts constituted one of the most powerful weapons held by the Church, enabling it to exclude women from the world of religion and education. The humanists, especially Calvin, were strongly in favour of better and broader education regardless of birth, sex or wealth and believed that everybody should have free access to the Bible texts.

Albrecht Dürer, *Portrait of Desiderius Erasmus of Rotterdam*, 1526, engraving.

Luther, a Catholic priest of an Augustinian order, had tried to reform the Church from within, but the 95 theses that he nailed to the castle church at Wittenberg on the eve of All Saints Day in 1517 were too confrontational for the Catholic authorities. Although they tolerated him for a while, trying to persuade him to moderate his position, in the summer of 1520 a papal bull was issued declaring him a heretic and giving him 60 days to recant or be excommunicated. Luther refused and was outlawed in 1521, while his books were commanded to be burnt. Although he failed to achieve a reformation from within, his initiative led to further protestations and eventually to a new movement, Protestantism. Central to its belief is that grace or salvation is not obtained from the Church or through it, but by the individual through faith alone ('sola fide'), without the need of good works.

Only on November 1st 1999, after 482 years, did representatives of the Lutheran and Roman Catholic Churches sign a twenty-page document in Augsburg, marking the end of the difference of opinion and agreeing that grace can be achieved through the love of God only.

Luther's emphasis in the new movement was on simplicity, eliminating the whole Church collection of relics and saints. Monastic life was also abolished; compulsory celibacy for priests was ruled out, and Luther himself married a nun, partly in order to set an example.

Luther was the first to translate the Bible into the vernacular, published in Germany in 1534, for reading by everybody. As printing techniques of the movable type that Gutenberg invented around 1450 had been fully developed by that time, the spread of the German translation was quite broad and had a considerable influence on the German literature of the 16th century.

Although Luther had many humanist followers and in the beginning was also supported by Erasmus, his theology and methodology were in the end not compatible with humanist views, and Erasmus left him alone.

At the same time the Catholic Church had to react and strengthen its position against the various new movements that threatened its survival.

A counterattack was launched defending its fundamental beliefs and institutional organization through a contra-reformation which was confirmed by commitments made at the Council of Trent in 1545-1563 to a rigorous reinforcement of Church discipline.

A central role in this campaign was played by the Society of Jesus, or Jesuits, an order created by Ignatius Loyola (1491-1556) in 1539 and approved by Pope Paul III in 1540. It is the only Catholic order that does not have a female branch.

Loyola, originally a soldier, had a vision which led him to choose a lifetime of service to Jesus. He later published The Spiritual Exercises, a work that reflected the basis of his religious experiences. The organisation of the Jesuits was very orthodox and disciplined, virtually a military operation headed by Loyola with the rank of general. They did not reject experimental science; on the contrary, they studied all fields of doctrinally sound scientific enquiry in order to understand their import and how to reconcile them with Christian teaching, accepting the possible consequences in a progressive way. They were also dedicated mystics and did not shy away from controversy with Church officialdom.

The Jesuits played a major role in the fight against heresy through rigid implementation of the Inquisition. They were heavily involved in the surge of witchhunting, condemnations and burnings that took place during the 16th century counter-reformation.

The Council of Trent, the 19th ecumenical council of the Roman Catholic church, was held at Trent in northern Italy between 1545 and 1563. It marked a major turning point in the efforts of the Catholic church to respond to the challenge of the Protestant Reformation and formed a key part of the Counter-Reformation.

All in all, the Renaissance was a confusing period when Greek antiquity, hermetic traditions, Catholic orthodoxies, humanist ethics, the Protestant religion and mathematical sciences were all competing to guide the individual heart and mind into modern times.

When we look at this brief and selective overview of the history of what amounts to a transformation from a medieval to a modern world-view, one wonders where the women were in this process and what humanism and Protestantism had to say on gender issues.

Were not women, as we have seen in the previous chapter, the original reformers and innovators in the earlier part of the late Middle Ages?

We saw a return to antiquity and a resulting humanist movement. Were these not events that could and should have offered a unique opportunity for the rehabilitation of the women in social, political and religious life?

Did not the revival of alchemy and magic contain elements likely to restore the equality between male and female?

Was not the radical confrontation with the traditional, patriarchal Catholic institutions an obvious occasion for mounting a critical attack on their prejudiced and ill-argued anti-feminine attitude?

I found some answers to these questions in the literature cited in the bibliography. In addition, based on my own interpretations, I will present some clues gathered from mathematical science, humanist views, hermetic traditions and the Protestant movement.

First mathematics.
As discussed earlier in this chapter, the return to antiquity included the rediscovery of methods of describing the physical world in quantitative terms, numbers and ratios, while not dismissing qualitative interpretations of divine mysticism.

The core of the theories of Pythagoras (580-500 BCE) consisted of the numbers 1, 2, 3, 4, 5, etc. (the concept of zero was not yet known) which he considered holy, especially the numbers from 1 to 10, the so-called decade, which he identified with abstract gods. The non-quantitative properties of numbers could serve as ethical archetypes, and the study of mathematics could therefore provide an insight into human behaviour. In this context, the school of Pythagoras considered not only odd numbers masculine and even numbers feminine, but also odd numbers good and even numbers bad, which put women on the side of evil.

In this simplistic cosmology, the number 1 represented the highest masculine principle, closely connected with spirit, the non-material realm. The number 2 represented the highest feminine principle, closely connected with matter ('mater'), the substance of the earth.

These Pythagorean dualisms reflected the Mesopotamian and Greek polarities of the Heavenly Father and the Earthly Mother.

According to the Pythagorean school of thought, the ultimate destiny of the immaterial soul was to escape from the material world and enter the immaterial kingdom of the Heavenly Father. The philosophical context in which they placed the male/female dualism, reaching the ultimate masculine, non-material or spiritual world and leaving behind the feminine, material world, meant for them that studying mathematics with its extrasensual god-numbers was typically a task for the male element of humanity, as the earthly female element was left behind.

Although women did study in the school of mathematics of Pythagoras in Kroton, they were supposed to abandon their femininity and become mathematical men.

When mathematics and the laws of God were rediscovered in the Renaissance, these subjects were, in line with Pythagoras, considered to be male territory. Women were excluded from this part of the current renewal in thought. Margaret Wertheim argues in her book *Pythagoras's Trousers, God, Physics and the Gender Wars* that the link between mathematics and masculinity has had a profound influence in Western culture.

Even today a woman studying mathematics is considered odd.

It was probably because of this mindset that the Renaissance academic world was a world without women. They were simply not accepted as part of the scientific and philosophical mainstream of the time.

Now Humanism.
The humanist movement of the late 15th and early 16th centuries CE contained clear feminist elements, such as the promotion of equal rights to education and learning, based on the ideological principle of individual education as a vehicle of Christian virtue, regardless of class or gender. Humanism also emphasized the right of access of every person to the original sources of the Holy Scriptures, as well as to the revelations of the natural world, the 'book of nature', without doctrines or dogmas. All this implied an anticlerical and revivalist trend that opened up opportunities for female involvement in the renewal of religious practices.

Erasmus in Holland, Thomas More in England and Juan Luis Vives in France strongly defended both the principle of education and that of returning to the original sources of the Bible and nature. Although their views promised a more liberal approach to the feminine dimension in nature and human society, in reality their attitudes towards women as such remained incredibly conventional. They went on stressing the physical and moral weakness of women, maintaining with Aristotle that women were by nature intellectually and biologically inferior. The principle of equality of men and women in the spiritual realm, prophesied by Aristotle, St Paul, St Augustine, Aquinas and now by humanism, was never translated into the material world. *L'histoire se répète.*

The result of the ambiguous position of the humanists was that neither in the universities, not even in the new neoplatonic academies, nor in the churches did women have any hope of active participation.

As had often occurred in the past, aristocratic and intellectual women were keenly interested in understanding and materially supporting new movements. They did so again in the case of humanism. Catharine of Aragon and Margaret of Austria were such women. This meant that in aristocratic and intellectual salons the new thinking was debated and discussed, including the position of women. But still, none of this led to women having any part in academic, public or religious institutions. There were rare exceptions, such as Costanza Calenda, daughter of a medical professor, who received a degree in medicine in Naples in the 15th century, but here again exceptions confirm the rule.

In private family circles, women were receiving a better education but mainly with the aim of making them more intelligent and expert within the household, not outside it.

All in all, the humanist movement held great possibilities for changing gender roles, but they were never realized. The old Greek concept of the structural inferiority of women remained intact. Again a heritage from antiquity.

How About Magic?

As discussed earlier, the revival of alchemy and magic contained positive elements with regard to the equality of male and female, but the 'intellectual' hermetic movement was male in composition, esoteric in spirit, ascetic in lifestyle and secretive in attitude. As its devotees were experts in astronomy, mathematics, metaphysics and medicine, they distanced themselves from the 'popular' magics practised by women, which were linked with witchcraft and heresy.

This split into two kinds of magic, good and bad, angelic and demonic, benevolent Christian and malevolent heretical, learned and unlearned, philosophical and bestial, put women again in the wrong corner. In the end, the magical movement as such did not survive, being condemned by Catholics, Protestants and scientists alike. In any case, the positive impulse it could have given to a re-alliance of masculine and feminine values was made impossible by its division into male and female magics, radically opposed to each other, both socially and intellectually.

Finally Protestantism.

The views of the Protestant movement with regard to marriage had a positive effect on the position of women. Sexual intercourse was accepted as a normal and beneficial

part of married life. Being a virgin was no longer considered the preferable state. Celibacy was abolished. Men and women were equally eligible for grace and equally responsible for sin; they both had access to the text of the Bible and were both bound by individual faith.

Luther amongst critics and other reformists (second on the right the French reformer Calvin).

The wife of a minister could play an informal role in the Church community, and in the early days of Protestantism discussions were started to reinstate the position of a deaconess. Women performing this function were committed to a life of service to the Church, assisting the sick and the poor, working for a charity or serving in a mission field.

On the other hand, Luther, who believed in the original equality of men and women, maintained that Eve was to blame for the structural subordination of women because she had sinned. In his opinon, women were punished by being confined to household tasks and keeping their husbands off the streets, thereby protecting them from sins of the flesh. For both Luther and Calvin, as in the model of Aristotle, the subordination of women fitted in with the natural order of Creation.

Furthermore, when in the 16th century women indeed started to play a more active role in religious matters and to interpret the scriptures, acting for instance as prophets and preachers in the radical left-wing Anabaptist movement, the Protestant leaders hurriedly backed out of supporting female participation in Church matters.

The possibilities for women promised by deaconship were dropped, and the restricted fields of motherhood and domestic work were again earmarked as the proper activity for women.

In England a law was passed in 1543 that restricted the right of women to read the Bible. The lower classes were forbidden to read it altogether. Middle-class women were allowed to read it only in the presence of men, and the higher-class women, if alone, only at home.

As monasteries were abolished, they no longer provided an escape route for women who did not choose motherhood and domestic servitude to men; the only activity remaining open to them was missionary work. Over the course of time, Protestant women became heads of substantial missionary organisations.

Although some individual protagonists of gender equality balance remained, such as Jacob Boehme (1575-1624) who wanted to see spiritual equality reflected in the formal organisation of the Church, the official Protestant position eventually boiled down to women being inferior and subordinate to men.

Thus in the creative turmoil and religious confusion of the Renaissance, women finished, with some ups and downs and with exception the art of painting, at the bottom of the ladder once more, waiting for the next chance to improve their lot.

It was not until the end of the Enlightenment period that a new impetus was given to the position of women, as we shall see in the next chapter.

XIV

Enlightenment: For Men Only

In the last chapter we saw how a change in the cosmological world-view was initiated by Copernicus in the 16th century. He was responsible for a shift from the prevailing Ptolemaic concept of the (feminine) earth as the centre of the universe to a new view of the (masculine) sun as the centre. He went so far as to praise the sun as the master of the universe. 'The earth conceives of the sun'; and 'The sun rules the family of the stars,' he wrote in *De Revolutionibus Orbium Caelestium* (On the Revolution of the Heavenly Bodies) published in 1543 CE.

Although both Luther and the Catholic Church refuted this observation, which was officially condemned by the Holy Office in 1616 until corrected in 1620, it marked the beginning of a new world-view that eventually led to the scientific revolution of the 17th century CE.

Meanwhile in 1572 a new star had been observed as having entered the constellation of Cassiopeia, and it remained the brightest star in the sky for two years. A similar phenomenon occurred at the turn of the century and was studied by Protestant astronomer Johann Kepler (1571-1630). He concluded that the heavens were changeable, contrary to the existing views of astronomy and astrology.

Kepler went one step further than Copernicus and propounded three mathematical laws describing the motion of the planets, which he published in *Astronomia Nova* in 1609 and in *Harmonices Mundi* in 1619 CE. The laws related to the elliptical paths, the varying speeds and the movement of planets relative to each other.

Another important step towards identifying the facts and mathematics of the movements in the sky was an understanding of the mechanics of motion.

Galileo (1564-1642), when observing the regular swings of the lamps during a service in the cathedral of Pisa in 1583, concluded that the timing of the pendula was independent of the swing and the weight. This inspired him to formulate the law of gravity between 1604 and 1609 CE. In essence the law states that a ball rolling down a slope from rest covers a distance that is proportional to the square of the time it has been travelling. He demonstrated that this law is true whatever the mass of the object, thereby refuting Aristotle's opinion, endorsed by Thomas Aquinas, that a heavy object falls faster than a light one.

Galileo translated his findings into the movement of celestial bodies and created confusion in religious circles because he was turning visible cyclical phenomena into non-visible mathematical logic. When he published his *Dialogue on Two Principal World Systems* in 1632, the Church ordered the printer to stop selling the book within 6 months and two months later Galileo was called to Rome for trial. At the age of 70 and in ill health, he was forced to recant in abject terms. He died blind and in solitude in 1642 under house arrest in Florence. It was only in 1992 that the Pontifical Academy of Sciences declared the Church's stance to have been an error of judgement and rescinded Galileo's condemnation.

Galileo's position had always been that 'God does not disclose himself less admirably to us in Nature's actions than in the Scripture's sacred dictions.'

Thus, the Book of Nature was introduced in parallel with the Book of the Bible.

The strength of the combined theoretical ideas of Copernicus and Kepler and the practical science of Galileo proved resilient enough to establish, irreversibly, the basis for a new world-view. Nearly 50 years later, in 1687, Isaac Newton put the crown on this achievement when he published his unified theory in *Principia*. By integrating all previous visions and his own discoveries about the laws of gravitational forces, he celebrated a scientific triumph with his explanation and prediction of celestial movements, applying differential and integral calculus, a mathematical methodology of which he and Leibnitz were, independently, co-inventors.

◄ Astronomy, one of the oldest and most esteemed exact sciences in antiquity, flourished in the Islamic lands from the ninth century, when major Greek astronomical texts were translated into Arabic. Many astronomers served the court, as in this depiction of the observatory established by the Ottomans in 1575 at Istanbul.

The Enlightenment was driven to investigate the Book of Nature as a source of inspiration, objective information and liberation from ancient traditional assumptions. This could have led to a more balanced and natural view of male and female roles and relationships than the intellectual doctrines revealed in the Book of the Bible, especially in view of the fact that the new cosmology was unfettered by the hierarchical organic world-view of the Middle Ages and the Renaissance .

Unfortunately, once again, this opportunity was not seized, because the fascination with the discovery of mathematical and mechanical laws applying to the heavens motivated scientists to speculate that maybe the same kind of laws were applicable on earth. So the investigations into the natural world were primarily aimed at finding evidence of these laws in that world. Although this approach ushered in new concepts of nature, as I will show further on, outdated assumptions about the male-female hierarchy went unchallenged.

One of the first to undertake the search for laws in nature, even before the celestial laws were discovered, was Francis Bacon (1561-1626 CE). His aim for mankind was to regain the dominion over Creation that it had lost after the Fall.

It was the Calvinistic Reformation that taught that the Book of Nature once revealed God through Creation, but that the Fall had destroyed this revelation. More than Lutherism and Anglicanism, Calvinism radically split humanity from nature and denied its sacredness, opening the way for the manipulation and physical exploitation of a purely material earthly world.

Bacon developed his experimental philosophy in order to discover the hidden laws of nature, so as to be able to use them to turn nature into an unlimited resource for the benefit of mankind. He introduced a new so-called inductive method to investigate and probe natural processes by making experiments, drawing general conclusions from them and then testing these conclusions in further experiments, without preconceived theories or concepts. This differs from the deductive method, typically Aristotelian, where theories are intellectually conceived and tested in mental exercises.

Francis Bacon was of the opinion that nature had to be the servant of the exploiter, who would turn her from a teacher into a slave, kept under control and moulded by the mechanical arts. He wrote several books based on these ideas, such as *The Masculine Birth of Time* and *The Advancement of Learning*. His two major works were written in the latter part of his life, *Novum Organum* in

◄ Copernicus. Although his name is now associated with heretical concepts rejected by the Vatican, he spent his life as a cleric. In fact, his great work, *On the Revolution of the Celestial Spheres*, was not banned by the church until 1616, more than a half a century after his death.

163

1620 and an utopian work, *New Atlantis*, unfinished and published in the year he died, 1626.

Bacon had great respect for the powers of nature, which he compared with witchcraft. His works express a metaphorical identification of nature with female, and he was convinced that the chaotic (female) forces of nature could be contained and ordered to advance human progress. He was a great supporter of the Inquisition.

The combination of inductive methodology and an increasingly mathematical and mechanistic world model were not very conducive to the restoration of a male/female balance in the mindset of 17th century Europe.

An interesting example of the inventiveness of the time was William Harvey's discovery of the circulation of the blood, published in 1628. His analogy of the heart as a pump not only influenced Descartes's mechanistic physiology but also led Harvey to become a promoter of mechanistic thinking, especially in the field of biological reproduction. In his book *De Generatione*, he treats this subject as a purely material and mechanical process, degrading the female role to the mere functioning of imperfect matter in obscure passivity. In this respect he followed the old Aristotelian view, including (though less pointedly) assigning the major role in procreation to the male.

The scientific revolution continued a pace contributing to the invention and manufacture of fine instruments in many fields such as optics and medicine. It also improved the technologies of milling, weaving, mining, forestry and agriculture. In addition, the increasing wealth derived from the exploitation of resources in the new colonies was having a great impact on the materialistic aspirations of political and commercial leaders in Europe. Capitalism was born.

The Puritan and Huguenot movements in England and France in the 16th and 17th centuries had only a temporary effect in select circles in tempering the zeal for material welfare.

Meanwhile, the centre of gravity of power in Europe was shifting from the Mediterranean to the Atlantic. England, France and Holland had taken the lead over Italy, Spain and Portugal as seafaring nations, conquering new territories in the Americas, Africa and Asia.

Innovations in philosophy, politics, science and technology were also clearly becoming preponderant in the north. In 1662 The Royal Society of London for the Promotion of Natural

◄ A seventeenth century illustration of Copernicus' heliocentric universe. The Polish astronomer accounted for the apparent movement of the sun, moon, and stars form east to west by postulating that the Earth spins on its own axis while also orbiting the sun.

Knowledge was created with Charles II as its patron, and 1666 saw the institution of the Academie Royale des Sciences in France under the patronage of Louis XIV.

These two all-male institutions were deeply influenced by Bacon's experimental philosophy and were to play prominent roles in the advancement of the scientific revolution during the Enlightenment period. The first secretary of the Royal Society, Henry Oldenberg, made it the highest priority of the new organization to establish a 'Masculine Philosophy', with the aim to root out 'The Woman in us' as he put it.

Although writer and scientist Margaret Cavendish, Duchess of Newcastle, became the first woman member of the Royal Society in 1667, no other woman was admitted until 1945 when Kathleen Lonsdale (1903-1971) became a Fellow for her outstanding research into the structure of crystals.

Unfortunately, the academies contributed significantly to a more and more simplistic, mechanistic, reductionist, male-dominated and female-negating world-view. They ignored the fact that this one-sided orientation would affect the integrity of Creation, even though the founders believed that God operated through nature, albeit in simplicity. It was apparently not recognized that Creation was not a purely divine concept, but that it involved the complexity of the natural environment and that humanity as such was becoming an increasingly major factor in the ecology equation; ecology in the traditional scientific sense as the dynamics of survival of living organisms in natural surroundings. The inclusion of (more) women in the membership of the academies could probably have prevented them from ignoring the ecological dimension in their perceptions of reality.

I will not go into much more detail of the new world-view, except to mention some famous scientists of the 17th century, many of them members of the above-mentioned societies, who were instrumental in shaping it. They included Pascal, More, Locke, Hobbes, Boyle, Hooke, Huygens, Descartes, Newton and Leibnitz. These men all contributed individually not only to new philosophical concepts, but also to specific scientific achievements, methodologies and practical instruments. One could say that the foundations for our present traditional scientific and technological heritage were all laid around the 17th century CE.

Comparatively, the foundations for our present male-dominated traditional religious and philosophical heritage were all laid around the 6th century BCE.

The interesting thing is that the men mentioned earlier who were instrumental in developing a new world-view were still traditionally religious. They differed greatly, however, as to whether the empirical method

Francis Bacon (1561-1626), English philosopher and statesman, one of the pioneers of modern scientific thought. ➤

(mainly followed by the English scientists), or the theoretical method (mainly supported by the French), was the preferred route to the revelation of the divine laws of the universe. They also disagreed about whether one or the other method would lead to the ultimate and universal knowledge of everything. Pascal and Leibnitz did not believe they could. Newton and Descartes believed they would. But they all believed in God, either as the prime mover of a clockwork continuum or as being actively involved in an ongoing creation.

Today we believe that both inductive and deductive methods have to be used in combination in order to achieve scientific results that are realistic and orderly, but the question of whether we will ever understand the whole universe through a unified law still remains unanswered.

There was some resistance to the new world-view, for instance from Cambridge Platonists and from vitalists who often turned to Quakerism, a Protestant sect giving women and men full equality. Poulain de la Barre championed the idea of strict equality of men and women, based on the Cartesian philosophy of the unity of mind, publishing *De l'Egalite des sexes* in 1673. Women were actively involved, too, such as Anne Conway (1631-1679), a former disciple of Henry More who shared a monist view with Leibnitz, both of them opposing Descartes and his radical dualism of spirit and body, of soul and nature.

Anne Conway wrote a book on these views that she actively disseminated during her life. Called *The Principles of the Most Ancient and Modern Philosophy*, it was edited and printed 11 years after her death, in 1690, and not always recognized as her work as her name was withheld from the original Latin title page.

Other women were also writing on the gender issues raised by the new philosophies, arguing that differences in male and female achievements did not stem from feminine intellectual inferiority but from education, social position and child-rearing practices. These authors, such as Hannah Wooley, Bathsaa Makin, Mary Astell, Margareth Cavendish, Marie de Gournay (*On the Equality of Men and Women*, 1622) and Madame de Sévigné (*In Defence of the Female Sex*, 1696) and Antoinette de Salvan de Saliez (*La Comtesse d'Isembourg*, 1678) were mostly 17th century upper-class women, and their ideals were apparently more ambitious than those of the women we know in the Renaissance. They were active and devoted forerunners of feminism.

Intellectual women, ridiculed by their contemporary Moliere in 'Les Femmes Savantes' and in 'Les Precieuses Ridicules', were an interested audience of the new thinking, just as they were in time of the Reformation, trying to grasp its threats and opportunities in their 'salon' gatherings. They even joined egalitarian sects founded in response to the underlying tensions resulting from the mechanistic world-view.

All in all, however, the voices of women went unnoticed except in rare cases where they were invited openly to demonstrate their abilities and rose to the challenge. This usually took the form of anonymous participation in demonstrations, riots, protests and general dissidence. Such a collective response to unacceptable conditions in society happened quite regularly in both the Renaissance and the Enlightenment. There were also some opportunities for individuals of prominence in politics and the arts to make their voices heard.

In politics, Elizabeth 1 of England, Catherine of Russia and Maria Theresa of Austria were able and powerful queens and empresses.

In the arts, along with the women writers mentioned earlier there were, as in the previous 100 years, some famous female painters in the mid-17th century. One was Elisabetta Sirani (1638-1665) of Bologna, who invited her doubting accusers to watch her painting a portrait to disabuse them of the suspicion that she was being helped by a (male)painter. Others include the Dutch Maria van Oosterwijck (1630-1690), who did portraits of the kings of France, England and Poland; Mary Beale (1632-1697), the first British professional woman artist; and Charlotte Vignon, a French still-life painter. Working in the 1600s, Anna Maria van Schurman, poet (called the Sappho of Holland), scholar and painter, was ranked with Rembrandt by art critic Houbraken in 1717 in his publication on 17th century painters. Judith Leyster, influenced by Vermeer and Frans Hals, won acclaim with her paintings of embroidering women and cheerful scenes, comparable to the old masters. In the late 19th century at least eight pictures formerly attributed to Frans Hals were re-attributed to Leyster.

Clara Peeters, one of the earliest group of famous still-life painters at the turn of the 17th century, is an example of a Flemish professional woman of that period.

When the Academie Royale de Peinture et Sculpture was opened in 1648 by Louis XIV, he declared it accessible to all gifted artists regardless of sex. In that same year French still-life painter Catherine Duchemin gained entry. Later, painters Genevieve and Madeleine de Boulogne were admitted in 1669, Mary Beale and Charlotte Vignon in 1670 and Catherine Perrot in 1682. However, when more women became eligible for admission, the Academie established a limit of four women members in 1706. Later, in 1723, Dutch painter Margareta Havermans was expelled from the Academie because her pictures were 'too good to have been done by a woman' and were supposed to have been done by her (male) teacher.

It is clear that the road to equality in the art world, as everywhere else, was not strewn with roses.

As for the academic disciplines of science and mathematics, they functioned with practically no women at all from the outset. The absence of prominent female scientists and philosophers during the Enlightenment period is, therefore, not surprising. The French Marguerite de Chatelet, an expert on Newtonion methods, the Italian mathematician Maria Agnesi of Bologna, the German astronomer Caroline Herschel and insect expert Maria Sibylla Merian, all living in the second half of the 17th century, are on record as scientists with some stature, but they were not pioneers.

So we end up at the end of the seventeenth century in Europe with a male-dominated scientific revolution in a male-dominated religious and political environment.

The emergence of the Enlightenment did nothing to remedy the subordination of women and nature. Men and culture remained on top.

The movement did not have a positive influence on gender relations. On the contrary, the erroneous assumptions dating from antiquity about the inferiority of women persisted and were even institutionalized. The result was that, once again, humanity suffered economic and intellectual loss through not being able to profit from the benefits of a more balanced contribution to society and the individual by the feminine element, counteracting masculine rational and intellectual attitudes. This was all the more regrettable as the trend towards a mechanistic and exploitative approach to nature could have been prevented from going as far as it did if the active participation of feminine intuition and common sense had been given a fair chance.

When we move now to the 18th century and look into the heart of the world-views of the men who shaped the philosophical, scientific, social and political thoughts in the next phase of the Enlightenment movement, we

◄ Judith Leyster, *Self-Portrait. c.* 1630.
Oil on canvas, 72,3 x 65,3 cm, National
Gallery of Art, Washington.

find that their discourses were all based on reason. The scientific revolution of the 17th century had demonstrated the supremacy of reason in describing and explaining how the world works. Whether we look at Locke, Diderot, Montesquieu, Rousseau or Kant, we recognize a historic pattern of ambiguity between, on the one hand, theoretical, idealistic and universal analyses of the human mind, and on the other hand, splitting this mind up into male and female in the practical world of human society. While all these men argue that every human individual is free and spiritually equal to every other, which implies that there is also equality between men and women, they stumble over the sexual and biological differences. They then translate those differences into social and political instruments that lead to the sort of sexual discrimination that has dominated the thoughts of men with regard to gender for the past 3000 years.

One of the problems inherent in the male-oriented world-view, also showing up in the Enlightenment movement, is language.

It is the language of men discussing men and men discussing women; it is a language that speaks of 'we', meaning men, and 'the other half of humanity', meaning women, assuming tacitly the primacy of the first half; it is about men's ideas on the incapability of women to go beyond the intelligence of daily routine and the superiority of men in creating, inventing, conceptualising and establishing new boundaries in the fields of philosophy, politics, science and the arts. It is, once again, the identification of nature with female and culture with male.

All of the above elements of men's view of women in the Enlightenment can be found in the article entitled 'Woman' in the *Encyclopedie*. The *Encyclopedie* was the famous and influential record of the French Enlightenment's cultural, philosophical, scientific and political achievements, edited by Diderot and d'Alembert and published in 17 volumes between 1751 and 1765. 'Woman' was written by three men: an anthropologist, a moralist and a naturalist, who all pronounce from their own particular disciplines upon the inferiority of women. But they also warn of that strength of the woman which is belied by her apparent weakness, emphasizing how she exploits her influence on men through her sexual seductiveness, her unpredictability and her control of the family through her role as wife, mother and mistress of the household.

At least two men in the 18th century, however, Helvetius and Condorcet, vehemently opposed the views of the encyclopedists. Helvetius in *De l'Esprit* (1756) emphasizes the identity of the brains and minds of all men and women, claiming that all inequalities, and not only those between the sexes, are the result of social and political factors that have shaped the human race throughout history. His book was condemned in

◄ Queen Elisabeth I at the age of 51. The portrait was painted by Nicholas Hilliard.

1759 by Pope Clement XIII and burned on order of the Paris Parliament and the Sorbonne's faculty of theology.

Condorcet challenged what we would today call the sexist attitudes of his male contemporaries and maintained that women were as equally capable as men in all respects, including the fields of philosophy, politics, science and the arts if only they would be allowed equal opportunity and equal facilities. He quoted examples of prominent women who had been given the chance to show their true capabilities and who were not, as his colleagues claimed, just rare exceptions to the rule.

Condorcet was of the opinion that reason was either universal or nonexistent, and that in the matter of reason there was no valid argument to assume that women were inferior to men. As reason was usually guided by self-interest, maybe sometimes women and men would reason differently at the level of intention, but this did not mean differently at the level of quality. He strongly advocated equality for men and women in education and civil rights, subjects he wrote and spoke about often and clearly. He declared that what people mistook for female nature was the result of a long history, an insidious accumulation of customs, designed by men. In 1790 he published an article *'On Granting Civil Rights to Women'* in the Journal de la Societe de '89.

Rousseau, on the other hand, stressed in all his works the inherent natural inequality of men and women based on sexual difference, although he acknowledged their equality in the spiritual sense. He subscribes to natural inequality as a fact of life, but in his *Discourse on Inequality* (1754), he objects to those resulting from privileges for the elite, authorized by convention. His view was also that science, letters and the arts had a degenerating effect on the human individual and that we had to return to our pure and natural origins. This viewpoint could have made a case for also returning to a natural balance between masculine and feminine, both individually and in society. But advocating a return to the natural life as opposed to the cultural life, and the need to include this in education, did not prevent Rousseau from confirming at the same time the natural superiority of men over women in society. His classic *Emile* (1762), all about education (of a young man), sets out this philosophy clearly. The first four chapters are devoted to the new kind of education that Rousseau considers necessary for a better humanity, but it is directed solely at the education of young males. The fifth and last chapter describes the kind of woman fit to be the companion of this man, within the context of her important but inferior role of serving him. This approach is very similar to that of the encyclopedist philosophers, although later on Rousseau distanced himself from that movement. He disapproved of their utilitarian and materialistic world-view, on the way, as he was, to becoming the inspiration of the Romantic movement which chose sentiment, emotion and nature as the preferred guidelines to a new society, where feeling is more essential than reason. This shows the ambiguity of Rousseau's thoughts about woman and man, about male and female.

In the 18th century, the ranks of women writers increased considerably, as did the number of salons where Enlightenment ideas were discussed. Well-known names such as Mme de la Fayette, Mme de Scudery, Anna Maria van Schurman, Jane Austen and Sophie von La Roche all touch carefully upon gender issues, avoiding taking up radical positions. In a study of 18th century women's fiction, Katharine Rogers suggests that the authors may have been deliberately repressing their sexuality in favour of their intellectuality. In the delicate transition to the acceptance of women writers in a man's world, it was apparently neither appropriate nor wise to hint at equality of the sexes in erotic aspiration and satisfaction. This was still the world of 17th century Richelieu, Corneille and Malherbe who ignored female sexuality and where Molière had made mock of female 'intellectuals'.

Jean-Jacques Rousseau was the most influential political philosopher of the eighteenth century. In his hostility to many aspects of science, and in his passionate nature-worship, Rousseau was a precursor of the Romantics. He died in 1778.

In the journalistic field we see the *Female Spectator* in the mid-18th century in England and the *Journal des Dames* in France, both distributed all over Europe and the North American east coast and both with considerable circulations, over 300,000 subscribers. These and other publications in Europe were all run by professional female journalists.

Statistics from different European countries reveal a considerable amount of literature written by women and a wider spread of fields of interest. In Venice for instance, women published 49 works in the 16th century, 76 in the 17th century and 110 in the first half of the 18th century. These consisted mostly of novels and poetry, but they also included works of history, philosophy and science, as well as plays and opera librettos.

With regard to the arts, at the end of the reign of Louis XIV in 1710, Europe's cultural trend had turned from classical to neoclassical and Baroque. This signalled a change to a more sober and religious lifestyle, especially in the middle classes, fitting high standards and performance to a more introvert and contemplative mood. In music, the disciplined, intellectual works of the early 18th century composers, somewhat mathematical but at the same time movingly beautiful, illustrate this mood. Bach and Handel, Scarlatti and Vivaldi, Couperin and Purcell all mark the cultural change, which was also reflected in architecture and furniture.

The 18th century, like the 16th and 17th, again produced an impressive number of excellent women painters. Angela Muratori, Lucia Torelli, Rosalda Carriera (who became a member of the Academie Royale in 1720), Catherine Read, Mary Delaney, Lady Calverly, Francoise Duparc, Marie Loir, Elisabeth-Louise Vigee-Lebrun, Anna Vallayer-Coster (a member of the Academie Royale from 1706 when the limit of four was imposed), Adelaide Labille-Guiard, Marguerite Gerard, Angelica Kauffmann and Mary Moser. The last two, both natives of Switzerland, were among the founding members of the British Royal Academy in 1768; Kauffmann had been elected to the prestigious Academy of Saint Luke in Rome in 1765 and was hailed as the successor to Van Dyck on her arrival in London in 1766, being associated with the decorative and romantic strain of Neoclassicism.

All these women met with criticism and skepticism from the male-dominated establishment and had to fight for their integrity. They managed to achieve a place in his-

tory, however, even though many art experts today still do not wholeheartedly welcome them into the male pantheon of famous painters. It was more than 150 years after 1768 before another woman was granted membership of the British Royal Academy.

LEFT Elisabeth Louise Vigée Le Brun, *Self-Portrait*, c.1782. Oil on canvas, 64,8 x 54 cm, Kimbell Art Museum, Fort Worth.

RIGHT Isabelle de Charrière, in the Netherlands known as Belle van Zuylen, 1777.

In music, we have few women composers on record in the 18th century. In my primary search I found one woman (harpsichord) composer, the Swiss-married-Dutch Isabelle-Agnes-Elisabeth Charriere (1740-1805), who was a prominent feminist writer in the Netherlands known as Belle van Zuylen.

I wonder why it was that although women gained considerable visibility in the arts of painting and writing, they were seemingly absent from the world of music composers.

Also in politics women were not very prominent in the 18th century, apart from appearing sometimes as the woman behind the man (Marie Antoinette and Madame de Pompadour).

So we approach the end of the Enlightenment and the beginning of Romanticism towards the latter part of the 18th century. Here is a world where women have advanced in the fields of art and literature, have continued their mostly secondary role in politics and religion, and have been virtually inactive in shaping philosophy and science and in composing music.

Although the Enlightenment inspired people in the 18th century to reform society in the direction of a more egalitarian and liberal community, the effects on gender relations were very limited. But the seeds of more gender equivalence had been planted, and three revolutions would provide a fertile soil for nurturing those seeds, as we will see in the next chapter.

XV

Revolutions Coincide: Women Arise

The Enlightenment period saw a change to a world-view based on reason, individual liberty and creativity as well as the universal principle of equality. As we have seen in the previous chapter, this prompted a fundamental discourse on the equality of men and women and thus prepared the ground for a thorough review of previously held opinions and practices. All the same, there were no real changes touching upon this issue for most of the 18th century. However, the new world-view definitely did lead to changes affecting power relationships in society, paving the way for a shift away from divine monarchy and feudalism, and towards secular democracy and capitalism.

In England this transformation started at an earlier stage than in the other European countries. The English Revolution (1642-1660) and the Civil War between Parliament and Charles 1 on matters of authority and religion led to his deposition and beheading in 1649, when Cromwell took over. During the Revolution women actively campaigned for their share in the Petition of Right, which dealt only with the equal rights of men, but unsuccessfully.

Cromwell's protectorate was not a success, and after his death (1658) Charles 11 was called to the throne in 1660. Eventually, a substantial turnaround was effected when his successor James 11 was accused in 1688 of endangering religion, laws and liberties. The Bill of Rights was passed in 1689, proclaiming Parliament as the only legal body for political decision-making. William of Orange and his wife Mary Stuart had agreed in 1688 to this Bill as a condition of their becoming the new King and Queen of England in 1689.

The Bill of Rights was an Act declaring *'Rights and Liberties of Subjects and Settling the Succession of the Crown'*, the last part referring to the continuity of Protestantism in England.

John Locke, champion of natural rights, liberty and equality, had been the architect of the Bill of Rights, and one would have expected that, in view of his criticism of the patriarchal government system, he would also have taken up the matter of gender equality, but that was not on his agenda. In his *Two Treatises of Government* (1689) he did not discuss women's votes and citizenship; he merely concluded that, within marriage, differences of understanding or conflicts of will between husband and wife should be finally decided upon by the man 'as the abler and stronger'. He drew a parallel between the family, civil society and government, and in the same year, 1690, a treatise on parliamentary law explicitly stated for the first time that women were not eligible to vote. Locke, like many of his enlightened contemporaries, was in favour of education for women, but for the sole purpose of helping them to serve well as their children's first teachers. For him, equality and liberty in the broader sense were matters that concerned the male population only. Such a view was held consistently throughout the 18th century in other European countries, guided by Les Lumieres in France and Die Aufklärung in Germany.

In the British Constitution women were not eligible for citizenship because, as William Blackstone, a distinguished professor of law at Oxford, argued in his *Commentaries on the British Constitution* (1758), married men and women formed a unity of which only men were the political representatives. This principle has been called the 'civil death' of woman in marriage.

The Enlightenment philosophies of the English, based on the same experimental principle as their inductive approach to science, impressed people like Voltaire, who was largely instrumental in introducing them into France. The English approach had a substantial influence on the encyclopedists, who were actually inspired by the *Cyclopedia*, a multi-volume work published in 1729 in England expounding the new world-views of the Enlightenment movement in that country.

Although Britain had been ahead with restrictions on the powers of the monarch, its Parliament was still a very elite group of men, representing not more than 0.5 percent of the adult male population. In the view of Montesquieu, Blackstone and Burke, the British Constitution was designed to maintain liberty through respect for rank and for the special privileges of the nobility in exchange for its protecting the Crown and the people. As for Parliament, the Lords and the Commons were autonomous, and their power was safely beyond the reach of the King or the people. The Great Reform Bill of 1832 was needed to repair this anomaly, and in this respect England lagged behind North America and France where constitutional transformation had been achieved by that time.

In the meantime, in 1770, the revolutionary mood had spread to the British colonies in North America. Here it was not the protest of a parliament against a king, as in England, or the protest of a middle class against an elite, as later on in France, but the protest of one country against another oppressive country.

John Trumbull, *The Declaration of Independence, July 4, 1776*. 1787-1820. Oil on canvas, 53,7 x 79,1 cm, Yale University Art Gallery, Trumbull Collection.

In 1776 Thomas Jefferson had drafted the Declaration of Independence. It was approved on July the Fourth of the same year by the Constitutional Congress, which represented 13 colonies. Interestingly, only New York abstained from voting, the other 12 being in favour.

The Declaration states: 'all men are created equal, are endowed by their Creator with certain inalienable Rights, among which are *Life, Liberty and the Pursuit of Happiness* and to secure these Rights government institutions are instituted among men, deriving their just powers from the consent of the governed'. The document only deals, however, with the equal rights of men (meaning the white male section of the community) and not those of women. There is the record of a letter from Abigail Adams (née Smith) to her husband, congressman John Adams, who was involved in drafting the new code, urging him to 'not put unlimited power in the hands of husbands', but Adams ignored her petition. Voting rights for women were also denied, and where they had existed, in New York and New Jersey, they were set to be abolished. Compared to England and France at that time, women in North America were not yet very politically aware. That would come after the French Revolution.

The Declaration contains a long list of complaints about the misconduct of the Americans' British brethren in matters relating to the rights of men and concludes that the colonies will become independent as defined in the agreed Articles of Confederation.

The Declaration was the credo of a new age, as is stated still on one side of the US one dollar bill: *Novus Ordo Seclorum Annuit Coeptis*, written around a pyramid with an all-seeing eye, the symbol of the masonic cult.

The contents of the Declaration clearly derive from the European Enlightenment movement, reflecting the principles and even some of the literal texts of Hume, Locke, Montesqiueu and Rousseau.

When the British were defeated in 1783, the Articles of Confederation were changed into the American Constitution, and George Washington became the first President. The Constitution reflected a more centralized style of federal authority, because the Articles provided too weak a structure for government. Conversely, this weakened to a certain degree the liberal principles that were fundamental to the Declaration, based on natural rights. Constitutional civic rights implicitly refer to men only, as women are considered subordinate to men.

In France, pressures were mounting within the middle classes, directed not primarily against King Louis XVI, but against the power of the greedy and decadent elite establishment. A revolution was inevitable.

The spirit of the French Revolution in 1789 is reflected in *the Declaration des Droits de l'Homme*. It was based on Locke's principle of natural rights *(Two Treatises of Government, 1690)*, on Montesquieu's principle of the separation of legislative, executive and judicial powers, the trias politicas *(l'Esprit des Lois, 1748)* and on Rousseau's principle of the sovereignty of the nation *(Le Contrat Social, 1778)*.

The text states in article 2 that all men are born free and have equal rights as regards liberty, property, inviolability, participation in legislation and access for the middle classes to all governmental offices and positions.

Whilst a year later the name of the declaration was changed to the *Declaration des Droits de l'Homme et du Citoyen*, it was Condorcet who objected to the absence of explicit reference to the civic rights of men *and* women. Olympe de Gouges, in protest, published the *Declaration de la Femme et de la Citoyenne* in 1791, replacing all references to 'l'Homme' by 'la Femme'. Still, when the French Constitutions were approved in 1791, 1793, 1795 and 1800, they were based on the unchanged version of the Declaration of 1789. Although a clear improvement of the position of women was secured in the first draft Civil Code of 1793 by Cambacérès, providing women and men equal rights and obligations regarding communal property, parental authority, marriage and divorce, inheritance and for instance witnessing public documents and contracts, the civic, political rights of women that would be the necessary consequence of the acceptance of female individuality were not included.

The new government in France aimed at securing happiness for all, and Talleyrand stated in a report in 1791 that this concerned 'women above all', provided that 'they do not aspire to excercise political rights and functions'. The men of the French Revolution began to be afraid that the civic emancipation of women, which they had favoured, would run out of control. They therefore reverted to the laws of Nature to remind the citoyennes that it was in their own homes that they would fully and honourably benefit from the Revolution. According to Talleyrand, women needed to assert their civil personality and 'the moment they renounced their political rights, they would gain the certainty that their civil rights would be consolidated and even expanded'.

Olympe de Gouges strongly opposed this view. She also voiced severe criticism of Robespierre, the leader of the Revolution, and was subsequently executed in Paris in 1793, around the same time that Louis xvi was beheaded.

The Jacobins' anti-feminine attitude led to the repression of all women's political societies in 1793. They argued that women were intellectually and morally inequipped for political life, thereby throwing the initial intentions of the Revolution overboard.

In that same year the French Revolutionary Convention declared that women, minors, the insane and criminals were not citizens. End of story.

Endless discussions on draft Civil Codes between 1793 and 1799 never led to an approved version until Napoleon instituted the Code Napoleon in 1804, deleting most of the original clauses of the draft that would have improved the position of women.

What remained was reflected in David's sculpture of the goddess of Liberty, created in 1793. It was dedicated to the regeneration of France and based on Rousseau's ideal of the pregnant and nursing mother.

The only group of women to derive any lasting benefit from the Revolution were female artists. Midway through the early years of social unrest when the debate over the political rights of women raged, Academie Royale member Adelaide Labille-Gurard, mentioned in the previous chapter, addressed a meeting of that body on the subject of the admission of women, at that time still limited to four. She insisted that the only acceptable limit was no limit, but she was not successfull, and the limit remained four. However, women won the right to exhibiting at the Salon, and after the Revolution this led to an ever increasing number of women exhibited and significant progress for women artists in general. All this regardless of the fact that they were not admitted to the Ecole des Beaux-Arts and the Class of Fine Arts until the end of the 19th century.

> Although the three revolutions (the British, the American and the French) were each different in character, they all embraced the ideals of liberty and equality. But they were all drafted and approved by men and led in the end to only minor improvements in women's rights.
>
> All three glorified the principle of basic human rights, but they neglected to translate these into equality for both men and women. They ended the day with legislation that denied women's eligibility to vote, and in spite of all that was written and said in the 18th century on gender equality in principio, little was done in facto.

The ghosts of the 'Triple A' (Aristotle, Augustine and Aquinus) still seemed destined to inspire men and haunt women for ever, without end.

Meanwhile, Romanticism in Europe had progressed around the turn of the century towards the idolatry of female spiritual and moral qualities.

Beethoven's *Sonata Pathetique*, Goethe's *Faust*, Blake's *Marriage of Heaven and Hell*, Goya's *Caprichos*, Kant's *Critique of Pure Reason*, Schiller's *Wallenstein* and Wordsworth's *Lyrical Ballads* are all examples of the Romantic Movement in the latter part of the 18th century, which opposed the rationalist attitudes of the Enlightenment and emphasized feeling and passion, a trend that would continue well into the 19th century. The new movement, however, failed to promote the political equality of women and men as the male-invented romantic image of the feminine blurred the real issue.

As Balzac would declare bluntly a few decades later, in 1835, 'woman is a slave whom we must be clever enough to set upon a throne'.

One of the greatest English publicists for freedom was Thomas Paine, the author of *The Rights of Man* (1790). But while he devoted only a few critical lines in one of his writings to the subjection of women, it was Mary Wollstonecraft, who for the first time applied the 1790s call for freedom and liberty to women, with her *A Vindication of the Rights of Women*, published in 1792 and dedicated in protest to Talleyrand. Before Wollstonecraft, only such changes as the reform of female manners or improved education were proposed. Other women reformers throughout the 18th century, ranging from Mary Astell to Hannah More and including 'bluestockings' like Elizabeth Montagu, Mrs Thrale and Mrs Barbauld, more or less accepted the prevailing social and economic system with a double standard for male and female and avoided at all costs contamination with what we today call feminism. Mary Wollstonecraft initiated, in my opininon, a major breakthrough with her single-minded stance on gender relations, although it would take a long time before the depth of her perception would penetrate Western thinking. Her approach was of a different order, what we today would call a 'second order' as opposed to a 'first order' approach. Whereas the latter gives rise to incremental changes within an existing perception of reality, the former introduces a discontinuity leading to a radically different perception of reality. Due to the usual resistance to revolutionary innovative thinking which threatens the presumed security of existing models, first order changes are the norm, and second order changes take a long lead time for them to break through, if ever.

In the case of Mary Wollstonecraft, the point is that she was concerned not so much with the legal improvement of women's lot within the family and society, but with the fundamental and equal rights of all human beings, male or female, to choose

Mary Wollstonecraft painted by her friend John Opie in 1796.

their own civic responsibilities and to achieve economic independence based on learning, intelligence and occupational skills.

In previous periods and up to the time that she proclaimed her message, the relationships between women and men had been mostly governed by practical conditions of survival, by legal and moral standards, by opportunistic conventions, power, class or political establishments, occasioning ups and downs as we have seen in earlier chapters. Mary Wollstonecraft went to the root of the matter: allowing women to reason about their own vocation, as mistress of the household, as republican mother and as private citizen.

The men and women who had been actively struggling to improve the female condition had mainly concerned themselves with achieving a better deal for women in a man's world, whether in the institutions of religion, marriage, education, arts and crafts or commerce.

Mary Wollstonecraft rejected in principle the premise of the man's world and all its implications for society.

She was herself a controversial personality, first as an unmarried mother and a passionate lover while at the same time rejecting love as a threat to independence, then becoming actively involved in what we today call 'alternative' lifestyles, including not bothering to dress particularly well. She embraced Rousseau's romantic ideals and his rejection of the inequalities brought about by establishment privileges, but sharply attacked his views on the subordinate role of women. Unfortunately, she died very young, in 1797 at the age of 38. Had she lived longer, surely her clarion call would have had more impact in the nineteenth century. She would have continued addressing specifically the middle classes, because she considered the upper classes degenerate, out of touch with reality and a lost case anyway, and although she detested the phenomenon of poverty, she also did not feel that gender issues could be tackled effectively at that level either. The middle classes, however, were to her mind in a 'natural state' where women had the time and the ability to do more, over and above their responsibilities as wife, mother and mistress of the household; time they could, according to Mary Wollstonecraft, use to achieve economic independence and pursue vocational opportunities instead of wasting it in gossip and conversation, pleasing men, spending money and passing the days in idleness.

On the other hand, the Victorian period would not exactly have been the ideal time to cultivate sympathy for such a rebellious, unconventional person as Mary Wallstonecraft. And many women in the middle classes seemed to be quite comfortable and content with their protected condition.

Nevertheless, I think her vision represented an irreversible step in the march towards gender equality, even if the discontinuity she demanded will have to wait for the 21st century to be realized. Her outcry was a lasting signal to women to arise and take control of their own fate.

In the meantime the population of Europe exploded between 1750 and 1800, up by between 50 and 100 percent in the leading countries due to better diets, more food (the potato had been introduced) and a temporary decline in epidemics. Production and trade were booming, and next to the three political revolutions a fourth revolution, the Industrial Revolution, started to have a substantial impact on economic and social conditions and on the division of labour between men and women outside their traditional communities. Adam Smith had published the *Wealth of Nations* in 1776, and capitalism and democracy continued their progress. This was the time when most of Europe's forests were felled due to the fast-growing need for wood and farmland. It was also a time when in Britain and on the Continent, the expanding population began a relentless attack on ecological balances.

Another aspect of the time around the turn of the 19th century was that during the Romantic Movement, as a sort of precursor to the 20th century revival, the Great Goddess, Mother Goddess or Earth Mother of neolithic times came back into the spotlight after having been replaced by the many functional mythological goddesses of patriarchal Greek and Roman times such as Venus, Diana and Minerva. Whereas in the Renaissance and even in the Enlightenment these goddesses had been popular in European letters as patronesses or allegorical figures of civilisation, in the Romantic Movement the growing interest in the divine feminine caused a shift towards identifying goddesses with nature and eventually towards acknowledging Nature herself as the single divine mother of living beings. Hence the return of the nameless Mother Goddess.

At the same time there appeared a widening gap between religion and science and between divine spirituality and secular materialism. This resulted from the Scientific Revolution on the one hand and the revival of the Romantic Movement's feminine idolatry on the other, and led to the Catholic Church placing renewed emphasis on the worship of Mary, the Mother of God. This second wave of the Mary cult would raise her to an ever more elevated status and would climax, after mature reflection, in the 1854 proclamation of the Immaculate Conception of Mary herself, implying that apart from Jesus being conceived without sexual intercourse, Mary was conceived without the transmission of sin. This was proclaimed during the reign of Pope Pius xi as what we might call something of a 'media coup', being clearly a conscious move to regain support for the Catholic Church. Its architects were building on the revival of female spirituality promoted by the Romantic Movement, much to the dismay of the supporters of radical change in gender relations.

In the wake of Wollstonecraft's call for women to arise, the 'Woman Question', as it became known over time, was to blossom into a central issue of the 19th century, as the growing and maturing European population came to realise that it could no longer avoid coming to grips with correcting the unfair and unreasonable treatment of 'the other half' of society.

Nineteenth Century:
The Woman Question

The revolutionary events described in the previous chapter had provided a solid platform for launching a programme inclined towards gender equality in Europe and the USA in the 19th century. But it would take more than a hundred years of small, incremental improvements for the cherished aim of national voting rights for women to be achieved. The Woman Question had to compete with many other issues – political, philosophical, religious, industrial and social – that were preoccupying people's minds for most of the century.

Politically speaking, the post-revolutionary periods were restless times, with many warring factions in France, Germany, Austria, Italy, Spain and Russia. In Britain the situation was more stable but very conservative, while the USA was struggling to put its new house in order.

Differing and compromising constitutional frameworks were emerging in the various confederations, republics, principalities and semi-monarchies in Europe as they searched for new identities. They were not exactly favourable circumstances for a gender revolution.

It was only in the last quarter of the nineteenth century that the political cards were sorted out, and an era of relative stability was created.

In France there were counterrevolutionary movements, and hostilities broke out with coalitions of the monarchies of Prussia, Austria, Spain, Piedmont and Britain, joined by emigrés from France itself. There were also conflicts with the Catholic Church whose local possessions had been confiscated by the revolutionary forces.

Internal and external tensions in the early years after the French Revolution had, since 1793, led to the so-called Reign of Terror by the Committee of Public Safety, headed by the Jacobin Robespierre and instituted to keep the new situation under control. The resulting massacres and tyranny and the wars with other parts of Europe created conditions for a new balance of power in France between a republican and an absolutist leadership which eventually produced the phenomenon of the Emperor Napoleon in 1804.

Napoleon is credited with having innovated the organisation of the state through the Napoleonic Civil Code. It was a model for continental Europe, but it represented a serious setback in the context of gender relations.

By reverting to patriarchal standards and strengthening the prerogatives of the husband and father, the Code wiped out the substantial gains women had made during the Revolution and under the original draft of the Code Civil. Wives were again barred from signing contracts without their husband's consent, the wife's portion of the family property fell completely under husband's control during his lifetime, and the father's disciplinary hold over his children was increased.

The new Code also curbed the right of equal inheritance and rolled back the Revolution's extremely liberal divorce legislation. Divorce was now only possible in cases of cruelty resulting in grave injury and of adultery on the part of the wife. Adultery by the husband was recognized as a reason for the wife's demanding a divorce only 'when he shall have brought his concubine into their common residence'. This gave licence to the men in Napoleon's armies when at war away from home, although admittedly this may not have been the sole reason for this legislation.

In general, Napoleon's policy was a reaction to the Revolution's liberal individualism. It introduced monopolistic state regulation of occupational groups, extreme centralisation of administrative authority and a concordat with the Vatican, reversing previous trends towards secularization.

All the Napoleonic innovations and reversals endured through the subsequent political upheavals of the 19th century in France. In 1815 when the Bourbons took over, most of the remaining women's rights, including the already limited right of divorce, were eliminated altogether.

It was only in 1879 when the Third Republic was established that France entered a period of greater stability, and more attention could be paid to gender issues.

In Germany, Austria, Italy, Spain and Eastern Europe, the various states were busy organizing themselves in a spate of revolutions and counterrevolutions. Also here, gender issues were not high on the agenda in a time of political unrest.

In 1871 King Wilhelm 1 of Prussia became Emperor of Germany as Chancellor Bismarck completed his mission of aligning all the German states to form a strong and wealthy German Empire under paternalistic and despotic Prussian leadership.

Other major powers were also consolidating their positions in Europe. The Austro-Hungarian double monarchy crowned King Franz Josef in 1867. Russia completed its territorial establishment under Czar Alexander 11 in 1881. Italy became one nation under King Victor Emmanuel of Piedmont in 1860, and Spain reached a compromise between (royal) Carlist absolutism and republican anarchy in 1876.

The political climate in these nations, again, hardly led itself to considerations of social renewal, let alone gender issues.

Although the political situation in England under Queen Victoria was quite stable, the process of improving women's rights and incorporating them into a socially and legally acceptable system was extremely slow and piecemeal.

In the USA the effort of forging the principles of the Declaration of Independence into a workable Constitution and the energy that went into the Civil War were higher on the political agenda than gender issues. These had to wait until after the War was finished in 1865.

But after the political map was more or less settled in Europe, there were still other major factors that were very much occupying the agenda of the leading nations (England, Germany, France and Italy). In a further effort to strengthen their position as nation-states, they were expanding their military power but also their colonial power. In the latter part of the nineteenth century they each established colonial domination (dominions) in Africa: England and France in west and east Africa, Italy in north Africa and Germany in southern Africa. Portugal joined the scramble for colonial expansion by acquiring territories in East Africa, and France built up its colonial base in Indochina.

Clearly, also these developments did not help to devote much attention to the position of women in Europe, let alone in the new territories.

Nevertheless, the concept of a radical renewal of gender relations proved to be resilient, but it took more than a hundred years to adequately address the Woman Question in Europe and the USA after it had been raised at the end of the 18th century.

This was due not only to the political and legal preoccupations mentioned above, but also to influences stemming from philosophical, industrial, social, religious and scientific developments.

Philosophically speaking, the Romantic Movement had produced many influential 18th and 19th century thinkers such as Kant, Fichte, Feuerbach, Schopenhauer, Nietzsche and Hegel in Germany; Kierkegaard in Denmark; Rousseau, Comte, Fourier, Leroux, de Saint-Simon and Proudhon in France; and Stuart Mill, Owen and Spencer in England, all of them men.

They were heavily involved in the gender debate in controversial ways, all searching for new avenues of approaching the Woman Question in the spirit of a new era. 'It was obvious that a reconsideration of sexual inequality seemed a matter of some urgency as the nineteenth century dawned Fichte is quoted as observing'.

The preoccupation of the philosophers was with questions of dualities and their relationships, starting from the duality of Enlightenment, reason and Romantic emotion and following through to the duality of male and female. Some considered dualities as radical and separate, others as complementary and hierarchal; some as complementary and equal, others as dynamic and evolving. In terms of male and female, this led to different perceptions of gender relations, marriage, individuality and society.

The German thinkers were, with important nuances, mostly in favour of models that positioned women in the inferior position of wife, mother, daughter or sister, responsible for domestic life and reproduction, and men in the superior position of a person responsible for public life and wealth production. Within these models they would differ as to whether a marriage was a union (Fichte), a contract (Kant), or a moral act (Hegel). Some identified male with pursuing the infinite and female with explaining the finite (Kierkegaard). Some associated male with character and female with intelligence (Schopenhauer), character being connected to the immortal soul and intelligence to the mortal mind. Some considered the female or the feminine in man as the origins of evil (Nietzsche) which had to be eliminated. Nietzsche wrote in *Thus Spoke Zarathustra*: 'Thou goest to woman? Do not forget thy whip.'

The dualistic distinctions these philosophers made sprang from the biological, sexual differences. From that point on, they constructed their social and political models of the male and female roles. The spirit of Aristotle, Augustin and Aquinus lived on.

In all probability these models had a profound influence on the 19th century's insistence on a strict separation of the male/female roles in European and North

American society. More and more men spent most of their time outside the family home, in factories, in offices, travelling or at war, and the women stayed and worked at home. As a result of this separation and of puritan and post-revolutionary attitudes within society, the century produced the well-documented Victorian culture. Sex and affection were suppressed, and widely different roles were designated for women and men, with exclusive representation of men in all political and public functions.

André Collin, *Sewing Studio*, 1890, oil on canvas, 120 x 144 cm, Paleis voor Schone Kunsten, Brussels.

The exaltation of the female role of Motherhood, the worship of feminine moral qualities and spirituality in the Romantic Movement, the rediscovery of the Great Goddess and the further upgrading of the Virgin Mary by the Catholic Church were described in the previous chapter. Each helped to improve the status of women, compensating for and disguising to a certain extent the imbalances inherent in the model, where women were still objects and men still subjects. To repeat Balzac's pointed quotation: 'Woman is a slave whom we must be clever enough to set upon a throne.'

In France de Saint-Simon (whose work led to the term socialism around 1830), Comte (inventor of the term sociology at the same time) and Proudhon, all coming from the natural sciences, developed more or less similar models to those of the Germans with their dualistic concepts of the position of women in marriage and society. They conceived them, however, within the broader context of the social and economic upheavals of the industrial revolution which were starting to influence the political and philosophical conscience. Socialism was born.

194

> Feuerbach in Germany, Fourier and Leroux in France and Stuart Mill in England had begun to recognize that humanity was on the wrong track as regards its own human gender. They detached the issue from the purely biological outlook that had prevailed in previous thinking and started to concentrate once again on the freedom of the person, the individual human being regardless of sex.

They argued that the individual is primarily a self-sufficient and absolute entity in itself, whether male or female (Feuerbach). It can fulfil different roles, according to its capabilities, free choice and appropriate education (Stuart Mill). So a woman can choose to be a wife, a mother and/or a person in public life, just as a man can be a husband, a father and/or a person in public life. Only in the relationship between woman and man, with love and affection, are they male and female (Leroux). Consequently, economic independence in public life should be accessible to every woman and man. The voice of Wollstonecraft could be heard loud and clear in these messages.

The revival of the fundamentals of equal rights for women and men coincided with growing tensions that were becoming apparent in the process of industrialisation, associated with unacceptable social and economic conditions of the working classes and with slavery in Europe and the USA. This coincidence led to enduring connections between socialism, feminism and abolition, all originating in the same period of the 19th century.

Two classic works dealing with these issues, *The Capital* by Marx (1848), the bible of socialism, and *The Subjection of Women* by John Stuart Mill and his wife Harriet

Taylor (1869), the bible of feminism, were both published in that period.

LEFT In the second half of the nineteenth century anti-feminine opinions were strong, the Catholic Church backed the renewed emphasis on Motherhood and the exclusive role of women as mistress of the household.

RIGHT Women working in a factory.

Socialism and feminism also crossed paths at the level of labour relations as more women joined the workforce in the factories. The connections were sometimes quite ambivalent. On the one hand, steps were taken and laws passed to protect women from unreasonable working conditions and working times. On the other hand, actions and reforms were proposed for achieving equal treatment of men and women in the workplace. Moreover, while the state was not supposed to interfere in industrial relations, the trade unions were coming into existence in the second half of the 19th century, and they were not at all happy with the influx of women, who might take jobs away from men at lower cost. In these circles there were strong anti-feminine opinions on the inferior capabilities of women, both physical and mental. Women were unable to do a man's work. Women should stay at home. Very often, however, the income of the man was not sufficient to maintain the family, so the woman had to go to work as well.

The strain on women must have been enormous, caught up in these conflicting trends as they travelled the road towards equality, liberty and economic independence. All the more so as they strove to stay mistress of the household while remaining restricted in their marital and civic rights.

On top of all this, the Catholic Church intervened in the debate by issuing conservative statements rejecting the emancipation of women. It backed the renewed emphasis on Motherhood and the exclusive role of women as the centre of family life.

Pope Pius IX published in 1864 the *Syllabus of Errors*, accompanying the encyclical *Quanta Cura*. It denounced liberalism and nationalism, insisting on the duty of Roman Catholic rulers to protect the established church. The proclamation of papal infallibility in 1870 also signalled a firming-up of resistance to change.

Adopting a slightly more ambivalent tone, the Church responded in 1880 to the lay attack against marriage with the encyclical *Arcanum*, in which Leo XIII confirmed male marital authority: 'The man is the head of the woman, as Christ is the head of the Church'. The wife 'must be subject and obedient to her husband, not as handmaid, but as companion, such that the subjection that she shows him is devoid of decorum and dignity'.

In the encyclical *Rerum Novarum* of 1891 Leo XIII urged Catholics to accept political institutions such as parliaments and universal suffrage; it was understanding of the actions taken by trade unions against the excesses of capitalism, but vigorously denounced socialism.

Between the lines of the encyclicals one can read the patriarchal and absolutist attitude of the Church leadership, far removed from what was happening in the real world.

Another important development in the 20th century that influenced minds was the wave of substantial further advances in science. At the beginning of the century science had been the source of advances in knowledge which had led to the widespread use of 'hard' technologies such as textile machines, steam engines, steel manufacturing and railroads. Now, however, it was turning its attention to 'soft' technologies in the fields of electricity, chemistry, and biology.

Whereas in the first stage of practical scientific development the emphasis had been on discovering systems and mechanisms external to matter, the emphasis was now shifting to the discovery of structures and potent forces within matter.

The reader will have to bear with me in what may seem a far-fetched digression from the subject we are investigating, but there is to my mind a close link between the new findings in science and a new way of looking at the male/female dualism, as I will try to show.

Science-based industrial technologies had been developed as the result of human (male)-designed laws, formulae and equations based on simplicity, reversibility and linearity. Although these laws, such as the conservation of energy and the mechanical equivalence of heat, were only valid within restricted models, they could be successfully used to create human (male)-designed machines. In a way this success added to the growing confidence that the universe could be explained as a mechanistic model designed by reason and that no metaphysical or religious dimension existed. Man(kind) had the potential to become the master of the universe; at least that is what many believed.

The botanist Linnaeus with his *Systema Natura* in 1750 explained how the plant world is systematically organized. The geologist Lyell in 1832 said his findings showed that the earth must be many millions of years old instead of 6000 as suggested by Genesis. Darwin came with his theory on the origin of species in 1859, denying separate creation and fixity of species. Mendel revealed the mechanism of heredity in living organisms in 1866, and Mendeléjev produced the *Periodic System* of chemical elements in 1896. All these scientists seemed to confirm that mankind was on the way to understanding the systematic organization of the universe.

And although Linnaeus had emphasized that nature changed slowly, 'Natura non facet saltus', it was the element of continuous creative change over the course of time, the phenomenon of evolution in nature, the rediscovery of Heraclites's 'Panta Rei' that was dawning on the horizon of philosophical and scientific thought during the 19th century.

Buffon (*Histoire Naturel*, 1750) and Lamarck at the turn of the century had speculated and elaborated on the idea of evolution, but now it seemed to be turning into a credible story.

Evolution was believed to lead to lasting and beneficial progress by slow and small degrees, and the European mind was becoming aware that the mechanistic model of fixity, regularity, reversibility, linearity and radical dualisms could not explain evolutionary cosmology. Both Kant and Hegel saw the consequences of these lines of thought and were instrumental in preparing the ground for a fundamental rethinking of the mechanistic approach. Kant by integrating into his world-view both the material and the non-material phenomena we observe and experience, and Hegel by introducing the logic of things in movement and progressive change instead of static and cyclical. 'Thesis and antithesis lead to synthesis', a dynamic, interacting and evolving dualism.

Although it would take the best part of the 19th century before the evolutionary world-view and the relativity of dualisms would become embedded in scientific and philosophical thinking, they gave a new dimension to the understanding of progress other than in economic, cyclical and mechanical terms. As we will see in the next chapter, the gradual disappearance of the mechanical model and the related habit of thinking in radical distinctions were opening up ways of rediscovering the interaction and interdependence of reason and emotion, physics and metaphysics, science and religion, subject and object, economy and ecology, and last but not least, male and female.

Regardless of the main focus of the nineteenth century on the political, social, religious, industrial, philosophical and scientific developments described above, women had not been sitting still, and towards the middle of the century they started to make themselves collectively heard.

Inspired by the vision of the original ideals of the French Revolution and of Mary Wollstonecraft's *Vindication*, women were organizing themselves into movements and associations all over the Western world, including the USA and Eastern European countries. They were determined to achieve social and political improvements in their civil and civic rights. As far as they were concerned, the Woman Question remained on the agenda in this century of political, industrial and social revolutions, with the gaining of national voting rights for women as a priority.

In America as early as 1798 Judith Sargent Murray wrote, 'I expect to see our young women forming a new era in female history'. She represented the new generation of survivors, the 'republican' women who had emerged from the Revolutionary War, faced with the need to provide for their families after the men had gone to fight. As they had become aware of their individual strength and courage, Judith tried, through the medium of numerous essays, to convince people of women's intellectual capacities and their need for better education. Although at that time the new American women did not aspire to public duties, the Revolution had given a new meaning to their familial role; it had introduced a civic element into the domestic function.

After that, nineteenth-century America saw dramatic changes in women's educational opportunities in common schools. The teaching profession became the quintessential work outside the home for educated women, replacing men within a generation, but at half or less of a man's salary. But the feminisation of the teaching profession gained women increased respect for their intellectual abilities.

Interestingly, when de Tocqueville travelled through North America to prepare his famous *De la Democratie en Amerique* (1835), he attributed the prosperity and growing strength of the American people to 'the superiority of their women'. Noting significant differences between the status of women in America and in Europe, he commented: 'In Europe there are people who, confusing the divergent attributes of the sexes, claim to make of man and woman creatures who are, not equal only, but actually similar'. He criticised this notion and was of the opinion that such forced equality degraded both sexes and produced feeble men and unseemly women. He then went on to declare that this was far removed from the American idea of democratic equality between men and women, which consisted of allowing their diverse faculties diverse employment and applying the great principle of political economy to the two sexes, carefully tracing the clearly distinct spheres of action for each of them.

So the republican woman was apparently not yet very visible!

It would be nearly 50 years after Judith Sargent Murray's statement before the increasingly unfair conditions for women in marriage and industry (mainly textiles) provoked the first national protest: the National Women's Rights Convention in Seneca Falls, N.Y. on July 19th, 1848.

> A Declaration of Sentiments made by one of the leaders of the gathering, Elizabeth Cady Stanton, and read out at the Convention says in part:
>
> 'The history of mankind is a history of repeated injuries and usurpations on the part of man toward woman, having in direct object the establishment of absolute tyranny over her – he has created a false public sentiment by giving the world a different code of morals for men and women, by which moral delinquencies which exclude women from society are not only tolerated, but deemed of little account in man. He has endeavoured in every way that he could to destroy her confidence in her powers, to lessen her self-respect, and to make her willing to lead a dependent and abject life.'

Many of the women present considered the Declaration too daring, and it was adopted only by a narrow margin. Attended by 300 all-white delegates, the Convention ended after two days with resolutions to fight for women's suffrage and legal equality in marriage, work and education, and to secure for women equal participation with men in the various trades, professions and commerce.

Two years later, in 1850, the first International Women's Congress was held in Worcester, Massachusetts.

Elizabeth Stanton, leading the first wave of American feminism, was the first woman to run for Congress in 1866, despite the fact that women could not yet vote. In 1869 she and Susan Anthony founded the National Woman Suffrage Association, which became the National American Woman Suffrage Association in 1890 after a merger with a rival organization.

A US constitutional amendment to grant full suffrage to women was introduced in Congress for the first time in 1879. Regrettably, Elizabeth Stanton did not live to see the Nineteenth Amendment to the Constitution in 1920 finally consecrating women's right to vote, but she had paved the way for women's participation in politics in the twentieth century on a scale of which she could only have dreamt. She did, however, after the end of the American Civil War (1861-1865), see the end of slavery for which she had fought so hard and in pursuit of which she had co-founded the Woman's Loyal National League in 1863.

French women, supported by Pierre Leroux, made their demands on voting rights public when universal male suffrage was established in France in 1848. In 1866 the first French feminist organization, aiming for better education, equal pay and the prevention of prostitution, had been created by Louise Michel.

The claim for voting rights was turned down, and even in 1879 when the Third Republic was in place it was rejected again, on the grounds that the new regime was too fragile to permit innovations of this kind. What also seemed to have played a role is that women were by far the largest group of faithful churchgoers and the authorities were afraid that their votes would increase the influence of the Catholic Church in politics. Only in 1944 did France endorse legislation for women's voting rights, long after many other European countries, but before Belgium, Italy, Portugal, Greece and Switzerland (being the latest, in 1971).

In Britain the various Reform Bills, in 1832, 1835 and 1867, increased voting rights for ever greater sections of the population, the last including urban workers but not women. In 1867 Dame Millicent Garrett and other British feminists formed the National Society for Women's Suffrage.

John Stuart Mill was the spokesman for feminists in Parliament at that time, but his efforts were not successful, regardless of the fact that his *Subjection of Women*, published in 1869, caused much concern and upheaval. Municipal and county suffrage was gradually introduced in England and Scotland before the turn of the century. In 1918 national universal voting rights for women were approved, although women over 30 years old. Lowering the age to the same as for men, 21 years old, at the national level did not get through Parliament until 1928.

Italy was a very different case in point. The most renowned representative of Italian feminism was Anna Maria Mozzoni. Under the Restoration she linked emancipation to the Catholic feminine model, which found expression in *La Donna Cattolica*, written in 1855 by the priest Gioacchino Ventura. It designated woman as the centre of the family, more important than man because of her moral virtues and superior character. This idealistic nineteenth-century Catholic feminism was exclusively that of the wife and mother, without affectionate aspects of conjugal love, in a way in line with the Victorian model. It had very little to do with feminism as it developed in other European countries. Still, many Catholic women in Europe were attracted by it.

The struggle to get votes for women, led by Mrs. Pankhurst and her daughter Christabel at the head of the militant suffragists, convulsed Britain from 1905 to 1914. In Britain, so proud to claim 'the Mother of Parliaments', universal suffrage, including women's, was granted only in the year of her death, 1928.

Also in other parts of the Western society women were taking initiatives to fight collectively for their rights: in Germany the General Association of Women (1868), in Denmark the Danish Women's Association (1871), in Switzerland the Association for the Defence of the Rights of Women (1872), in Norway the Women's Suffrage Society (1885), in Australia the Women's Suffrage League (1888) and in Britain the National Union of Women's Suffrage Societies (1897).

Ingenious propaganda.

The only country in the world to approve legislation giving national voting rights to women on equal terms with men before the end of the century was New Zealand, in 1898. In all the rest, women had to wait for the 20th century.

In this chapter, dealing with some of the major developments affecting the Woman Question in the 19th century, the subject of the arts has not been touched upon. I decided to leave it out because the participation and visibility of women in the creative arts gradually improved along the lines observed in the previous age. Hence, the number of women writers and artists increases to the extent that it becomes nearly impossible to make an acceptable selection. In other words, to my mind this is not the worst arena when considering the male/female imbalance, except that in the field of musical composition the seemingly nearly total absence of women remains puzzling. Only recently has Luba Timofejeva, a contemporary Russian pianist, brought a few excellent women composers borne in the 19th century back to life on a CD: Louise Farrenc (1804-1875), Agathe Backer-Grondahl (1847-1907), Mel Bonis (1858-1937) and Germaine Tailleferre (1892-1983).

As to education, I prefer to deal with that subject in more detail again in the next chapter. Suffice to note at this stage that the steady spread of primary education significantly increased female literacy in Western Europe and the USA, bringing it almost up to male levels by 1900. A growing minority of middle-class women had entered secondary schools, and by 1870 a handful reached universities and professional colleges. From then on, women slowly started entering the liberal professions as medical doctors, lawyers, scientists and, as mentioned earlier in America, teachers.

Before moving on to the next chapter I would like to remark how frequently in the literature, including in this book, the word feminist is used. It actually appears for the first time in the April 27th, 1895, edition of *Atheneum*, an English literary weekly, describing a woman who 'has in her the capacity of fighting her way back to independence'.

Back from when, I wonder?

XVII

Waves and Wars

In the previous chapters I have tried to present an overview of how, in both the public and the private domains, male/female relationships developed through the ages in Western society, based on historical data and references.

Now that we have reached the 20th century, I will occasionally include my own perceptions and impressions of what has happened over the past hundred years, sometimes explicitly, sometimes implicitly.

The reasons for doing this are threefold.

In the first place I myself am of the 20th century. I belong to the four generations that have occupied it. I have known and continue to know those four generations. My father was born in 1897 and my mother in 1900. I was born in 1928 and my children in 1955, 1958 and 1962. My grandchildren were born in 1984, 1987, 1998 and 2000.

So for me this is not an age of history, but an age of memory and experience. I can search in my own past and my own present for clues to the male/female issue. Therefore, I am sometimes able to interpret events in this century in a different way from that applied to previous centuries, although probably with less objectivity, if objectivity is at all possible in the study of history.

Secondly, as we started the 20th century with a world population of 1.6 billion and are ending it with 6 billion, the sheer number of people involved in male/female relationships has increased substantially, and the scope of the issue has also become much greater, both locally and globally. But in addition to this expanding volume of male/female life experience, more people have been working, writing and communicating on the subject and producing an ever growing mountain of books, articles, opinions, conference proceedings, academic publications and documentaries. A full coverage of all the events, ideas, movements and legislation relating to feminism and gender in the

20th century would thus become very tedious, and I had to make my own subjective selections. I must admit that I had to go through much of the relevant literature of our times in order to arrive at this selection. But as matters of gender are very much in the limelight today, I imagine the reader is broadly familiar with them and may not always agree with my choices.

In the third place, enormous changes have occurred and are occurring in gender relations over the past 25 years. The intensity and speed of these changes and the way they are communicated, more or less on-line, through TV, the Internet, e-mail, air travel and specialized journalism, make a comprehensive assessment of the state of the art at any point in time volatile and short-lived.

While political stability prevailed in the Western world at the end of the 19th century, there existed an urge for cultural renewal, a movement away from Romanticism and all its subsidiary-isms, away from Victorianism towards what we now call Modernity.

Scientific and philosophical renewal was also in the air. Materialistic and deterministic modes of thinking were giving way to more relativistic and evolutionary ideas. New world views based on these ideas were being developed, mainly by men, although some women were also contributing significantly to advances in various fields of science – Madame Curie in physics is a prime example.

The renewals in science and philosophy influenced concepts of male/female, as I will briefly explain from my own perception of scientific theory.

When I studied chemical engineering at Delft Technical University in the late 1940 and early 1950, I had difficulty with the still mainly mechanistic world view that prevailed in the curriculum. Not convinced that everything in the world can be predicted, measured, regulated and controlled when we have discovered or invented laws, I started to look for other mentors, intrigued by Einstein's, Heisenberg's and Bohr's ideas concerning relativity, uncertainty and complementary dualism in the early decades of our century.

At university the philosophical aspects of these theories were not discussed. They were considered relevant only to the extent that they might assist in the advancement of technology.

In the same period Bergson in France, Whitehead in England and Heidegger in Germany propounded new philosophies on the driving forces in the evolutionary

Marie Curie. Together with her husband Pierre, she isolated the element radium. ➤

process, matching science and metaphysics and introducing the relativity of linear time. The perception of developmental time in addition to cyclical time in observing the march of evolution linked science with religion, a link that had gradually got lost over previous ages.

> Bergson appealed to me because he introduced the notion that events in nature follow laws that are very different from the laws of science. Today we know that in contrast to traditional technology-related science, which is based on predictability, linearity, reversibility and simplicity within closed systems, natural processes are unpredictable, non-linear, irreversible and complex, operating in open systems. Although this is perhaps stating the case rather too simply, it nevertheless pictures the essence of the difference between the world of technology and the world of Nature.

I first started to understand this when I read Bergson's *Evolution Creatrice* (1920) and the French biologist Lecomte du Nouy's *Human Destiny* (1943). Ilya Prigogine, Nobel prizewinner and co-author of *Order out of Chaos* (1985), supplied further scientific proof by adding that while natural processes are never in complete equilibrium, traditional technology-based science always assumes equilibrium. In coming face to face with him at a dinner in Copenhagen in 1997, I met a man who studies the link between science and life and is an artist as well as a scientist, a living example of the link himself.

Man-made perceptions and models of reality are thus limited and not universally applicable. Oh yes, they may be when applied to man-made machines and technologies, but not when they are applied to nature, life and human destiny.

Maybe we should keep all this in mind when we come to consider the nature of masculine and feminine, and avoid pressing them into a (literally) man-made mould that does not represent reality and could lead to wrong conclusions and distorted relations, including human relations.

Unless we can fully appreciate the unpredictability, irreversibility, non-linearity and complexity of natural processes, mixing nature and man-made models is a risky venture.

It was much later, after my career in business, that I became aware of the fact that when man-made machines and technologies are put to work in a massive way in the service of an exploding world population, then they become inevitably linked with nature and human destiny. Obviously, an exploration of that link leads one to the investigation of the interdependence of economy, technology and ecology, until recently a non-subject in a male-dominated economy that produces these machines and technologies. I will come back to this in later chapters.

Apart from new ideas in science, the first half of the century also produced new ventures in the field of the arts. In architecture, music, literature and poetry there was an explosion of creativity, a cosmopolitan 'Modern Movement' that pervaded the whole of Europe, with its stronghold in Weimar. In the visual arts we saw the introduction of Cubism, characterized by Picasso as 'paint not what you see, but what you know is there', and later of Symbolism and Impressionism. I do not feel qualified to express an opinion as to what effect these renewals had on the subject of male and female because I have no expertise in this field. It strikes me that the exponents of renewal were all men. Was this because men are more innovative or because women's innovative powers could not come to bloom in a man's world?

There is one aspect of the new movement, having to do with psychology, I would venture to comment on. From what I understand of Sigmund Freud's psychoanalysis, his contribution to the male/ female debate seems devastatingly simplistic. He was obsessed with the fact that women differ from men because they lack something, namely a penis, which is unsatisfactorily substituted by a clitoris. On this premise he bases his theory that a man is complete and a woman incomplete. Thus, almost unbelievably, Aristotle's view of woman as a mutilated creature comes back again, even in the twentieth century.

Freud also theorized that all libido is masculine and that between all mothers and sons the Oedipus complex is a dormant problem. But regardless of these strong opinions, he still felt insecure about femininity. It was this insecurity that, towards the end of his life in the mid-1930's, led him to pose the celebrated question to Marie Bonaparte: 'What does a woman want?' (Was will das Weib?).

Born on May 6, 1856, Sigmund Freud was an Austrian physician, neurologist, and the founder of psychoanalysis. His ideas and theories, especially those with respect to such notions as the 'Oedipus Complex', have been widely accepted, as well as widely argued, since their introduction.

In the Netherlands, universal suffrage was introduced in 1919. Women voted for the first time in 1922.

Although this is merely a hint at some aspects of Freud's psychoanalysis, I have always been highly suspicious of this method, and I am sure it has had a very negative impact on the integrity of relations between men and women, including fathers and daughters and mothers and sons.

I will now return briefly again to the course political and social history was taking.

When, on June 28, 1914, Gavrilo Princip, a Serbian nationalist, assassinated the Austrian Archduke Franz Ferdinand, the illusion of the stability, creativity and strength of Europe fell to pieces. Germany rushed to help Austria-Hungary against the Serbs; Russia refused to abandon Serbia; France maintained its alliance with Russia, whilst Germany, sensing a major power struggle, launched a surprise attack on France and Belgium, whereupon Britain stood by a defence treaty with Belgium and declared war on Germany.

This situation marked the beginning of a dark age in our culture, including a severe setback to the process of improving the political and private status of women in continental Europe.

By 1920 women had gained the universal right to vote and other legislation granting them public and private rights in respect of inheritance, custody, property and labour had been implemented in 24 countries in the Western world and Eastern Europe.

However, a severe depression and five dictators, Franco, Salazar, Hitler, Mussolini and Stalin were temporarily to ruin the chances of women advancing towards more equal treatment in the period 1919-1945.

The new political situation in Europe marked the end of the first feminist wave that had started in the second part of the 19th century.

The second wave was not to launch itself before the 1960's, 100 years after the first wave began and 25 years after the beginning of World War II.

Although the first wave had produced legislation that raised woman's formal status in society in Western and Eastern European countries at the beginning of this century, this by no means implied that her position had noticeably improved when it came to the roles played by the sexes, where men's rights remained the standard by which all rights were judged.

This ambiguous situation could have changed as a result of the war experience, just as it could have done, but eventually failed too, after the revolutionary wars of the 19th century. In wartime women prove that they can do men's jobs, handle economic independence and take part in public activities while still managing the home front.

I have myself seen how strong and courageous women can be in critical and challenging periods of political suppression, such as the occupation of the Netherlands by the Germans in World War II. A first cousin of mine, seemingly low-key both in appearance and attitude, worked all through the war years helping Jewish people and guiding them personally through the German lines to freedom. And there were many more women doing such things. As a member of the underground resistance, I met women in that movement who made a lasting impression on me through exercising springs of resourcefulness and courage without showing off or indulging in macho behaviour. After the war it seemed as if these women, who had perfectly well managed roles stereotyped as male, simply disappeared, submerged again in 'normal' society.

This apparently also happened after 1918.

In the turmoil after World War I, women's movements were either dissolved or allowed to become inactive, while the Communists, the Fascists and the Nazis were engaged in taking over political leadership in five European countries: in 1917 Lenin in Russia, later succeeded by Stalin; in 1922 Mussolini in Italy; in 1932 Hitler in Germany; in 1936 Franco in Spain and, at about the same time, Salazar in Portugal.

Each of these countries' dictatorships had a different background, as I will briefly summarize.

Originally, Marxism had postulated equality of men and women, economic independence of every citizen, and public ownership of the land and means of production. After the Revolution in 1917, Russia and its later communist-aligned neighbouring countries developed the most advanced systems of legislation and education towards gender equality seen in Europe at that time.

Although at first Lenin and then Stalin appointed women to the top positions affecting feminine and family matters, this policy was subsequently abandoned or

LEFT Jozef Djugashvili – Stalin – the sole
Bolshevik leader of peasant stock, was
born the son of an impoverished Georgian
shoemaker in 1879. He became a Communist Party Secretary in 1922. The eleven-year-
old girl Mamlakat Nakhengova traveled
from Tajhikistan to present him a Tajik
translation of his book *Stalin about Lenin*.

RIGHT Chamberlain's policy of appeasing
Hitler pleased some, not least, of course
the Führer himself, who fêted him at no
fewer than three conferences in September
1938.

watered down, due to the vested interests of the male
culture.

Alexandra Kollontai, who was the only woman
ever elected to the Communist Central Committee in
1917, headed the Women's Department of the Committee Secretariat which was created in 1919. She
urged a redefinition of the sex roles, different from the
existing male model, and progress towards women's
emancipation based on a new model, not unlike the
idea of Wollstonecraft. But she did not succeed. Her
office could never really have had any function other
than conveying the wishes of the male-dominated hierarchy. The Department was abolished in 1929.

Italy fell under Mussolini's fascist power following a paternalistic regime. He promised improvements in the private position of women, but within the context of a
family-centred ideology in line with Catholic dogma and morality. He made it very

clear that he considered women to be different from men, and by this he meant different according to the old Mediterranean and Catholic tradition of subordinate to men.

Mussolini never even admitted any female members to his hierarchy. There existed some women's organizations such as Fasci Femminili, but they were powerless to represent women's issues.

Patriarchal Germany had been subjected to severe financial penalties by the international community and had been in no mood to consider a gender equality policy. When Hitler came to power, he emphasized the importance of women in both the public and private domain in developing the Aryan super race. Building the super race also meant the annihilation and banishment of 'unworthy life', including old, handicapped, mentally incurable, homosexuals and Jewish citizens.

The 'Reich Women's Leader', Gertrud Scholtz-Klink, was listed in the Nazi hierarchy, starting in 1934, and she also led the DFW (Deutsche Frauenwerk). Although she initially represented a voice for women against male domination, over the course

LEFT Francisco Franco (1892-1975), Spanish military leader who rose to power during the Spanish Civil War and went on to rule Spain as dictator from 1939 until 1975.

RIGHT Mussolini's rise to power was rapid; his Fascist Party Blackshirts marched into Rome in 1922, a year before Hitler's failed first attempt to seize power.

of time the Nazi regime put all matters of family, motherhood and women under the Party welfare organization and thereby under male leadership.

Although lack of genuine intention, failure to understand the 'woman question' and the macho nature of totalitarian systems all contributed to the degradation of women's role under the new dictatorships, a significant additional factor came into play.

Eventually Stalin, Mussolini and Hitler were all confronted with a pressing need for more people to supply cheap labour for their state-controlled or state-directed economies, to back their military build-up and to add to their demographic 'weight' in Europe.

But at the same time the Soviet Union, Italy and Germany all had to cope with a 'population problem' relating to declining birth rates since the turn of the century, caused by improvements in women's education, the practice of contraception and abortion and the consequent greater influence of women on family planning.

As a result of this paradoxial situation, the leadership resorted to imposing regulations and laws against abortion and contraception, and to exalting motherhood in order to foster not only the quality but also the size of the nation's population. This led to the responsibility for population policy being centralized in state institutions directed by the male Party hierarchy.

Spain was a special case. It had experienced a change from a monarchic dictatorship to a socialised Republic in 1931. The latter proclaimed strong support for women's rights in contrast to the anti-feminine attitudes that had prevailed under King Alfonso XIII. In the year it was elected, the new government set in motion the necessary legislations for achieving women's universal voting rights.

But strong reactionary forces persisted, led by General Franco and backed by the Church. Franco led a coup in 1936, and after his winning his Civil War with the help of Hitler and Mussolini, all moves to improve the position of women were nullified with the support of the Catholic authorities, and women were sent back to where they belonged: running the household. There had been active and strong anti-fascist participation in politics by Marxist-oriented women's organizations before and during the Civil War, but their cause was defeated with Franco's victory.

Franco worked with the rightist movement called 'Woman's Falange', but its members were dedicated to serving the army, motherhood and God. They supported the army in its Civil War battles, where women were also actively engaged in the fighting on the Republican side. In total more than 100,000 women died.

The woman question in Spain died with them.

I have given this summary of how the first feminist wave died out in some major European countries after World War I in an effort to drive home the resilience of the male domination model and how during crises it can return to full power, annihilating all previous progress.

In the period immediately before and during World War II, more than 50 million lives were lost as opposed to 4.5 million in the wars of the 19th century and 8 million in World War I.

This is not ancient history; it happened before my eyes, and I can still see the faces and hear the voices of Mussolini, Hitler, Stalin and Franco. We had no television then, but the radio and the newsreels in the cinemas conveyed the messages only too well, and they were frightening. Especially Hitler yelling psychotically at those massive rallies in Germany, culminating in 'Deutschland über Alles; Sieg Heil', and the masses responding 'Heil Hitler'. During the War the German soldiers would be always marching through the streets of Amsterdam, mechanically chanting their loud war songs in an aggressively self-assertive way, their boots pounding out a regular drumbeat. It made you say to yourself: these are no longer human beings, they are robots without a human face, their personal integrity gone, lost in the Nazi system. Since the War I have seen many armies and witnessed many parades and music, but what the Germans did at that time represented something quite different. It was not just a matter of instilling courage and discipline, vital to a soldier's survival; it was the expression of supreme arrogance. These men were conditioned by the system to believe that they were a superior race. It never consciously occurred to me then that it also represented a male domination culture in one of its most ugly forms. As I see it now, my confrontation with this reality during my teenage years, literally on my own doorstep, probably contributed to a built-in abhorrence within me of mass gatherings, mass singing, the idolizing of male leadership and the violation of individual integrity.

These are the very elements that caused the disappearance of the feminist movements in totalitarian systems. They relate directly to the fundamentals of the male/ female issue.

This part of European history shows that, even if you have universal voting rights – as Russia had since 1917, Germany since 1919 and Spain since 1931 – that in itself does not guarantee the sort of resilience needed in society to achieve women's emancipation.

Even those countries that remained democracies began to lose interest in the woman question. After more woman-friendly legislation had been set in place, most people felt that was enough. At the same time, the image of the Western housewife

came back in a different setting, with modern domestic equipment and gadgets making her job more pleasant, efficient and clean. Hollywood's romantic movies, songs and music conditioned people to the desirability of traditional motherhood, the housewife happy in a bright new home with the children and the husband out earning money, status and praise. For formerly occupied Europe, especially, this vision of the American Dream was very appealing after the hardships of the war.

Before and after the war I grew up subjected to this kind of conditioning and had a great time. It never occurred to me, either when observing my parents or when contemplating my friends, that there was such a thing as a 'woman question'. Everything, after the war, seemed to be safe and in order, with a clear road to an early married life, a job, a home, children and a garden. Man busy in his big world and woman in her small one.

And although this remains an expectation of many people today, not least in the developing world, a lot has changed since the inevitable second feminist wave came rolling in during the 1960's and 1970's.

The well-known books that accompanied and triggered these changes such as Simone de Beauvoir's *The Second Sex* (1953), Betty Friedan's *The Feminine Mystique* (1963), Germaine Greer's *The Female Eunuch* (1971), Marilyn French's *The Women's Room* (1977) and many others will not be reviewed here in detail. Rather, I will give the reader my bird's-eye impression of what changes were sought and which of them produced this second wave in the subsequent decades.

Put simply, I think three major drives inspired the second feminist wave in the Western world.

The first was that the achievements of the first wave, namely voting rights and equal legal rights for women and men in many areas, were not matched by equal opportunities for employment and comparable salaries, and this applied at all levels within the institutions of society.

The second drive, directly related to the first, was the persisting perception in traditional society that men were the natural and salaried players in the outside world of culture, politics, business, technology, war and serious talk, whilst women were the natural unpaid players in the world of nature, domesticity, children and small-talk.

The third drive was the fact that everything being undertaken to further women's emancipation was done according to the standards of a man's world.

◄ The latest gadgets for household use.

Russian women decorated for service in the Second World War march through Red Square on a Victory Day Parade.

Second-wave pioneers have all been trying in their different ways to resolve these issues, and the above-mentioned writers each had a different view. Typically, this new feminism, although generally known as women's liberation, did not lead to large new organisations such as the suffrage movement. There were many different women's groupings, ranging from radical activists to modest reformers, and whereas the second wave more or less coincided with a surge in environmentalism and anti-capitalism, some groups were closely related to leftist ideological and ecological campaigns as well. As a resul, feminist activities were often characterized as being 'anti' in outlook, including anti men. The new feminism was more negative and problem-oriented than positive and solution-oriented. In the 1980's this generated a backlash both from men who felt threatened and from women who felt increasingly uncomfortable with the feminists' style.

My impression is that most second-wave activities were directed at infiltrating the male-dominated model of society by political actions and private pressures, coming from two main positions, one based on distinct differences between men and women, the so-called feminism of difference, the other based on complete equality of men and women, the so-called egalitarian feminism. The complication with these two approaches was that they could lead to radically different positions on issues of reform. An interesting example is the failure (to this day) in the USA to get the Equal Rights Amendment passed through Congress in the 1970's and 1980's, the differentialists opposing the egalitarians on the grounds that existing privileges for women would be scrapped by approval of the amendment. Ironically, therefore, the law in the USA does not comply with the Universal Declaration of the Rights of Man (1948), which does not fail to mention equality of the sexes as well as equality of the husband and wife in marriage.

Another illuminating case arose recently in France. In March 1999 the French Senate was divided over a proposal to create equal opportunities for men and women in politics. Differentialist feminist Agacisky (independent from her husband Prime Minister Jospin) backed it, but egalitarian Badinter (author of *The One is the Other*, 1986) argued fiercely against, especially because it would result in quota systems, which she considered humiliating for women. The law was finally approved, after nine years of resistance by its opponents who claimed that, according to French republican ideals, all citizens are equal.

But however diverse the various feminists' attitudes, the results of their efforts are plainly visible in modern life. After 25 years of hard work, the increased presence of women in the institutions of society becomes clear if we look at the figures.

Volumes of detailed statistics are available showing such improvements in most Western countries, far more than can be quoted in this book (for references see the bibliography).

The following give a rough idea: the workforce in these countries consists for up to 45% of women (mostly in the growing service sector), of which 70% are full time; up to 70% of women with one child working full time; up to 35% female members of parliament (the USA, Britain and France lagging behind with less than 10%); up to 50% female enrolment in universities; 10-25% female cabinet ministers and several women prime ministers.

On the less positive side there are still under 10% women in better paid management positions, under 5% in top management positions and fewer than 10% full university professors.

In addition, women's comparable wages and salaries, with a few exceptions, are still between 60% and 80% of those of men.

I will come back on these subjects in chapter IX.

In matters of religion there have been some positive achievements, such as the ordination of women priests in Anglican and Episcopal churches since 1976 and in the Church of England since 1992. In a remarkable document published after the 34th General Congregation of the Society of Jesus in 1995 in Rome, charting a course for the 23,000-member male order for the 21st century, the Jesuits officially formulated their regret at 'having been part of a tradition that had offended against women, reinforcing male domination'. In the coming century the members all over the world are urged to listen 'carefully and courageously' to the experience of women and 'to align themselves in solidarity with women'.

On the other hand, in that same year, 1995, Pope John Paul issued a *Letter to Women* on the occasion of the forthcoming Fourth World Conference on Women in Beijing. In it, he exalted in familiar fashion all the excellent qualities of women as helpers of men (referring to *Genesis* 2) and the significance of womanhood as manifested so sublimely by Mary. Although extremely flattering to women in many ways, the Pope signalled no change with regard to the traditional role of women in the Church. The European Women's Synod, made up of 1,000 women from 54 countries and different denominations gathered in Austria in 1996, gave him a clear answer, requesting equal rights to positions of authority in the Church hierarchy.

So all in all, the present situation of women in the Western world is a mixed bag of encouraging indications and disappointing realities.

As to the rest of the world, the fourth UN Conference on Women in 1995 in Beijing, attended by 40,000 women from more than 160 countries, highlighted the global dimension of the issue as it had developed over the previous 20 years since the first World Conference on Women in 1975 in Mexico. These conferences have taught us how diverse the conditions of women are in different parts of the world and how careful one must be not to translate Western experiences into other cultures. In this book I have concentrated on European and North American history, but in chapter XXI will briefly touch upon the global situation, as obviously this will be an important debate for the 21st century.

Coming back to the three drives powering the second feminist wave in the Western world, it is now clear that the relative improvements achieved in the first, i.e. women's conditions in the world at large, are still not matched by improvements in the other two, i.e. role division and masculine standards. It would therefore seem to me that, having gained voting and other legal rights during the first wave and improvements in womens' presence in the world during the second wave, more progress is now anticipated towards the reshaping of roles and values in a new gender model.

When I meet the new grown-up generation of today (born, let us say, after 1955) and read current popular books, newspapers, magazine articles and interviews about the roles played by the sexes, I get a definite feeling that all, men and women alike, are engaged in developing cooperative divisions within the family and at work and in replacing the man-dominating model by new gender relations based on both difference and equivalence. We will return to this subject in Chapter XIX.

At this point in time it would be interesting to investigate what caused the loss of momentum in both the feminist waves. Probably, lack of a good understanding or conflicting opinions as to what is meant by male and female and masculine and feminine and what is meant by gender equality and gender difference, considering them as opposites instead of complementary.

As long as men only wonder, as Freud did, what a woman wants, and women only wonder what a man wants, we shall keep on running into two traps: first, looking at the question from either a male or a female point of view, and second, assuming that these points of view are universally shared by both men and women.

If we could start wondering what the human being, man or woman, wants, each with differing masculine and feminine traits, the question should be, and Freud should have asked, 'Was will der Mensch?'.

Maybe Alexandra Kollontai, that member of the Central Committee in Russia in 1917 responsible for the Women's Department of the Committee Secretariat, was right when she proposed replacing the male domination model of traditional society before going to work on women's emancipation. Her problem was that nobody in the male hierarchy would accept such a thing, and neither Marx and nor Lenin had ever given it a thought in their utopian ideologies.

Consideration of what is meant by male and female and by masculine and feminine is so central to the future coexistence of the sexes in a new society that the next chapter will specifically address this question.

XVIII

The Stereotype Trap

After having digested the essence of the previous chapters on the past and present, and before speculating about options for the future, it may be useful to ponder a while on the meaning of the words woman and man, female and male, feminine and masculine, gender and sex, and to what extent they represent difference or equality. It appears that people give different meanings to these notions, leading to equally different viewpoints and all contributing to confusion and misunderstanding. When I discuss these notions with others, we often find our-selves falling into the trap of subjective interpretations and personal experiences, confusing for instance the words woman with feminine and man with masculine.

Based on my own life experience and my selective reading of the substantial number of recent books and articles on the subject, examples of which are listed in the bibliography of this chapter, I will try to clarify and integrate the various perceptions of these notions.

The fact that *Time Magazine*, *New York Times* and *Scientific American* all issued extensive special editions on women and men and feminity and masculinity between March and June 1999 shows how much this subject is at the forefront of public interest.

In the previous chapters we have seen the persistence of the classic viewpoint, developed and maintained by men, that man is radically different from woman and that this difference compels the superiority of man over woman in an asymmetrical and hierarchical model. We have also seen that one group of feminists have tried to remove the asymmetry and hierarchy without denying the principle of radical difference, while others have rejected asymmetry, hierarchy and difference altogether, claiming perfect equality.

All three models have been and still are being defended on the basis of a variety of conflicting theories, and there has been a hardening of positions, both by adherents to feminist movements and by adherents to male superiority, the masculists.

They all tend to assume universally stereotyped women and men all over the world.

Just recently, some new approaches by feminist writers have focussed on the female person, her unique biology, her physical, mental and intellectual abilities, and the value of her feminine qualities for a healthy society. But there is still a tendency to separatism and to offensiveness touching upon male attitudes.

Let us look first in a little more detail into the background of the conflict between biological nature and cultural nurture.

As an example, at the one extreme, E.O. Wilson claims in his *Sociobiology, a New Synthesis* (1975) that all the differences between women and men originate from the genetic codes that determine their attitudes and roles. At the other extreme Simone de Beauvoir declares that women's characters and conduct (and implicitly men's, although she focusses on women) are completely shaped by socio political conditions. She asserts in *The Second Sex* (1952) that women are 'not born but made'.

As regards sociobiology, recent scientific research into the configuration and functioning of the human brain has shown that there are indeed differences between women's and men's brains, resulting from genetic and hormonal inputs. It is true that the average man's brain is about 10% heavier than that of a woman, and this has often been used by masculists as proof of man's superiority. The fact that on average a man is 10% taller and 20% heavier than a woman, however, must surely have something to do with it.

But recent findings have also revealed other differences, such as that female brains have a higher neuron density and activity and that they possess a larger corpus callosum, the part that connects the left and right hemispheres.

According to the so-called 'organization theory', these differences can be related to prenatal hormonal activity, and they confirm mental and biological differences between women and men. They do not, however, reveal asymmetrical or hierarchical differences, nor do they indicate a radical difference in cognitive functions, because tests in these areas have shown a great many similarities between the sexes.

Then there is the question of female xx versus male xy sex chromosome pairs. Men have suggested that the xy configuration contains the potential of creativity while the xx represents more of a sameless, fitting the general (man-made) consensus that a woman is a human being lacking things that men have, in this case the Y chromosome. It recalls Aristotle's theory of the lacking soul and Freud's idea of the lacking penis, all indicating that woman is incomplete and man complete.

A happy family as the cornerstone of our society. ❯

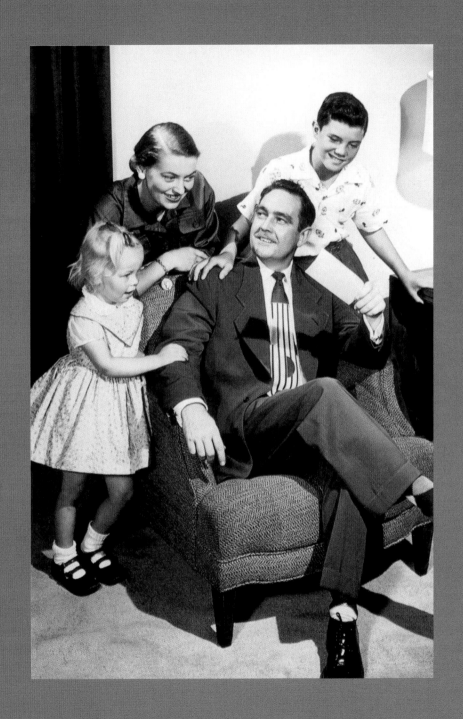

LEFT Dutch swimmer Inge de Bruijn wins her third gold medal on the 50 metre free-style at the Olympic Games 2000 in Sydney.

RIGHT The American athlete Marion Jones succeeded in reaching her goal of five medals (three gold and two bronze) at the Sydney Games in 2000. She won more medals than any female track athlete ever had at a single Olympics.

Meanwhile, we have found that the Y chromosome is very much smaller than the X chromosome. In fact, as mentioned in chapter XI, genetics scientists have recently discovered that the Y chromosome evolved from the X chromosome. It has also been discovered that only the female egg cell contains mitochondrial DNA, the 'powerhouse' of the cell, that provides the energy for all the cell's activities by converting food. Sperm cells contain tiny traces of mitochondria, but they do not participate in the chromosome exchange mechanism of meiosis. As a consequence of two large X chromosomes and of mitochondria in female cells only, the egg cell of a woman has a greater genetic DNA variety than the simple sperm cell. It would have been better if Aristotle had known this before he launched his 'scientific' theory that woman only contributes matter to procreation while man exclusively provides soul, character and quality. It now appears that the Y chromosome induces many deficiencies which are detected and mostly corrected by the female system. Although there are more male foetuses than female at conception, by a factor of between 1.3 and 1.5, many male foetuses are not viable because of genetic deficiencies, so that there is still a roughly 50/50 division of the sexes at birth.

The fact that in all birds and butterflies and in some fish, amphibians, reptiles and insects the sex chromosomes are arranged the other way around (XX in male cells and XY in female cells) shows that nature does not function according to a rigid model.

The same holds true for hormones; in the recent past it was still thought that androgenic hormones were exclusive to men, giving them superior qualities over women.

We now know that women and men both produce androgenic and oestrogenic hormones, albeit in different proportions, and that for instance oestrogenic hormones are indispensable for the development of the male brain.

It has also recently become clearer how prenatal and postnatal hormones affect the individual's awareness of being a woman or a man and behaving as such, and that these feelings and expressions overlap and interact with social and cultural influences.

Biology alone does not necessarily fix the identity of humans; environmental and social factors come into play to allow a certain flexibility and choice in shaping the balance between masculine and feminine in the individual person. When this is socially recognized and politically accepted, interesting things can happen.

> In the field of sport, for instance, marathon running times for women have dropped 34% since 1964, compared to 4.2% for men, theoretically indicating that their performances could match by early in the 21st century. In practice, this will not happen because of the physiology of the female body, that has less muscular mass, more fat and lower blood volume, whilst the female heart can pump around less blood per minute than a man's. In one field, however, women excell over men: women already swim farther and faster than any man. Here the relatively higher level of fat makes floating easier and avoids undue cooling.

In many other sports, too, women are currently performing better than men did a few decades ago. In the Netherlands more than 20,000 young girls from the age of 13 are enrolled in football training, and they are at least as good or better in tactics as boys and have no difficulty in coping with physical endurances. Both sexes have their own advantages and disadvantages; their differing anatomy and physiology tend towards different performance, but given equal chances for development both can be winners and losers.

In today's world the potential of the female body is being rediscovered. The myth that women are generally and inherently weaker than men is set to disappear; women are about to escape the stereotype trap. And so can men.

In general, when comparisons are made of the mental, intellectual and physical qualities of men and women, it is increasingly evident that there are broader areas of similarity than was previously assumed. Carl Jung long ago proposed that female elements in man (Anima) and male elements in woman (Animus) are archetypically and subconsciously present, and that if through life experiences and stereotyping these elements are unconsciously suppressed, it leads to unbalanced personalities and relationships.

Within society we have a better understanding these days of how the cultural environment influences behaviour and role playing. There is clear evidence, for instance, that children can be conditioned before the age of five by their parent's or teacher's perception of what it is to be a girl and what she likes, and similarly for a boy, and that this influences the child's preferences for specific toys, games and behaviour very much more than only genetic codes. The symbolic blue and pink colours are painted on boys and girls at such an early stage that they will know no better than to conform to the adult stereotype woman or man of their culture. In other words, the original integrity is lost. Literature on this subject, mostly from female authors, has concentrated on girls and the effects on their lives, but if we want to eradicate the stereotype trap, we shall have to acknowledge that the effects on boys and their lives are equally important.

Another example of a stereotype trap is the persistent idea, held for more than 2,000 years, that women are structurally less talented than men in technical and mathematical disciplines. The statistics that support this premise must be regarded with suspicion, now it has been shown that they appear to derive from the different attitudes of women and men towards teaching and learning methods rather than from asymmetry in their brains. The techniques employed in science and engineering education have been developed over the ages, starting with Pythagoras, by male teachers for male pupils. When they are replaced by techniques that focus on female pupils, the performance of women substantially improves, often to levels better than those of men. In Germany this has led to renewed debate about separate schools for boys and girls, or at least separate classes for science disciplines. The co-educational system was introduced in the Federal Republic only in 1965, as both the Catholic Church and the Nazi regime had been strongly against co-education for sexist reasons. Now, for non-sexist reasons, separate education could return in specific fields!

In Britain and the USA, too, in the later years of the 1990, specific classes for boys and girls in physics, mathematics and engineering are being reinstated, or even separate schools.

In Italy, co-education was never introduced. Interestingly, Italy is the only country with a considerably higher percentage of female academics in technical disciplines than other countries, except Russia. In Russia the status of technical disciplines has not been high and therefore fewer men chose that profession.

After a sharp decline in popularity as a result of feminist pressures, women's colleges in the USA have made a substantial comeback in the 1990's. The Seven Sisters, the most traditional of the women's universities, are booming with enrolment soaring up to 100%. Not only is teaching for girls qualitatively more effective without boys; the students are no longer demotivated from entering traditionally masculine-stereotyped courses. Women graduating from these institutions are displaying a high degree of self-confidence and are successfully entering the world of business and industry.

So it seems that there are few radical distinctions between the sexes and few perfect equalities either. The reality lies in a broad spectrum in between.

Within this broad spectrum we find the great diversity of human beings, each with a unique sex identity and masculine and feminine qualities on the one hand and a gender-neutral soul, mind, spirit, intellect and creative urge on the other. Out of this complex of properties and qualities arises the integrity of the personal identity. It seems only logical to accept that if that personal identity is forced to conform to unrealistic roles and stereotypes, its integrity can be affected, leading to all sorts of internal and external conflicts.

> Maria Montessori was one of the first persons to become aware of this, which is why she developed her educational system offering minimal interference with individual identity and character. Unfortunately, she engaged her ambitions in the ideology of Mussolini's regime, but her concept has persevered up to today in many Western countries.

The endless variety of women and men in our world is inimical to individual identities being defined in distinctive stereotypes. Human individuals have personal identities that result from an unpredictable mixture of their genetic and cultural codes, of which the sexual element is an important but not the only part.

The United Nations conference on Women in Beijing in 1995 brought home the clear message that the 40,000 attending women represented a huge diversity of races, cultures, religions and sociopolitical conditions, each with a different approach to the issue of women.

If there is no stereotype 'woman' or stereotype 'man' in this world, what is there?

In this book, as I am investigating the identities, roles and relations of women and men and their influence on sustainable development, I cannot escape the necessity of addressing this question.

It is useful at the outset to try to understand how the notions of woman and man, female and male, feminine and masculine and sex and gender interrelate. These notions partly overlap, which is an inevitable consequence of the complexity of the issue, but for the purpose of clarifying our thinking, I will make use of a simplified scheme or model. In doing so I realize that models never represent reality and are only helpful for spotlighting coherence or incoherence in our reasoning, leading to new insights for new models that could bring us nearer to reality.

I am not presenting here definitions of the notions involved, but their interconnections offer a way of understanding how they relate to each other.

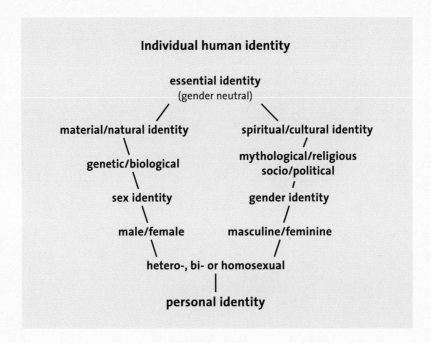

Dr. Maria Montessori when director of the Orthophrenic Institute, Rome. ➤

The model represents the various levels of identity of a human being focusing on sex and gender.

The first, essential level is gender-neutral; the next levels represent the material and spiritual manifestations, leading to sexual and cultural differentiation. All levels interact in a dynamic and organic fashion, integrating at the ultimate level of the individual person, a unique product of chance, choice and necessity.

In the model the word genetic is used with reference to the specific chromosome pairs xy and xx in the cells of an individual organism that fixes its sex identity.

The word biological is meant to cover the physical sexual appearances of the organism, its hormone chemistry and nervous system, including the brain.

One could call these two categories material and natural manifestations, which are indeed more or less 'facts of life' and usually identified with male or female.

On the other side, the religious/mythological aspect refers to mysticism, myths, stories, dreams, metaphors, fantasies, projections and perceptions of the human mind bearing on sex roles in a cosmological context.

Sociopolitical is meant to represent a mindset of what in human societies at some point in time is perceived and constructed as characteristic of feminine and masculine behaviour, style, function and performance and for sex roles in a secular context.

One could call these two categories spiritual and cultural manifestations, governing gender relations.

It is interesting to note that there seems to be no need to have woman and man in the model, as each human individual identity is in reality such a unique composition of female and male and of masculine and feminine properties that narrowing down to woman and man would reduce the diversity of individuals to unrealistically simple proportions. A human being cannot be reduced to a sum of parts. Therefore, you cannot de-link or isolate certain parts of an individual for the purpose of categorizing these parts in a sociological context.

When you ask a person who he is, the usual answer makes reference to a category, such as I am a housewife, I am an artist, I am an engineer, I am an ambassador. Sometimes people say it is better to keep one's professional and private life separate, or that a comment on one's performance should 'not be taken personally'. These habits all deny the integrity of a person and can lead to confusion about identity and relationships, including sex and gender.

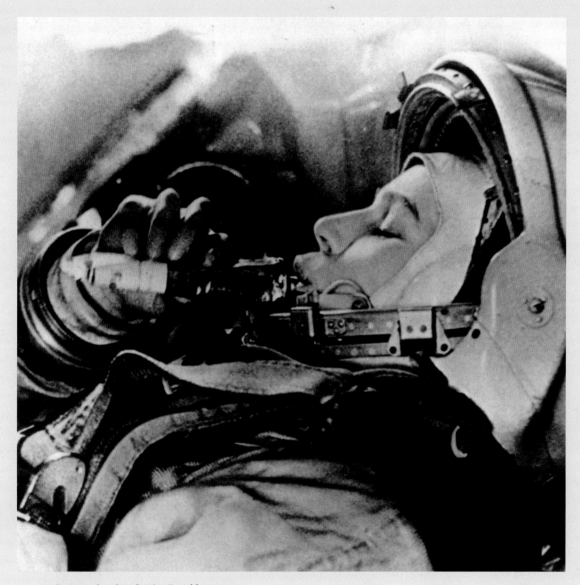

On June 16, 1963 Valentina Tereshkova was
launched into space aboard *Vostok 6*. She
became the first woman to travel into space.
Valentina Tereshkova made 48 orbits of Earth.
She spent almost three days in space.

In other words the dichotomy between what one is and what one does is too simple and radical for the description of a human individual. This also applies to the dichotomy between a woman and a man.

In human cultures, languages and social institutions, however, we have become accustomed to using the words woman and man as if they do identify the person, whereas in reality sex identity consists of many components: personality, interests, capabilities, social roles and sex-role behaviour.

I believe the linguistic and cultural misinterpretation of the human condition to be one of the major reasons for the persistent assumption of radical differences between men and women based on biology alone.

Aristotle, Augustin and Aquinus laid a solid base for this misconception, and Protestantism, the Enlightenment, Romanticism and Modernism did little to modify the doctrine of biological, radical distinction, as we have seen in the previous chapters.

In the last few decades various attempts have been made to find out how, in different cultures and civilisations, human qualities are viewed as being male- or female-associated, to what degree people incorporate these qualities in their self-perception, what they make their idol and what they consider the proper sex-role relationship between women and men to be.

One of these studies, published by John E. Williams and Deborah L. Best in 1994, covered 15 years and 30 countries. This is how they worked: – using 300 adjectives (e.g., aggressive, emotional) there was a high degree of pancultural agreement on the characteristics differentially associated with women and men. The table on page 233 shows the 100 adjectives that were deemed to have a differential connotation. The other 200 were considered neutral. It would actually be interesting to know these adjectives as well, because they would indicate the apparently vast overlap in attributes considered common to both men and women.

I will briefly summarize their observations:
- The male stereotype characteristics were more favourable in Japan, South Africa and Nigeria, the female in Italy, Peru and Australia, but cross-culturally the stereotypes of women and men were equally favourable.
- In the countries studied, self-perceptions were as expected more masculine for men and more feminine for women, but they encompassed both and revealed only a slight echo of the stereotype characteristics. Differentiation in self-perception was greater in poorer, rural, non-Christian countries.

The 100 items of the pancultural adjective checklist

Male- Associated

Active	Loud
Adventurous	Obnoxious
Aggressive	Opinionated
Arrogant	Opportunistic
Autocratic	Pleasure-seeking
Bossy	Precise
Capable	Progressive
Coarse	Quick
Conceited	Rational
Confident	Realistic
Courageous	Reckless
Cruel	Resourceful
Cyrical	Rigid
Determined	Robust
Disorderly	Serious
Enterprising	Sharp-witted
Greedy	Show-off
Hardheaded	Steady
Humorous	Stern
Indifferent	Stingy
Individualistic	Stolid
Initiative	Tough
Interests wide	Unfriendly
Inventive	Unscrupulous
Lazy	Witty

Female - Associated

Affected	Modest
Affectionate	Nervous
Appreciative	Patient
Cautious	Pleasant
Changeable	Prudish
Charming	Self-pitying
Complaining	Sensitive
Complicated	Sentimental
Confused	Sexy
Curious	Shy
Dependent	Softhearted
Dreamy	Sophisticated
Emotional	Submissive
Excitable	Suggestible
Fault-finding	Talkative
Fearful	Timid
Fickle	Touchy
Foolish	Unambitious
Forgiving	Unintelligent
Frivolous	Unstable
Fussy	Warm
Gentle	Weak
Imaginative	Worrying
Kind	Understanding
Mild	Superstitious

- Both genders described the person they would like to be as more masculine-natured.
- The most egalitarian sex role ideologies were found in the Netherlands, Germany and Finland; the most male-dominant or traditional in Nigeria, Pakistan and India. The USA fell towards the middle of the range.
- In most countries women have somewhat more modern or egalitarian views than men.
- In each of the countries studied, children's learning of gender stereotypes generally begins before five and continues through childhood and adolescence.

234 My conclusion from these observations is that people all over the world apparently have a similar view as to what constitutes masculine and feminine characteristics, and all cultures have developed generally accepted gender stereotypes, but that individual self-perceptions do not match these stereotypes. On the other hand, sex-role relationships between men and women can and do differ greatly between cultures and races. Finally, male characteristics are viewed as more desirable throughout all cultures.

My guess is that the gender stereotypes and the preference for male characteristics are all a direct consequence of the prevalent male-domination ideologies appertaining to women and men all over the world. So far in this book, it has been demonstrated that these ideologies have been developed and defined predominantly by men and that they suffer from misconceptions backed up by scientific and social theories that are now out-moded but maintained by the vested interests of 'men in power'.

The question in the beginning of this book was whether these ideologies were based on people's experiences of ways of life in their communities, under certain economic and practical conditions, for instance in early civilisations – and if so, they can and will be readjusted and reconstructed under new and quite different conditions – or whether male domination is a law of nature.

The research mentioned above indicates this is not a law of nature. People have a pretty good idea of who they are, how they experience being a woman or a man and which gender stereotypes and sex roles are embedded in their cultures. But they also recognize that these types and roles do not correspond to their personal self-perceptions. The stereotypes for male and female usually imply that being a man is exclusively defined by the characteristics associated with men as listed in the table on page 15 and conversely that being a woman is exclusively defined by the characteristics associated with women. This misleading and unrealistic radical distinction is a crucial point in shaping male/female relations and personal identity, because the occasions when men and women experience themselves as different from cultural stereotypes will either force them to comply with the stereotype against their inner feelings or lead them to deviate from 'normal' behaviour as woman or man, with subsequent social tensions. I cannot judge for women or other men, but I know from my own experience, and especially in my business career, that the macho behaviour so often encountered in the business world ran against the grain as far as I was concerned. I thus found myself either participating uncomfortably or refusing to join in with the bragging and the brawling, sexist jokes and the man-dominating power games. In either case, no doubt, I was often considered odd. But at the same time I was able to observe the strain on people who preserve an unnatural attitude and constantly force themselves to suppress their real identity. Maintaining an outward appearance that clashes with inner feelings is bound to result in split personalities, leading to mental and physical stress. I am convinced that, for both women and men, this is a major cause of unhappiness and poor health, although it will be rarely admitted because the stereotype forbids it.

The logical conclusion from the above is that there is apparently something fundamentally wrong with the perceptions of sex identity, gender and sex roles that we still cling to in our modern societies.

Stereotypes are models, paradigms, and what we need in the 21st century, in today's jargon, is a paradigm shift.

If this is the right conclusion, we can and must redefine our perceptions of reality, replacing present gender stereotypes and sex roles with ones that are more in tune with the way we experience ourselves in today's real world. A world of intensive and global communication, with increasing openness, individual liberty and universal access to education and economic independence in many countries.

In fact, there is a parallel here with the paradigm shift that occurred in the field of the natural sciences, physics and mathematics in the 20th century.

It was pointed out in chapter XVII that when new theories in science concerning relativity, uncertainty, dualism, chaos and complexity achieved recognition, it became clear that they covered a much wider and deeper scope of reality than the traditional concepts. This is a familiar phenomenon in the history of science.

The traditional and the new models in science can now be characterized, as indicated in the previous chapter, by the following key principles:

traditional science	new science
(matter oriented)	**(nature oriented)**
linear	non-linear
simple	complex
reversible	non-reversible
in equilibrium	not in equilibrium
closed system	open system
predictable	unpredictable
compartmental	interconnected

It could be said that the principles on the left are from the world of reason and those on the right are from the world of nature. The intriguing point in these lists is that the left one seems to have more affinity to a masculine stereotype and the right one to a feminine stereotype. The first, mechanistic model has been the basis for all 'man'-made technologies, economics and social organization, while the second, natural model is at the heart of all biological and ecological processes in nature.

I am convinced that these two modes of orientation are at the core of the dichotomy between male and female and between economy and ecology in the present world.

Mechanistic models are and remain valid within a limited and man-defined range, but in a broader context, such as ecosystems and global interactions, they interfere with natural and social processes that follow very different laws. If we want to avoid serious clashes, the man-made models will have to be thoroughly revised in order to maintain a balanced co-existence with the laws of the natural environment.

For a while we have tried ignoring the tensions between the two models by keeping them apart and/or letting one dominate the other. But now that the earth's population has grown from 1.3 billion in 1900 to 6 billion in the year 1999, the sheer numbers of people and their increased standard of living no longer allows us this option. To survive, we need to integrate and balance technology, economics and ecology, but we also need to rediscover the natural balance between masculine and feminine in order to achieve this integration.

If the foregoing analysis is correct, we will have to fundamentally change our 20th century culture which sanctions technology

Madonna 'Express yourself'.

and economics interfering with the integrity of natural ecosystems and male domination interfering with the integrity of human relations. Making radical distinctions between economics and ecology and between masculine and feminine will have to give
way to a respectful and creative interaction.

This means that present perceptions of reality in the fields of technology, economics and social organization will have to be revised.

It means that both the ecological and the gender dimension will have to be integrated into the economic and social fabric of politics, finance, business, religion and
education. There are signs of a growing awareness of the need for such changes, but
it still lacks conviction and commitment, at the political and institutional level no less
than at the private and personal level.

The supposedly radical dualisms of economy and ecology and of male and female
are very resilient, precisely because we have lived with that model for so long.

Dualisms exist by the grace of each other. They are interdependent and their interacting polarities can be creative when operating from positions of equivalence. This
we can learn from the old Taoist philosophers. It is a truth we have forgotten or
ignored since Western thinking ran into the trap of radical dichotomies. The male/
female dichotomy is a classic example of how you can get lost if you use the wrong map.

As we have seen, outmoded gender stereotypes increasingly interfere with people's
self-perception in an age when globalization and the discrediting of old-fashioned
views of the world and society have liberated so many women and men from a
straightjacketed past.

The current paradigm in gender relations is closely linked to the mechanistic world model and has encouraged dualisms in which asymmetrical and hierarchical relations promote rigidity and discourage creativity. The new paradigm will be more closely linked to the natural model in which symmetrical and organic relations promote flexibility and encourage creativity.

The popular star Madonna symbolises this new approach, especially in her hit 'Express yourself' (1989) where she plays with gender stereotypes. This so-called gender-bending deconstructs masculinity and femininity, freeing the individual from the stereotype trap.

238

To my mind, the eventual removal of the stereotype traps will improve the chances of moving towards a sustainable condition of human society in the coming decades.

In effecting this change, women and men will cooperate, and both will benefit. It will be neither a feminist nor a masculist movement, but a movement of a different order, celebrating the sexes' creative values in difference and added values in equality.

XIX

Glass Ceilings and Walls

In debates on women's careers, the concept of the 'glass ceiling' has emerged, a metaphor for the assumed presence of a barrier in the way of women trying to reach the top positions in the worlds of business, academia, the civil service and other institutions. It supposedly results from the closed shop of an 'old boys' network. The USA even has a bipartisan Glass Ceiling Commission.

In this chapter I will explore this notion and conclude that in reality many other factors play a role in the career opportunities for women ambitious to reach the top and that eventually the glass ceiling, as it is perceived today, will disappear.

Only about 5% of the top jobs in business in the Netherlands are today held by women.

Also, what might be called the glass wall, a barrier that limits spontaneous communication between people in the hierarchy of organisations, and between women and men in particular, is then likely to vanish.

If one looks at the statistics, it is clear that in the Western world the percentage of women participating in all levels of education and in the workforce has increased markedly in the last 25 years, and especially in the last 15 years. This trend has now gained full momentum.

> In the Netherlands 25 years ago, only one-third of girls between 16 and 18 continued with high school education as against 50% for boys, while now it is two-thirds for both. Some 10% of university students were female; now the average is more than 50%, varying from between 60% and 80% in law, pharmacy, veterinary studies, agriculture, (soft) medicine, business administration and social sciences to less than 20% in (hard) medicine and technical and natural sciences. As for participation in the labour market, the percentage for women between 15 and 64 years old has increased from 35% to more than 50% over the last 15 years, mainly, it must be said, in part-time jobs and the service sector, while the figure for men in the same age range has remained stable at 70%. More than 50% of households now rely on income from both partners, up from 15% 20 years ago.
>
> On the other hand, when it comes to careers, only about 5% of the top jobs in business in the Netherlands are today held by women, and the same percentage applies to full professorships in universities. In government circles feminine participation is higher: 20% of the members of the prestigious State's Council and 20% of cabinet ministers are women, but at the top of the civil service, percentages are still close to 5%. On the other hand, more than 30% of the members of parliament are female, 18% of mayors and 18% of municipal county members.

In other European Union nations and the USA we see similar trends, although the percentages vary due to differences in culture and in social evolution. In ever more countries political parties are promoting better opportunities for women. The Democratic Party in the USA and the Labour Party in the UK both have what they call Emily's List, financially supporting women who aspire to become formal representatives in political institutions, including government, Congress and Parliament. The majority of incoming elite foreign officers in the UK are women, and 30% of senior American officials are women, including Madeleine Albright, the former US Secretary of State.

However, whereas in business, academia and the civil service the percentage of women at senior level is on the increase, up to over 30% at the present time, it would seem that there are disparities between the senior echelon and the top echelon, leading some commentators to assume that there must be a barrier, the glass ceiling, preventing women from reaching the very top. I think, however, that a very important reason for this discrepancy is the fact that the real momentum of substantially increasing numbers of women entering the world of professional careers did not really get started until 10 to 15 years ago, while the very top level positions are normally reached only after a period of 20 to 30 years of moving up the hierarchical ladder within organisations in a tough process of promotion through talent and performance. This time factor alone is a major reason why few women have so far got to the very top.

As educated women have now started entering the professional world in great numbers, this will profoundly change the situation within the next 10 to 15 years. And if one can believe the comments one hears, women are not only making their presence felt in quantitative terms but are outstripping their male colleagues in both performance and dedication.

The real life stories of women in the business world who have reached senior level in boardrooms have been the subject of recent extensive reporting and interviewing. Hundreds of career women have revealed their individual cases. The issues of *Fortune* of September 18th, 1995, and October 12th, 1998, provide a great amount of factual and personal information on how these women made their way to the top in the 500 largest corporations in the United States, where nearly 12% of board positions are at present held by women, an increase of 37% since 1995. In 1998 *Fortune* reviewed the top 40 women out of a selection of 400. *Time* of December 7th, 1998, the *Economist* of August 26th, 1995, the Dutch magazine *Elsevier* of December 12th, 1996, and numerous newspapers in many countries during the late 1990's all have articles on women entering the men's world, where they often have to cope with conflicting personal ambitions affecting motherhood and career, and with sexist attitudes in the workplace.

The interviews and career stories show that all kinds of women are reaching the top: married and childless or with their own or adopted children, divorced, single or living together either apart or in the same place, most of them in the age group 40 to 50 and all white. They are all trying to find a way, sometimes the hard way, to balance private and public life. There seems to be no standard formula. Some enjoy being single, some choose to be single mothers, some have husbands who co-operate, some find satisfactory outside help, some manage to work part time, some restrict their success careers to a limited period in order to raise the children and then return to the market as consultants, and so on.

On the other hand, more and more women are founding their own businesses, running their own companies and achieving their ambitions in that way. In the USA, companies created and run by women today employ as many people as three-quarters of all the 500 *Fortune* US companies do together. Two-thirds of newly created companies in the 1990's are owned and led by women, not only in the USA but in Europe, too.

In other words, one should not concentrate on the big corporations when looking at the female/male division in the world of business.

It is also evident that today's successful business women are just as clever and ambitious as men, but they do not imitate men's lifestyles or role playing, as was more the case in the very early phase of the career woman. They do not claim equality because they know they are different, and they do not claim different treatment because they know the strength of their talents. They are against positive discrimination and quotas, for the same reason as Edith Badinter is against quotas for the French parliament (see Chapter XVII, page 216): it degrades the position of women.

The sum of the talents of a successful career woman equals the sum of the talents of her male colleague, but the composition may be different, in both a professional and an emotional sense. The terms equality and equivalence are inappropriate here; these words were created when we were constructing gender relationships.

The feminist movements have used the words equality and difference in too radically distinctive ways, ignoring variety and diversity and considering 'women' as a well-defined and singular category. One of today's well-known Dutch writers,

Maarten 't Hart, has written a book on this misconception entitled 'The Woman Does Not Exist'.

To dogmatise about what women are, what women want, and what women do or should do is as far-removed from the realities of life as it is to categorise men as a singular group. In an ideal society free from poverty, prejudices and stereotypes, individuals can make choices to fit their personalities. In the West we do not live in an ideal world, but there is definitely more room for free choices than ever before, for both women and men.

Successful women in business, university or government are successful because they deliberately chose an ambitious career. Many women do not make such a choice because they would rather use their talents in other ways and play a different role in society, including giving priority to child care. I have a feeling, but this is in no way proven, that there are now and will remain in the future more women than men who make the latter choice, even if men allow themselves to adjust to new perceptions of femininity and masculinity, and some men also opt for child care. It follows that there will always be more men than women going in for full-time careers aiming to reach the top. More men than women ending up in the highest echelons, therefore, it will be a question not so much of a barrier as of a choice. And whereas that choice has been limited in the past, because of discrimination against women in all levels of society, this discrimination will soon be a thing of the past, at least in the Western world.

The fact that many more women today have a proper education, and many more do not choose motherhood or choose the combination of motherhood with a career, means that the number of women going into the senior echelons or creating their own companies will continue to increase.

If we assume, and statistics and interviews confirm this, that more than 50% of existing professional women will make the above choices and that women will eventually form more than 50% of the total professional population, it follows that in the not-too-distant future more than 25% of the higher positions in many institutions will be filled by women. The reason that this is not yet the case is simply because, as previously stated, in practice it takes between 20 and 30 years for anybody who enters the career world with talent and ambition to reach the top. As career women have substantially increased their presence in the outside world only in the last 10 to 15 years, in parallel with their liberation from the motherhood stereotype, it is no wonder that they are still scarce at the senior level. My prediction, therefore, is that within the next 10 to 15 years we will see the percentage of top women in the institutions of Western society rising to at least 25%.

If over that period there is an improvement in the physical, social and fiscal provisions for child care, in tax allowances for joint earners, in the social acceptance of part-time work for both women and men, and in the attitudes of men in relation to caring roles, then women's participation will undoubtedly be even higher than 25%.

> Although adequate child day care facilities are crucial and are in general still insufficiently available, countries like Norway, France and the USA are well advanced in affording satisfactory provision for this purpose. But the costs of day care are high: in the Netherlands, for instance, equivalent to between 8% and 15% of household income.
>
> At a conference in Washington DC on October 18 and 19, 1999, organized by the Business Women's Network, 1,600 women from 76 countries made an inventory of present and future opportunities for women in business. The presentations and discussions provided the arguments for the above assumption of a growing women's role in the top management of business institutions. They also confirmed the driving force of enterprises owned by women, the emergence of e-commerce and the accompanying increased flexibility in working times and working places.
>
> In the Netherlands a growing presence of women is noticeable in non-profit-making activities; an agency called Top-Link has a databank of nearly 2,000 women qualified for senior administrative positions in this sector. Close to 100 women are added to the databank annually, but the number they can place in the profit sector is still limited, because the candidates are not yet visible, and the attitude of the employers remains hesitant. However, all expectations are that this is a matter of time, given the positive experiences with women in management to date and the resulting improved recognition.

Projects like Opportunity 2000, initiated in the UK under the Major government in 1991, and a similar scheme launched in the Netherlands in the mid-1990's called

'Opportunity in Business', are successfully helping businesses to introduce certain cultural changes. These include establishing a proper balance between private life and work, improving the quality of life for working women and men, and creating better opportunities for women in the world of business.

In the Netherlands, government, employers and employee organisations are now seriously preparing for the institution of a four-day working week in the near future.

At least two reservations must be made with regard to the improved recognition of women and breaking through the glass ceiling. The first relates to women's careers in the academic world. It seems that the male culture is more closely knit in universities than in other communities and the stratagems employed for protecting this culture from female infiltration are particularly clever. I suspect, therefore, that it will probably take much longer for women to reach levels of 25% or more in the halls of academia than in other institutions.

Carly Fiorina, CEO of Hewlett-Packard.

The second reservation is in respect of the top executive officers or their equivalents in the larger corporations. My guess is that very few women will be willing to hold such exceedingly demanding occupations, on call for 24 hours a day and with heavy and unpredictable travelling schedules.

Today only one woman in the Fortune 500 US companies, Carly Fiorina of Hewlett-Packard, holds the chief executive position. I would be surprised if, when in 10 to 15 years' time the executive boards of large corporations consist of more than 25% women, more than 5% are chief executive officers. Another reason why I think the percentage will remain low is that women will not stay as long in the top position as men, because they will decide to retire earlier in order to devote their time to a more relaxed and less money-making-oriented activity.

I am convinced, however, that the stronger feminine presence in the boardrooms of corporations will lead to a better balance of financial, ethical, ecological and social considerations in decision-making. One of my male friends in a top position calls this a romantic and unrealistic observation. I am fairly sure he will be proved wrong in the long term. In fact, even in the prevailing male culture of many organisations, there are signs of change.

Concepts such as the 'triple bottom line', meaning attaching equal importance to financial, social and environmental performance, are being seriously entertained in many companies.

Institutions such as insurance companies, investors' funds, pension funds and even security exchange authorities are increasingly focussing their criteria on a mix of the financial, social, ethical and ecological performance of corporations rather than the merely financial. This is in paradoxical contrast to the recent hype on shareholders' value, which some companies interpret as a license to limit measures of performance solely to short-term profits per share. I am sure this hype will not last, in view of changing public perceptions of the responsibility and accountability of the private sector in society.

It is also a fact that, due to women having a longer life expectancy than men, shares are increasingly held by women (in the USA they command more than 70% of all shareholdings), and this will eventually have an effect on shareholders' choices and expectations as well.

At the same time, as more and more corporations are experiencing greater numbers of women entering their managerial ranks, they are beginning to recognize the need to change their male culture if they want to keep these women motivated.

In the Netherlands ABN/AMRO have seen the percentage of women in senior management positions rise from roughly 5% to 10% in recent years, although in their management training programme the participation of women and men is 50:50. In 1999 Royal Dutch Shell said it was their intention to have 20% women in the senior echelon of the company world-wide by 2005. Unilever is to make a concerted effort to adapt their corporate culture in order to keep more women in their organisation because, after having invested in their training, they find they lose many who feel uncomfortable with their very traditional style of management.

In Germany, Siemens completely transformed their company gender culture in 1999. They now offer flexible working times, part-time employment, work at home with complete IT equipment supplied by the company, and day care facilities and a free family advisory service for parents. To be sure Siemens were in desperate need of more professional personnel, but they also want more women at all levels of their organisation because they are convinced that the company culture and work – performance will benefit from a combination of male and female styles of leadership and human relations. Similar cultural changes are in process at companies such as Lufthansa and Volkswagen.

Another factor that facilitates the entry of more women into the world that used to be run by men is obviously the recent growth in the 'soft' service sectors of communication and information technology, including e-commerce, which offer unprecedented opportunities for women and feminine qualities. Actually, if one looks at typical success careers of women today, as published in *Fortune*, the majority occur in the spheres of marketing, communication and financial services.

At the same time the transparency of IT-based information systems leads to more horizontal decision-making through open network centres as opposed to traditional vertical decision-making through closed channels from the top. It is assumed that women are better at managing horizontal networks than vertical channels.

Thus, we have the phenomenon of triple bottom line objectives together with changing organisational concepts towards more transparency in the corporate world. When they start running in parallel with changing gender policies, these developments are likely to reinforce each other and become powerful driving forces towards a more sustainable state of the world in the 21st century.

Sceptics argue that present trends in gender relations will last only until there is a new and severe economic recession. My counter-argument is that before that occurs, the presence of women in the world that used to be run mostly by men will be so strong, and the change of attitude of many men so profound, that recession will not claim women as its primary victims. It might even be the other way around. With up to 40% women in most of the management levels in the next few decades, men will not be dominating the scene any longer and women may prove to be wiser in facing crises. The hero status of the male executive will not persist; the glass ceiling is already fracturing.

Other sceptics predict that where women enter a profession, the status and the monetary value of that profession will go down, as has been the case in the past. I would expect this phenomenon to change when women are well established and have a substantial share in the management market. Also, the new generation of women that have begun their careers in recent years have not seen the status and the monetary value of their professions decline, so unequal pay and unequal status may become a thing of the past when the present elder generation has left the market.

Let us not forget that in 1998 one in three working women in the USA, that is more than 10 million women, earned more than their husbands (or partners), while in the Netherlands one in six, or 400,000 women, did so. These figures are more than 60% higher than 20 years ago and are consistently on the rise.

As for the old boys' network, I believe that will also be a thing of the past when the present 'old boys', who are now in their sixties and seventies, are gone. Another 10 to 15 years at the most. In the meantime their influence, grossly overestimated by outsiders, will have faded. The marketplace for professional managers is becoming very large, both in numbers and in scope. It is easily accessible through the Internet, and soon headhunters will have taken over the field of identifying and approaching candidates for vacant top positions for both women and men.

Up to here in this chapter we have considered the female/male developments in a limited number of sectors of society. Let us now look at some random samples of developments outside these sectors, where bias against women is also disappearing and where women are successfully entering what used to be a man's world.

- Of the 43 women that have become prime ministers or presidents since World War II, 27 came into office after 1990;
- a woman, Sirrka Hamalainen from Finland, sits on the board of the new European Central Bank;
- a Canadian woman, Louise Arbour, was Chief Prosecutor for the Yugoslav Tribunal and her successor, appointed in 1999, is a Swiss woman, Carla Del Ponte;
- Gro Bruntlandt heads up the WHO, Mary Robinson UN Human Rights and Nafis Sadik the UN Population Fund;
- the first woman to command a US space flight, Eileen Collins, took off in June,

Carla del Ponte, chief prosecutor of the International War Crimes Tribunal. ➤

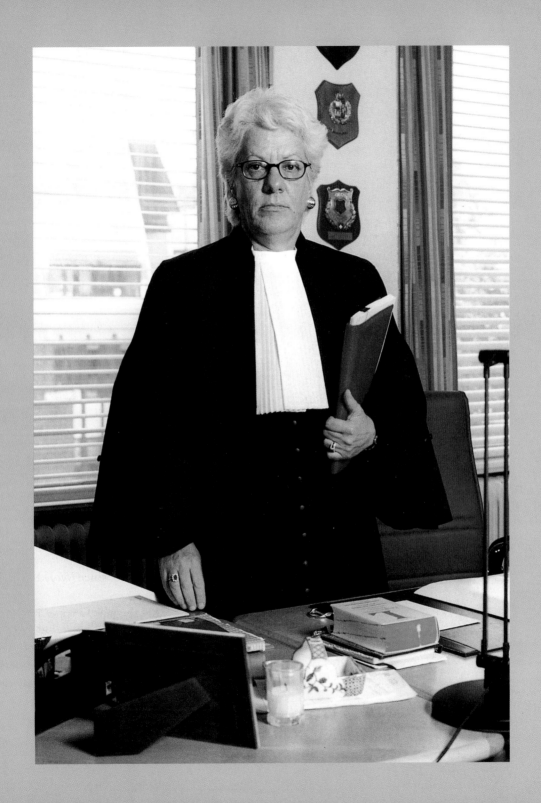

1999 and among the spectators seeing her and her crew off were First Lady Hillary Clinton and the victorious US Women's World Cup soccer team;

– in July, 1999 Nicole Fontaine from France was elected to chair the European Parliament;

– we see female policemen everywhere and soon the majority of judges will be women;

– law firms are finding out that they have to open up their male-dominated fortresses because the quantity and quality of the new female lawyers and their potential as valuable partners cannot be ignored any more;

– in September 1998, 69% of the 17,500 male members of the over-200-years-old all-male Marylebone Cricket Club voted to admit 'ladies' to their ranks;

– in July 1999, the four female ministers for development aid of the Netherlands, Britain, Norway and Germany spent a Sunday on a Norwegian island, Utstein, in order to set out new and joint policies for coordinating and stimulating the aid efforts of donor countries, highlighting the fact that women have a better feeling for the realities of life in developing countries than men.

– in Protestant and Anglican churches the bias against women priests has been disappearing in recent decades;

– in October 1999, an exhibition opened in the Royal Museum of Fine Arts in Antwerp, presenting for the first time more than 325 paintings and some sculptures by women from the 15th to the 20th century; a rehabilitation of their role as independent and unique artists.

One could continue citing such examples almost endlessly where biases against women are disappearing in sectors of society that are not specifically dealt with in this chapter.

It is still difficult to judge whether the changes mentioned are sustainable or whether they will be accepted only until such time as they reach limits of tolerance and are then reversed, as we have seen happen through the ages in the previous chapters of this book.

Nevertheless, I feel that in the world of business, with which I am more familiar, the changes are irreversible. They have been achieved with a comfortable degree of robustness, as I have tried to demonstrate.

A moot point raised by the vanishing glass ceiling that at least deserves mention is whether the genetic and emotional differences between women and men will influence the psychological climate in the workplace as more and more women reach top positions.

Whenever women and men are working together in some joint activity, there is a potential element of sexuality in their interaction that is mostly absent in relations between women and between men. Very often interactions are kept at a distance by what I would call the 'glass wall' with which people protect their privacy or their insecurity, but this wall also prevents sincere and spontaneous cooperation. In the particular case of a glass wall between women and men, professional relationships for women are complicated and career opportunities frustrated in a man-dominated organization, where women are not supposed to be too ambitious. When women become more prominent in the organization, however, chances are that the glass gender wall will disappear.

I would like to think that with a more powerful presence of women at the decision-making level, where they are no longer exceptions or even outsiders, being a woman will no longer be worthy of special note but as normal a state of affairs as being a man. This will no doubt reduce stereotype attitudes and may also do away with the need for a glass gender wall. The need for privacy will not disappear, but too formal a barrier blocking opportunities for frank and outspoken communication between women and men on sensitive subjects will no longer make sense. Maybe the lowering of the glass wall will indeed lead to more personal relationships between women and men in the workplace, with the inherent risk of their becoming too personal, but stricter social control will probably come to be accepted in a more open community.

In the long history of relationships in human society, interactions between women and men who work in related activities have always been the cause of various degrees of private involvement. This occurred not only in free professions but also in palaces, courts, parliaments, universities, bureaucracies and the private sector.

In the past, however, this usually took place in a different context from what we may face in the 21st century. In future, women will not only continue to fulfil an anonymous and often powerful function backstage, in the home and family, but will also increasingly play an independent and pronounced public role as well.

When women's share of senior posts in organizations exceeds 25%, this might lead not only to a better balance of financial, social, ethical and ecological considerations in decision-making, but also to a different atmosphere in human relations and personal relationships. The macho style that men inflict on each other, which is harmful to themselves and risky to their environment, will go out of fashion.

As has been noted in earlier chapters, the critical mass of women for acceptance of the equal authority of women and men in any kind of organised joint activity seems to lie around the 25% mark. It may be a coincidence, but that seems to be the level we will surpass in the institutions of the Western world in the early decades of the 21st century.

By the end of that period, the glass ceilings and glass walls will probably have disappeared from the scene, along with the old boys and the bias against women.

All this will change not only the position of women in society but also the position of men. That is why this book is about women and men, in contrast to so many books about gender that have focussed on women only.

I would even go so far as to predict that with a more balanced and mature participation of women and men in the institutions of society, there will be fewer victims of stress and depression. Both sexes will be well on the way to liberation from the straightjackets, stereotypes, radical distinctions and unnatural behaviour that have been a prime cause of inner tensions. They will be set to cast off ingrained misconceptions of femininity and masculinity, male and female, culture and nature, and indeed ecology and economy; misconceptions that have built up over the course of our cultural history, as I have attempted to illustrate in previous chapters.

XX

The Global Scene

Although this book is focussed on Western society, developments in some other parts of the world must at least be mentioned. They show that changes in gender relations are also taking place beyond our Western culture. Slower changes admittedly, but still significant.

Let me give some examples, in no particular order of priority and by no means exhaustive.

An important factor in the coming decades is the demographic shift resulting from a slowdown in the growth of the world population. If the United Nations 'low fertility' projection comes true, and several signs are pointing in that direction, the number of babies born into the world could fall below the number needed for replacement after 2010. This would lead to stabilisation at 7.5 billion people around 2040 and after that to a decline in the world's population. The effect will of course vary according to region.

In 61 countries, including all the nations of Europe and Japan, fertility is today at or below the replacement rate, the Italian being the lowest at 1.19, implying an almost depopulated Italy in 50 years' time.

In Africa and parts of Asia, however, it is still above the replacement rate, although this is now being increasingly affected by the AIDS epidemic. Of the 34 countries in the world, most affected by AIDS, 29 are in Africa, with life expectancy in some of them reduced by at least 10 years, to below the age of 50.

In general, however, the median age of the world population, close to 20 at the start of the 20th century, will in all likelihood rise to 40 by 2040 due to decreasing fertility. In Germany and Japan the median age is already around 40 and will rise to 50. In developing countries the average number of six childen per woman in 1969 has already fallen to three, probably due to the better education of women, better information on family planning and women's increased ability to make an independent choice.

254   A major consequence of this demographic development will be rising concern for the care of old folk, when there is insufficient money and not enough family to look after them because of the growing imbalance between the productive and the unproductive parts of the population.

This challenge will have to be addressed by women and men jointly, sharing the benefits and burdens of work and care on an equal basis, probably in very different social and political settings from those we see today. It will be a major issue in both the developed and the developing world, and it will undoubtedly affect gender relations. Employment and care will go hand in hand for women and men alike, as over-egotistical individualism in developed countries and over-dependency on children in developing countries will no longer be sustainable.

Nobody knows for sure when humanity will be faced with a decreasing world population, and for the immediate future we are still contemplating net increases of about 80 million people per year, for whom productive employment will be needed. We must prepare ourselves and our institutions for a soft landing at the turning point and avoid a scenario of overshoot and possible collapse.

I am convinced that over the next decades the balancing act between too many and too few and too young and too old will contribute to the eventual disappearance of traditional gender stereotypes in our various societies.

The annual report of the UN Population Fund, headed by a woman from India, Nafis Sadik, came out in September 1999 (at the time of the arrival of the sixth billion world citizen) and is called 'Six Billion: A Time for Choices'.

Choices that will be made by women and men.

Another phenomenon in the global scene is the fact that by the year 2006, again according to the same 1999 UN Population Fund report, more than half of the world's population, or three billion people, will be living in cities.

Cities have in the past always provided greater opportunity for women, with fewer obstacles to their freedom of movement and choice than in rural societies. As the trend towards mega-

Women count money at a weekly collection meeting where loans are repaid. Bangladesh, Maymensingh.

cities is most likely to continue, it is predicted that by 2025 five billion people will be city dwellers. In all probability this will contribute to a substantial increase in the active part played by women in the various institutions of society in the coming decades.

Another development that will support the changing balance in gender relations is the rise of women's movements within the global context of the UN Conference on Population and Development of 1994 in Cairo and the subsequent Fourth UN World Conference on Women in Beijing in 1995.

The main areas of concern at the conference in Beijing are summarised in the following agenda:

Areas of concern for the world

Conference on women in Beijing

Africa

Women's poverty, insufficient food security and lack of economic empowerment
Lack of access to education, training, science and technology
Women's vital role in culture, the family and socialization
Empowerment of women's health, reproductive health including family planning, and integrated programs
Women's linkages to the environment an natural-resource management
Women's involvement in the peace process
Political empowerment of women
Women's legal and human rights
Mainstreaming of gender-disaggregated data
Women, communication, information and arts
The girl child

Latin America

Gender Equity
Economic and social development with a gender perspective: women's equitable share in the decisions, responsibilities and benefits of development
Elimination of poverty among women
Women's equitable participation in decision-making and in the exersice of power in public and private life
Human rights, peace and violence
Shared family responsibilities
Recognition of cultural plurality in the region
International support and cooperation

Asia and the Pacific

The growing feminization of poverty
Inequality in women's access to and participation in economic activities
Inadequate recognition of women's role and concerns in environment and natural-resource management
Inequitable access to power and decision-making
Violation of woman's human rights
Inequalities and lack of access to health
Negative portrayal of women in the media
Inequalities and lack of access to education and literacy
Inadequate mechanisms for promoting the advancement of women
Inadequate recognition of women's role in peace-building

Western Asia

Safeguarding the right of Arab women to participate in power and decision-making structures and mechanisms
Alleviation of poverty for Arab women
Ensuring equal opportunity of Arab women at all levels of education
Ensuring Arab women's equal access to health services
Strengthening the capabilities of Arab women to enter the labour market and achieve self-reliance
Overcoming the impact of war, occupation and armed conflict on women
Participation of women in the management of natural resources and the protection of the environment
Elimination of violence against women
Effective utilization of communications to effect changes in roles in society and achieve equality between the sexes

Europe and Nothern America

Insufficient promotion and protection of women's human rights

Feminization of poverty

Insufficient awareness of women's contribution to the economy in the context of sustainable development and insufficient promotion of their potential

Insufficient de facto gender equality in employment and economic opportunity and insufficient policies and measures to reconcile employment and family responsibilities

Insufficient participation of women in public life

Insufficient statistical systems, database and methodologies to inform of policies and legislation and to secure equal treatment of women and men

Insufficient intra- and interregional networking and cooperation on the advancement of women

This summary illustrates how varied the issues are in the different regions of the world and, on the other hand, how some similar questions are coming up in all regions, regardless of the relatively advanced situation in Europe and North America. These common issues have to do with women and poverty, women and human rights, and women and participation in political, cultural, economic and environmental decision-making. It is rather striking that violence against women is only mentioned for Western Asia, when one would have expected this still to be a transcultural issue in all civilisations. Also in Western countries where statistics still show significant levels of violence against women within the home, not to speak of the violent behaviour of soldiers in territories of military conflicts.

The summary presents quite an impressive agenda for things to be improved and illustrates the need for a broader view on the subject of Woman and Man than that offered by the mere Western story focussed upon in the present book.

Taking this broader view would call for a separate book, but in order to avoid it being totally ignored in this one, I have decided to touch briefly upon at least three issues that will have a significant impact on gender and sustainable development in Third World countries in the 21st century, fully acknowledging that there are many more subjects worthy of consideration.

The three issues relate to fresh water availability, poverty, and the social and cultural transformation occurring in some Islamic countries.

Children collecting water, Burkina Faso.

First water. As long as there are still billions of people in the world living without adequate access to clean drinking and sanitation water, sustainable development is not achievable. Lack of water means poor health and shortage of food, and the potential resulting conflicts and migrations could be massive and could not fail to affect the developed world as well.

As we enter the 21st century, 21 countries and regions in Africa, the Near East and Asia are under water stress because the availability of water is out of balance with the need. If nothing is done to improve this situation, 15 more countries will be added to the list before 2025. Globally speaking, the natural annual fresh water supply due to evaporation from the seas and oceans covers total human needs many times over. Because the annual supply is a more or less stable volume, however, and the world population has grown from 1.6 billion in 1900 to 6 billion in 2000, the availability per person has decreased proportionally, while at the same time the average use per person has nearly doubled.

Nevertheless, there would theoretically be enough fresh water for eight or ten billion people if only rainfall and people were evenly spread over the world, which is obviously not the case. Seasons, geography and demography spoil the balance. In many regions of the world, water and people are not in the right place at the right time, and water is too cheap a commodity to ship all over the place, as can be done for instance with crude and vegetable oils, grain and minerals. Water is a regional problem and is not affected by the North/South debate, at least to the extent that the rich part of the world does not consume the water that should be available to the poor part. But the rich world has the money to extract, clean and recycle its water resources, while the poor cannot afford these facilities.

The link with the gender issue is that in those regions where the poor lack clean water and an estimated three to five million people (mostly children) die annually as a result, women carry most of the burden of finding and fetching water, while decisions on investments and distribution are exclusively handled by men.

No wonder women in developing countries have become rebellious in recent years over this state of affairs and voiced strong opinions at the World Water Conference in March 2000 in the Netherlands, claiming that they should occupy at least 30% of the decision- making positions in institutions that run the water business. This conference resulted in a framework for action, based on a thorough and ongoing assessment of the needs and supplies of water for nature, people and food, in order to reach a sustainable water situation in the world by 2025.

Typically, in the initial phase of the assessment studies, women were hardly involved in the consultations. This led to strong protests at an in-between meeting in Stockholm in the summer of 1999, after which the organizers (practically all men) hurriedly corrected this shortcoming.

Developed countries can contribute significantly to the alleviation of water scarcity in developing countries by introducing simple and proven methods for the more efficient supply and use of water for irrigation, drinking and sanitation and by involving men and women in training and applying these methods. This calls for more public/

private partnerships in which the private sector of developed countries can participate. Through the transfer of knowledge and experience and with the active involvement of women, they can make an economically and ecologically sound contribution to sustainable development and gender equality in developing countries and at the same time create a larger market for their products and services.

Of course these actions will cost money, and here is where the poverty factor, my second issue, comes in.

Financing poor communities is an issue that most Western people and specifically banks consider a *contradictio in terminis*. As an American friend told me cynically in 1998: 'Bankers don't give loans to people they can't have lunch with'. He is now actively involved in bridging the gap between local banks in developing countries and Western commercial banks in order to back up so-called *microfinancing*.

Microfinancing is a phenomenon that started many years ago on a small scale in Africa, Latin America and the Near and Far East, mainly for microcredits, by NGOS (non-governmental organisations), mostly funded by church and endowment charities and development aid programmes.

To cut a long story short, there is now a great volume of microfinancing operating in many developing countries in Asia, Africa and South America and involving a substantial number of well established microfinance institutes with good track records. The signs are that in the next decades this will become a major instrument for alleviating poverty. The experience is that well organized and well administered lending to poor people who have no employment, no collateral and no record results in over 95% payback, including stiff interest rates, as administrative costs are relatively high.

The link between poverty, microfinance and the gender issue is that, in general, poverty hurts women most, and most of the lending has gone to women. They handle money more carefully than men and through their micro-entrepreneurship (the loans vary from $100 to $500) gain economic independence, regain self-respect and become agents of economic growth. There is no doubt that if this instrument finds wider acceptance, and obviously it will extend increasingly to female/male partnerships, it will make an important contribution to reducing poverty and improving the gender balance. At present, about 500 million dollars of donor funds are earmarked for microfinance every year. When commercial financing is attracted, the scheme could encompass multi-billion dollars of revolving funds.

The link between microfinance and sustainability is that poor people often do considerable ecological harm by ruining the natural environment in their struggle for survival and their quest for water. This is especially true of those living in densely populated areas, as unfortunately is ever more the case.

A large international group of microfinance institutions called *The Microcredit Summit* has set itself a target of reaching 100 million people with microfinance projects by 2005.

If this can be done, it can be done only with the participation of women. This is quite an upside-down situation from the not-so-distant past in the West, when a woman who applied for a loan at a bank would have been asked: 'Does your husband know you are here?', even if the banker was gladly prepared to have lunch with her.

The third issue I would like to touch upon is the changing climate in gender relations in Islamic societies in recent years.

Islamic societies have a reputation of strong male domination. It is obvious, therefore, that their important cultural and political position in the global scene could present a major stumbling block to achieving a better gender balance in the world.

There are signs of change, however, in many Arab lands. Progress varies greatly from country to country, the pace is slow, and resistance by male vested interests is still considerable. Although we cannot compare the situation with the history of emancipation in the West, it could be said that initiatives for changes in attitudes, legal frameworks and educational opportunities for women are reminiscent of the first Western feminist wave, which occurred more than a hundred years ago.

The Economist of November 27th, 1999, gave an extensive survey of the struggle of Arab women for political and legal rights in their countries, varying from extreme liberalism in Tunisia to what is still extreme conservatism in Saudi Arabia. In between, slow progress is being made in Lebanon, Oman, Kuwait, Bahrain, Qatar and the United Arab Emirates, where the proportion of women in the workforce has doubled in the last 20 years. In Egypt, President Mubarak, who still decides who sits in parliament, was instrumental in getting new legislation through the male-dominated (99%) assembly in early 2000, improving women's rights in divorce proceedings. In Morocco and Jordan, the new kings have openly called for further women's emancipation. New legislation (200 amendments on gender issues) has been proposed by the socialist premier of Morocco, Youssoufi; in his 'plan for integration' he aims at 'developing a relationship between women and men from male dominance to partnership'.

There has been a recent shift from conservatism to liberalism in the elections in Iran. This trend is most likely to facilitate reforms in the direction of the emancipation of Iranian women as well. In all the above cases the initiatives meet with fierce opposition from fundamentalists who proclaim that the proposed changes are in conflict with Islamic law and endanger the foundations of family life. Arab women's organizations are pressing ahead with their agenda at an ever increasing speed, however, claiming, as I described in Chapter XII, that the essentially woman-friendly Koran has been falsely translated by men into a woman-suppressive legal, cultural and political system, not unlike the history of the Christian religion.

In the context of increasing globalisation and the transparency of information and cultural exchange, it seems to me that the transformation taking place in the Islamic world cannot be halted, although the road to a better gender balance will still be bumpy for decades to come.

With the above limited number of examples (I left out for instance what is going on in China and Japan), I have tried to show that in recent years the gender issue has increasingly become part of the global agenda. This agenda, illustrated earlier in this chapter by the summary of the Fourth UN Conference on Women in Beijing in 1995, is likely to become increasingly more and more pressing in the coming decades. It will contribute to an irreversible shift towards a new balance in gender relations in the world at large.

XXI

In Conclusion

After many ages of ups and downs in gender relations, are we now finally on an irreversible course towards a better balance?

Tracing the record from prehistoric times up to the recent second feminist wave in the Western world, I identified in the first seventeen chapters a number of events, in fact a dozen of them, that could have tipped the balance in the right direction, away from the male domination model that became firmly established 5,000 years ago. But in every case vested interests associated with male power suppressed the new trend.

Let me briefly summarize these events for you:

In Greek society after the Bronze Ages, upper class women were becoming better and better educated. Marriages with aristocrats had gained them increased influence in politics while they were still deriving some benefit from goddess mythologies, yet the tide turned against them when democracy and religion spirited away their hidden powers.

The views of Socrates with regard to women, deserving educational opportunities equal to men, could have helped to reverse the decline in respect for women, but the devastating theories of Aristotle on their subordinate biological and mental nature became the prevailing wisdom.

In Roman society women achieved greater influence and status, obtained more legal protection and received a better education. Some assumed civic offices, and the Goddess Isis cult was thriving. The end of the Roman Empire and the start of the Dark Ages, however, marked the end of this advance and of reverence for Isis.

Although the pronouncements of Jesus on the equal rights and values of women and men could have sustained the modest progress achieved for women in Roman times, the Church Fathers effectively undermined these teachings.

The doctrines of the Catholic Church that were formulated during the Dark Ages and supported by Augustin and later by Aquinas further reinforced the male domination model imposed by the Church on society.

Contrary to present perceptions, the Koran in the 7th century provided an opportunity to correct prevailing patriarchical traditions and to introduce fair rules on the equality of women and men and the protection of women in society against male domination. The Koran's wisdom was overruled, however, by the vested interests of men in power, and this led to Islamic traditions and laws that were quite the opposite of what was the intention of 'Gabriel's message' to Mohammed.

In the later Middle Ages women became visible once again. Notable influences included strong female personalities in mysticism, literature and the arts, the emergence of the Mary cult, the phenomenon of courtly love and the firm position of middle class women in trade and commerce. But the Inquisition and the exercise of political power, retained in the hands of men, stifled these developments.

The Renaissance could have reopened the gates to female participation in the outer world, as could the Reformation and Humanism. The resilience of the anti-feminine forces invoked by Aristotle, Augustin and Aquinas, however, prevented a breakthrough in gender balance in religious and political thinking. All this regardless of the increased visibility of women in the fields of literature and art.

In the Enlightenment female forces that had been suppressed in the past also showed signs of recovery and were given some hope of revival in a period that propagated natural rights, liberty and social equality. Although this led to the first awakening of feminism, the prevailing establishment did not fundamentally change any of its existing views on gender.

At the end of the 18th century there were again manifestations of an ongoing pressure for gender equality, and for the first time the orthodoxy was challenged by Mary Wollstonecraft. She rejected the male-dominated framework of society and, by definition, man as the measure for female emancipation. All the same, the Declaration of Independence in the USA, the Civil Code in France and the Bill of Rights in England were in essence designed to improve the lot of (white) men only.

At last, in the 19th century, regardless of wars and instabilities, addressing the 'woman question' became an unavoidable issue. Slowly and painfully the first feminist wave rolled in, leading eventually to universal voting and other legal rights for women in most Western and Eastern European countries by 1920.

The twentieth century started with a brighter outlook for more balanced gender relations in the political, academic, professional and artistic disciplines, but two wars and five dictators in Europe caused a serious setback that lasted until after the Second World War.

A new feminist drive after World War II, centred in the 1960's, was aimed at further improving the gender balance in society, as voting rights and legal protection for women were seen as not having fundamentally affected the male domination model. This second wave, which coincided with the introduction of the contraceptive pill, successfully opened people's eyes to the social and political shortcomings of the first wave and achieved a breakthrough for women's biological and economic independence. It unfortunately also led to occasional victim-oriented, anti-man and extremist attitudes which, although possibly necessary to make the point, eventually had an anti-feminism backlash effect on both men and women.

Then, in the last decades of the 20th century, we have seen in chapters XVIII and XIX that the distinctions between male and female were becoming more sophisticated, that the model with male as the yardstick was showing signs of breaking down, and that bias against women was starting to disappear in many sectors of Western society. This movement is gaining momentum day by day.

Then again, in non-Western parts of the world, as discussed in Chapter XX, a transformation is taken place, though more slowly.

I have argued that the new trend towards gender balance seems irreversible, for the first time in 5,000 years. I would therefore not call it a new wave, because waves roll in and out, but rather a revolutionary phase, because revolution rarely makes a backward move. Revolutionary in the sense that, whereas in all human history so far there has been a division of labour and function between woman and man, with male domination persistently creeping in, we are now entering a phase where the division is becoming optional, reversible and interchangeable, without domination. This new phase, to my mind, is not part of a recurring cycle, but part of a revolutionary step.

The characteristics of this process as I presented them in the previous chapters centred upon:

First, the breakdown of stereotypes.
Second, the increasing presence of economically independent qualified women in all institutions in Western society, which, over the coming decades, will exceed the critical mass of 30% participation needed to balance male power.

Third, changing political and social attitudes to gender balance in national policies and institutional reforms.

Fourth, a growing acceptance of the need for social, ethical and ecological considerations in decision-making over and above the economic factor, opening doors to new sensibilities that are rarely felt in the man's world.

Fifth, the third industrial (information) revolution and the emerging new economy, introducing opportunities that are more gender-independent than those offered by any industrial or economic advances in the past.

Sixth, the global and UN-supported women's movements that will increasingly press their agenda, especially with regard to gender issues in developing countries, including social and cultural changes in Islamic societies.

Seventh, the emergence of megacities where more than three billion people will live in 2006 and more than five billion in 2025, providing more opportunities for women to participate independently in the institutions of society.

Eighth and last, a dramatic demographic discontinuity occurring within 50 years from now, when the world population will in all likelihood have stabilized and of which the consequences are not yet understood, although they will undoubtedly affect relations between woman and man in the sense of stronger partnerships.

It is in the context of these coinciding challenges that I see an irreversible process gaining momentum, especially in the light of globalization, new economies and new technologies.

Let me offer a few thoughts on why I think there will be substantial interactions between the new challenges of this century and the trend towards a better balance of the sexes and of feminine and masculine values in society.

A remarkable shift has taken place in recent decennia in the sphere of economic activities, a shift in emphasis away from factories, machines, 'manpower' and instruments of rigid central control, and towards services, electronic control, 'humanpower' and decentralized flexibility.

Already today three-quarters of total economic activity in the world is oriented towards services and one-quarter towards production, with a growing concentration on individual performance and self-organizing enterprise. These trends are expected to continue over the next decade. At the same time traditional 'interaction management' costs are being dramatically cut by the application of advanced information technologies, resulting in substantial increases in productivity. Hence the new economy.

All this is significant for what is coming to be known as the third industrial revolution. The first was triggered by the invention of the steam engine, say 200 years ago; the second by the invention of electricity, say 100 years ago; and now the third at the end of the 20th century by the invention of information technologies. The next could soon be sparked by genetic engineering.

The so-called new economy gained momentum in the second half of the 1990's when the Internet and e-commerce grew over five years from practically zero to a multi-billion dollar business in an increasingly global market. Regardless of a recent 'shake-out' the high pace of development is likely to stay with us for the next decade or two; we have only seen the beginning as yet. The globalisation of the market is likely to see international trading rise from 20% to 80% of total trade in the next 30 years.

The shift from hardware to software, from formal centralization to informal decentralization, from inaccessibility to transparency of information, from 'manpower' to 'humanpower', implies new and 'gender free' opportunities for women and men alike, because the new style of management is based less on traditional male-oriented power cultures, as discussed in Chapter XIX. Contrast this with what happened in the first two revolutions, where employment opportunities in the new industries became available mainly for men, in strongly centralised organisations based on military concepts of command and control. And the changes in management style affect not only the business community; they also permeate many of the other institutions of human society.

Considering the profound impact the present revolutionary developments will have on the gender issue, it is surprising that today's leading professional management opinions have been slow to visualise this. The topic has hardly been debated so far, but should be high on the strategy agenda.

> *Time Magazine's* January 31st, 2000, edition devotes its *Viewpoint* column to the urgent need for new social and political concepts and a new generation of political role models while business is e-engineering and reinventing itself. 'Failing to integrate the social, psychological and ethical (and I would add gender) dimensions will invite a backlash from groups which will not easily accept that their values and their cultural diversity be sidelined.'

It is here that I see the need and the opportunity for a new process of decision-making where feminine and masculine sensibilities both come into play. And to my mind this will happen only if there is a fair mix of female and male participants in the process, leading to constructive corrections both ways. More than ever before, there is a need for such a mix at all levels, as society becomes more mature and critical in weighing values and addressing ethical, ecological, cultural and social issues alongside economic performance and financial analysis, not to mention the mounting debate on genetic engineering.

I would venture to speculate that making decisions with a balanced presence of both sexes will eventually change the attitudes of these women and men, allowing them to throw off the roles they have been accustomed to playing. They will achieve this by listening to each other, to themselves and to society concerning what drives them as mature human beings, instead of making relatively isolated judgements within a limited context. An illusion? I don't think so.

In the first chapter I wondered if we could change our perceptions of gender reality or whether we women and men are genetically destined to behave as we do.
My conclusion from the historical, cultural and biological evidence I have presented in this book is that we can indeed change our perceptions and that we had better do so soon.

Another question the first chapter raises is a crucial one. If we can and do change our perceptions and attitudes on gender while accepting certain biological and psychological differences between women and men, will that lead to a better world? A world with fewer wars, with economy balancing ecology, culture matching nature, less poverty and, eventually, no suppression of women and denial of feminine sensibilities? Again, my answer is yes.

Does it mean that we will no longer ask about percentages or quotas of women participating in the institutions of society, because that will have become irrelevant?
Once the presence of women and female qualities in decision-making has reached the critical mass, will there be no more talk about women's emancipation, suppression or struggle against bias?
Will there be no more women wanting to live up to the standards of men, nor men feeling embarrassed to show their feelings?

Will we stop referring to women painters, women writers, women composers, female prime ministers, female priests and female CEOS?

From what I have learned from my journey through history and what I sense is happening in the present real world, I am convinced that the answer to all these questions is in the affirmative.

Except maybe with respect to violence. In chapter three I have discussed the traits of violence in human and chimpanzee males, and although I think these traits can be socially controlled, this will probably be one of the toughest issues to deal with in a better gender-balanced world.

Achieving a better gender-balanced world will indeed be a balancing act and will not be without effort, fears, setbacks and disappointments, because there is no such thing as a free lunch. It will not be all in place tomorrow, nor in the next decade and not everywhere at the same time, but my guess is that it will be very near realisation by the time we will have a stabilized world population around 2050.

I won't be there to see it, but I believe that my grandchildren will have a fair chance of living in a better world.

A better world for woman and man.

XXII

Epilogue: A Balancing Act

This book has shown that some natural dualities in our society have become unnaturely separated over the course of human history.

Natural dualities may be perceived by us as radical opposites, but in fact most of them exist because of each other. They are born from unity. They need interaction, not isolation.

If dualities are radically separated, the result is a loss of coherence and integrity, an unwholesome state. This is what happened with our perceptions of male and female, culture and nature, and economy and ecology.

Philosophically and scientifically, the phenomenon of interacting dualisms has always been an intriguing issue. We find it back in Taoism's 'yin/yang', in Heracleitus's 'logos', in Bonaventure's 'Coincidentia Oppositorum', in Spinoza's 'meta/physics', in Hegel's 'thesis/anti-thesis', in Einstein's 'mass/energy' and 'space/time', in Bohr's 'wave/particle', in Jung's 'anima/animus', in Teilhard's 'complexity/consciousness' and in Prigogine's 'order/chaos'.

But also in more down-to-earth experiences such as dark/light, ugly/beautiful, low/high, body/soul or life/death.

All these dualisms are known to be interdependent; the one part does exist by the grace of the other; they are intimately connected.

In this book I have concluded that we can and must act to rediscover the natural balance between male and female, nature and culture, and ecology and economy if we wish to preserve a sustainable human society on this planet.

It will undoubtedly be a balancing act.

'A Hundred Years of Fortitude'. In: *The Economist*, November 1999.

'De fundamentele veranderingen worden niet onderkend: De nieuwe economie in de praktijk'. In: NRC *Handelsblad*, October 23 1999.

'The Truth about Women's Bodies'. In: *Time*, March 15 1999.

'The Shadow Story of the Millenium Women'. In: *The New York Times Magazines*, special millennium edition, May 16 1999.

'Unshapely World, Too Old or Too Young'. In: *The Economist*, September 25 1999.

'Winning the Talent War for Women'. In: *Harvard Bussiness Review*, December 2000.

'Zurück zur Mädchenschule Mehr Chancen für Frauen?'. In: *Der Spiegel*, May 6 1996.

6 Billion: a Time for Choices, UN Populations Fund report, 1999.

Ahmed, Leila, *Women and Gender in Islam*. Yale University Press New Haven & London, 1992.

Angier, Natalie, *Woman. An Intimate Geography*. A Peter Davison Book, New York 1999.

Anthony, Carol K., *The Philosophy of the I Ching*. Anthony Publishing Company, Stow, Massachusetts 1981.

Baalen, Anneke van and Marijke Ekelschot, *Geschiedenis van de Vrouwentoekomst*. De Bonte Was, Amsterdam 1980.

Badinter, Elisabeth, *L'un et l'autre*. Edtions Odile Jacob, 1986.

Badinter, Elisabeth, *The Unopposite Sex. The end of the Gender Battle*. Harper & Row, New York 1989.

Bancroft, Anne, *Weavers of Wisdom. Women Mystics of the Twentieth Century*. Arkana, 1989.

Baring, Anne and Jules Cashford, *The Myth of the Goddess. Evolution of an Image*. Arkana, Penguin Group, London 1991/3.

Basham, A.L., *The Wonder That was India*. Rupa & Co, Calcutta 1954/1992.

Blois L. de and R.J. van der Spek, *An introduction to the Ancient World*. Routledge, London 1997.

Boer, Esther de, *Maria Magdalena. De mythe voorbij. Op zoek naar wie zij werkelijk is*. Meinema, Zoetermeer 1996.

Bolen, Jean Shinoda, *Goddesses in Everywoman*. Harper & Row, New York 1984.

Bosma, Hanna and Patricia Pisters, *Madonna De vele gezichten van een popster*. Prometheus, Amsterdam 1999.

Braidotti, Rosi, Ewa Charkiewicz, Sabine Häusler, Saskia Wieringa, *Woman, the Environment and Sustainable Development*. Towards a Theoretical Synthesis. ZED Books, London, 1994. (In cooperation with Instraw Women's Studies Development/Environment)

Bronowski, J. and Bruce Mazlish, *The Western Intellectual Tradition from Leonardo to Hegel*. Harper & Row, New York, Evanston 1975.

Brunn, Emilyn Zum and Georgette Epiney-Burgard, *Women Mystics In Medieval Europe*. Paragon House, New York 1989.

Butterfield, Fox, *China Alive in the Bitter Sea*. Times Books 1982, New York, Toronto 1982.

Cels, Sanderijn, *Grrls. Jonge vrouwen in de jaren negentig.* Prometheus, Amsterdam 1999.

Chadwick, Whitney, *Women, Art, and Society.* Thames and Hudson, Ltd., London; second, revised edition 1997.

Chadwick, Whitney, *Women, Art, and Society.* Thames and Hudson, New York/London 1990/1996.

Chadwick, Whitney, *Women, Art, and Society.* Thames and Hudson, Ltd, London, second, revised edition.

Chamberlain, Jonathan, *Chinese Gods,* Pelanduk Publications, Kelana Jaya, Malaysia 1987.

Chang Chung-yuan, *Tao: A New Way of Thinking,* A Translation of the Tào Tê Ching with an Introduction and Commentaries. 1975.

Chang Po-Tuan, *The Inner Teachings of Taoism.* Shambala, Boston 1986.

Chittister, John D., *Heart of Flesh. A feminist Spirituality for Women and Men.* William B. Eerdmans Publicy Company, Grand Rapids, Michigan/ Cambridge, U.K.

Corneille, Catherine, *Vrouwen in de wereldgodsdiensten. Teksten tradities en recente ontwikkelingen.* Lemniscaat, Rotterdam 1994.

Dresen, Grietje, *Is dit mijn lichaam? Visioenen van het volmaakte lichaam in katholiek moraal en mystiek.* Valkhof Pers, Nijmegen 1998.

Duby, Georges and Michelle Perrot, *Storia delle donne in Occidente: II Novecento.* Editoria Laterza, Rome and Bari 1992. (English translation edited by Françoise Thébaud, *A History of Women in the West, V. Toward a cultural identity in the Twentieth Century.* The Bellknap Press of Harvard University Press, Cambridge, Massachusetts, London).

Duby, Georges, Geneviève Fraisse and Michelle Perrot, (eds), *A History of Women IV, Emerging feminism from Revolution to World War.* The Belknap Press of Harvard University Press, Cambridge, Massachusetts, London 1995.

Duby, Georges and Michelle Perrot, *A History of Women in the West III, Renaissance and Enlightment Paradoxes.* The Belknap Press of Harvard University Press, Cambridge, Massachusetts, London 1995.

Duby, Georges, *Edelvrouwen in de Twaalfde Eeuw.* Bert Bakker, Amsterdam 1997.

Ehrenreich, Barbara, 'Men. The Scientific Truth about their Work, Play, Health & Passions'. In: *Scientific American,* second quarter 1999, part 10, nr. 2.

Eisler, Riane, *The Chalice and the Blade. Our History, Our Future.* Pandora, Harper Collins Publishers, London, San Francisco 1987.

Engels, Friedrich, *The origin of the Family, Private Property and the State.* Penguin Books, London 1984.

Fausto-Sterling, Anne, *Myths of Gender.* Basic Books, New York 1985.

Ferino-Pagden, Sylvia, and Marina Kusche, *Sofonisba Anguissola. A Renaissance Woman.* Library of Congress Cataloging-in-Publication Data, 1995.

Fibbe, Arita and Mic Lansu, *M/V in evenwichtige organisaties.* Thema, 1999.

Fisher, Helen, *The First Sex, The Natural Talents of Women and How They are Changing the World.* Random House, New York 1999.

Fuldauer, Alice, 'Goochelen met sekseverschillen. Hoe wetenschappers de M/V-tegenstelling kunstmatig in stand houden'. In: *VB Magazine,* December 1995.

Gadon, Elinor W., *The Once and Future Goddess. A Symbol for our time.* Thorsons, London 1995.

Galdikas, Biruté M.F., *Reflections of Eden; My life with the Orangutans of Borneo.* Victor Gollancz, London 1995.

Gianini Belotti, Elena, *Little Girls.* Writers and Readers Publishing Cooperative, London 1975.

Gies, France and Joseph, *Women in the Middle Ages.* Herper Perennial, New York 1980.

Gimbutas, Maria, *The Language of the Goddess.* Harper Collins Publishers, San Francisco 1991.

Graham, A.C. (translation), *The Seven Inner Chapters and other writings from the book Chuang-tz.* George Allen & Unwin Ltd., London 1981.

Greenspan, Karen, *The Time-tables of Women's History. A Chronology of the Most Important People and Events in Women's History*. Touchstone, New York 1994.
Greer, Germaine, *The Female Eunuch*. Flamingo, London 1970.
Gruber, Elmar R. and Holger Kersten, *The Original Jesus*. Element Books, Shaftesbury 1995.

Hales, Dianne, *Just like a Woman. How Gender Science Is Redefining What Makes Us Female*. Bantam Books, New York, Toronto, London, Sydney, Auckland 1999.
Hart, Maarten 't, *De vrouw bestaat niet*. Geuze & Co. Drukkerij B.V., Dordrecht 1982.
Hassan, Riffat, *Women's Rights and Islam: From the I.C.P.D. to Beijing*. 1994 - 1995.
Holy Qur'an (translation M.H. Shakir), *Tahrike Tarsile Qur'an*. Inc. edition New York 1983.

Johnson, Geraldine and Sara F. Matthews Grieco (eds), *Picturing Women in Renaissance and Baroque Italy*. Cambridge University Press, Cambridge 1997.

Kaltenmark, Max, *Lao Tzu and Taoism*. Stanford University Press, Stanford 1969.
Kimura, Doreen, 'Sex Differences in the Brain'. In: *Scientific American*, September 1992.

Lahn, Bruce T. and David C. Page, 'Four Evolutionary Strata on the Human x. Chromosome'. In: *Science Magazine*, September 1999.
Lavinia Fontana of Bologna 1552-1614. National Museum of Women in the Arts. Electa Milan, 1998.
Leeming, David and Jack Page, *Goddess. Myths of the Female Divine*. Oxford University Press, New York/Oxford 1994.
Lehrman, Karen, *The Lipstick Proviso Women, Sex & Power in the Real World*. Double Day, New York 1997.
Lerner, Gerda, *The Creation of Patriarchy*. Oxford University Press, New York 1986.
Lerner, Gerda, *The Creation of Feminist Consciousness*. Oxford University Press, New York 1993.
Lipsitz Bem, Sandra, *The Lenses of Gender. Transforming the Debate on Sexual Inequality*. Yale University Press, New Haven and London 1993.
Lonner, *Psychologie and Culture. Cross-Cultural Views of Women and Men*, John E. Williams & Deborah L. Best, 1994

Mack, Burton L., *The Lost Gospel*. Element Books, Shaftesbury 1993.
Merchant, Carolyn, *The Death of Nature, Women, Ecology and the Scientific Revolution*. Harper Collins Publishers, San Francisco 1980.
Meyer, Marvin (translation), Hartold Bloom (interpretation.), *The Gospel of Thomas, The Hidden Sayings of Jesus*. Harper, San Francisco 1992.

Miller, Robert J., *The Complete Gospels*. Harper, San Francisco 1992.
Morgan, Evan, *Tao the Great Luminant. Essays from Huai Nan Tzu*. Reprint by Ch'eng Wen Publishing Company, Taipei 1974. Original publication by Kelly & Walsh Limited, Shanghai.
Morton, Tom, *Altered Mates. The Man Question*. Allen & Unwin, St Leonards NSW, Australia 1997.

National Museum of Women in the Arts. Library of Congress Cataloging-in-Publication Data, Harry N. Abrams, Inc. Publishers, New York 1987/1995.
Noble, David F., *A World Without Women. The Christian Clerical Culture of Western Science*. Oxford University Press, New York 1992.

Over, Raymond van, *I Ching. The New American Library*, New York

Pagels, Elaine, *The Gnostic Gospels*. Weidenfeld and Nicholson, London 1979.
Plant, Sadie, *Zeros + Ones. Digital Women + the New Technoculture*. Fourth Estate Limited, London 1997.
Pollack, Rachel, *The Body of the Goddess. Sacred Wisdom in Myth, Landscape and Culture*. Element Books Limited, Shaftesbury 1997.
Pomeroy, Sarah B., *Goddesses, Whores, Wives, and Slaves; Women in Classical Antiquity*. Schocken Books, New York 1975.

Power, Eileen, (ed. M.M. Postan), *Medieval Women*. Cambridge University Press, Cambridge 1975.

Radford Ruether, Rosemary, *Gaia and God. An ecofeminist Theology of Earth Healing*. SCM Press Ltd, London 1993.

Ronan, Colin A., *The shorter science & civilisation in China: 3*. A reduced version of the text by Joseph Needham. Cambridge University Press, Cambridge, New York 1986.

Ronan, Colin A., *The shorter science & civilisation in China: 2*. A reduced version of the text by Joseph Needham. Cambridge University Press, Cambridge, New York 1981.

Roszak, Theodore, *The gendered Atom*. Conari Press, Berkeley 1999.

Rousseau, Jean-Jacques, *Emile. Oeuvres Complètes de Jean-Jacques Rousseau*. Bibliothèque de la Pléiade, Gallimard, Paris 1969.

Rowbotham, Sheila, *A Century of Women. The History of Women in Britain and the United States*. Penguin Books, London, New York, Ringwood (Australia) 1999.

Russell, Bertrand, *History of Western Philosophy*. George Allen & Unwin Ltd, London 1961/1967.

Russell, Bertrand, *Marriage and Morals*. Unwin Paperbacks, London 1929/1976.

Sallberg Kam, Rose, *Their Stories Our Stories; Women of the Bible*. Continuum, New York 1995.

Schipper, Kristofer, *Tao. De levende religie van China*. Meulenhoff, Amsterdam 1988.

Schuurman, Anna Maria van, *De aanleg van vrouwen voor wetenschap*. Uitgeverij Xeno, Groningen 1996.

Seager, Joni, *The State of Women in the World Atlas*. Penguin Group, London 1997.

Sharma, Arvind (ed.), *Women in World Religions*. State University of New York Press, Albany 1987.

Shearer, Alistair and Peter Russell (translators), *The Upanishads*. Harper & Row Publishers, Inc., San Francisco 1978.

Shlain, Leonard, *The Alphabet versus the Goddess*, The Conflict between Word and Image. Viking, New York 1998.

Six Feminist Waves International Conference 7-10 June 1994 Amsterdam

Slavenburg, Jacob, *De geheime woorden, een ontdekkingstocht door vijfentwintig eeuwen verborgen kennis*. Ankh-Hermes, Deventer 1989.

Slavenburg, Jacob, *De verloren erfenis, Inzicht in de ontwikkeling van het christendom*. Ankh-Hermes, Deventer 1993.

Slavenburg, Jacob, *Valsheid in geschrifte*. Walburg Pers, Zutphen 1995.

Slavenburg, Jacob, *Een ander testament, onbekende geschriften over het leven van Jezus en zijn geheime leringen*. Ankh-Hermes, Deventer 1991.

Smith, Joan, *Different for Girls. How Culture Creates Women*. Chatto & Windus, London 1997.

Spretnak, Charlene, *Lost Goddesses of Early Greece; A Collection of Pre-Hellenic Myths*. Beacon Press, Boston 1981.

Steiner, Rudolf, *Het Vrouwelijke en het Mannelijke*. Uitgeverij Pentagon, Amsterdam 1987.

Stikker, Allerd, *The Transformation Factor; Towards an Ecological Consciousness*. Element, Rockport Ma, 1992.

Stone, Merlin, *When God Was A Woman*. Harcourt Brace & Company, New York 1976.

Sustainable Development and Water in International Gender Perspective, Conference Report Summary, Rotterdam 2-3 February 2000.

Tannahill, Reay, *Sex in History*. Abacus, London 1980.

The New Encyclopaedia Britannica, Fifteenth edition 1992

Thurow, Lester, *Building Wealth*. 1999.

Tiger, Lionel, *The decline of males*. Golden Books, New York

Trager, James, *The Women's Chronology*, A Year-by-Year Record from Prehistory to the Present. Aurum Press Ltd, London 1994.

Uitz, Erika, *Die Frau in der mittelalterischen Stadt* Herder Spektrum, Freiburg 1992.

Valian, Virgina, *Why so slow? The advancement of women*. The MIT Press, Cambridge, Massachusetts, London

Waal, Frans de and Frans Lanting, *Bonobo. De vergeten mensaap*. Natuur en Techniek Beek, Kosmos-Z&K, Utrecht/ Antwerpen 1997.

Walter, Natasha, *The New Feminism*. Little, Brown & Company, London 1998.

276

Wertheim, Margareth, *Pythago-ras' Trousers. God Physics, and the Gender Wars*. Random House, New York 1995.

Wilhelm, Richard, *Lectures on the I Ching, constancy and change*. Routledge & Kegan Paul, London 1980.

Wolf, Margery and Roxane Witke (eds), *Women in Chinese Society*. Stanford University Press, Stanford 1975.

Wolf, Naomi, *Fire with Fire. The new female power and how it will change the 21st Century*. Vintage, London 1994.

Wollstonecraft, Mary, *A Vindic-ation of the Rights of Woman*. Penguin Books, London 1992.

Wrangham, Richard and Dale Peterson, *Demonic Males. Apes and the origins of human violence*. Bloomsbury Publish-ing, London 1996.

Young, Louise B., *The unfinished Universe*. Simon and Schuster, New York 1986.

Illustration Acknowledgements

278

Cover Philadelphia Museum of Art, Philadelphia.

Page 2 Musée Rodin, Paris.

Page 10 In: Over, Raymond van, *I Ching, The definitive new rendering of the ancient Chinese book of divination* (New York: 1971).

Page 13 In: Russell, Peter, *The Global Brain. Speculations on the evolutionary leap to planetary consciousness* (Los Angeles: 1983).

Page 20 Frans Lanting.

Page 30 Scala, Florence.

Page 33 Goulandris Collection, Museum of Cycladic and Ancient Greek Art, Athens.

Page 43 In: Storm, Rachel, *Encyclopedie van de oosterse mythologie* (Lisse: 2000).

Page 47 In: Storm, Rachel, *Encyclopedie van de oosterse mythologie* (Lisse: 2000).

Page 49 Aegyptisches Museum, Berlin.

Page 50 Egyptian Museum, Cairo.

Page 51 Aegyptisches Museum, Berlin.

Page 52 Victoria & Albert Museum, London.

Page 55 In: Phillips, Charles, *De eeuwige kringloop. Indiase mythen* (Amsterdam: 1998).

Page 56 In: Storm, Rachel, *Encyclopedie van de oosterse mythologie* (Lisse: 2000).

Page 57 In: Littleton, C. Scott & Swieringa, Aleid C., *Oosterse wijsheid* (Amsterdam/Antwerpen: 1997).

Page 58 National Museum of India, New Delhi.

Page 60 LEFT Musée du Louvre, Paris.

Page 60 CENTER Musei Capitolini, Rome.

Page 60 RIGHT Archaeological Museum, Olympia.

Page 62 Archaeological Museum, Olympia.

Page 64 LEFT British Museum, London.

Page 62 RIGHT Glyptothek, Munich.

Page 66 Musée du Louvre, Paris

Page 68 EMB-Service, Lucerne.

Page 70 In: Chamberlain, Jonathan, *Chinese Gods* (Selangor Darul Ehsan: 1987).

Page 64 LEFT & RIGHT In: Storm, Rachel, *Encyclopedie van de oosterse mythologie* (Lisse: 2000).

Page 75 In: Storm, Rachel, *Encyclopedie van de oosterse mythologie* (Lisse: 2000).

Page 78 British Museum, London.

Page 84 Genève, Private Collection.

Page 87 Stanza della Segnatura, Vatican.

Page 93 British Museum, London.

Page 94 Scala, Antella, Florence.

Page 96 Bayerische Staatsbibliothek, München.

Page 100 Musée du Louvre, Paris.

Page 104 Galleria dell'Accademia, Florence, Italy.

Page 108 British Library.

Page 111 British Library.

Page 112 Philadelphia Museum of Art, Philadelphia, PA.

Page 118 Württembergisches Landesmuseum, Stuttgart.

Page 121 British Museum, London.

Page 123 S. Caterina, Pisa.

Page 124 National Museum of India, New Delhi.

Page 129 In: *Hildegard van Bingen, Spiegel van Hemelse geheimen*, Hoving, Jan (red.) (Ten Have: 1998).

Page 130 National Gallery of Art, Washington.

Page 133 Bibliothèque Nationale de France, Paris.

279

Index

281

284

285